The PIMS Principles ─────

The
PIMS
Principles _____

Linking Strategy to Performance

Robert D. Buzzell

Bradley T. Gale

THE FREE PRESS
A Division of Macmillan, Inc.
NEW YORK

Collier Macmillan Publishers
LONDON

The Free Press
A Division of Macmillan, Inc.
866 Third Avenue, New York, N. Y. 10022

Collier Macmillan Canada, Inc.

Printed in the United States of America

printing number

5   6   7   8   9   10

Library of Congress Cataloging-in-Publication Data

Buzzell, Robert D. (Robert Dow)
  The PIMS principles.

  Bibliography: p.
  Includes index.
  1. Marketing—Management.   2. Strategic planning.
I. Gale, Bradley T.   II. Title.
HF5415.13.B893   1987   658.8′02   87–416
ISBN 0-02-904430-8

Contents

Preface

"Why another book on competitive strategy?" would be a reasonable question to ask about this volume. A great deal has been written on the subject of strategy, especially during the past several years. Anyone who has followed the writings in this field might reasonably wonder if everything that could be said about strategy hasn't already been said.

It is certainly true that many business executives, consultants, and academics have expressed their views on competitive strategy. But we believe that in writing this book we are contributing something distinctive to the ongoing discussion of how enterprises can compete most effectively in today's global economy. Our "unique ingredient," as compared with other writers in the field, is factual *evidence* about the linkages between strategy and business performance. This factual evidence is drawn from the PIMS (Profit Impact of Market Strategies) data base, which contains financial and strategic information for around 3,000 business units.

The PIMS research program was initiated in 1972, for the specific purpose of determining how key dimensions of strategy affect profitability and growth. Since that time some 450 corporations have contributed annual data, for periods that range from 2 to 10 years, for their product divisions or other strategic business units. The PIMS program is housed at the Strategic Planning Institute (SPI), whose member companies include large and small firms, North

American and European, public and privately-owned. Many different types of products and markets are represented in the data base—among them consumer products, heavy industrial goods, raw materials, high-technology, equipment, and services.

Since the mid-1970s, the PIMS data base has been used by managers and planning specialists of the participating companies in many ways. Applications of PIMS-based analysis include developing business plans, evaluating forecasts submitted by division managers, and appraising possible acquisitions and divestitures, among others. We—and numerous other investigators at SPI and at academic institutions—have utilized the data base to investigate *general* strategy issues and relationships. In over 100 published studies (listed in the Bibliography) researchers have drawn on PIMS to explore such questions as:

- How important is market share, and how does it affect various dimensions of performance?
- When does it pay to be vertically integrated?
- Under what conditions should business invest in mechanizing or automating their operations?

Some management authorities doubt that there are meaningful answers to such broad questions. They believe that each situation has so many distinctive features that generalizations are virtually impossible. The basic premise of the PIMS program, however, is that useful generalizations *can* be developed about the linkages between strategy and performance; hence, the title of this book. This is not to say that situation-specific factors are not important: they almost always are. But, in our view, managers and managers-to-be can learn much about their individual problems from the experiences of others in *similar* situations.

The "PIMS Principles" summarized in this book reflect our views about the most important lessons to be drawn from the PIMS-based research. We haven't done all of this work by ourselves, of course, and we gratefully acknowledge the ideas and contributions of our colleagues, past and present. We've listed many of their names in the Acknowledgments section. We hope that practicing managers and planning specialists will find this book a useful source of ideas. We hope, too, that aspiring managers and their teachers—in MBA programs and elsewhere—will read and think about the concepts and research results summarized here. Finally, we hope that public policymakers will find our work useful in understanding the workings of modern economic systems.

Robert D. Buzzell
Harvard Business School

Bradley T. Gale
*The Strategic
Planning Institute*

Acknowledgments

Since the inception of the PIMS Program of research on competitive strategy in 1972, many organizations and individuals have contributed to the work on which this book is based. The corporations that have participated in the program, both past and present, provided the data and the financial support without which none of the PIMS research would have been possible. We gratefully acknowledge the help and the ideas of the hundreds of executives and planning specialists who have been involved in the program over the years.

Our special thanks go to the past and present chairmen of the Strategic Planning Institute's Board of Trustees—Bill Wommack (Mead Corporation), Jerry Weiss (Chase Manhattan Bank), and Worth Loomis (Dexter Corporation). The other current SPI trustees have also been very supportive. They include Arthur J. Ballard (Rohm and Hass); Georges Chazot (SAFT/CGE); Gunnar Dahlsten (Swedish Match); Richard Donofrio (SNET); John B. Frey, Jr. (E. I. du Pont de Nemours); Roger Gant, Jr. (Glen Raven Mills); Thomas Latimer (Chicago Pneumatic Tool); Robert L. Rain (Baxter Travenol); Donald R. Russell (Sonoco Products); Robert Saslaw (TRW); David K. Stout (Unilever); and James R. Utaski (Johnson and Johnson). The late Hermann Grabherr (Siemens) was a valued member of the Board until his untimely death in November 1986. Wilson Nolen of Becton Dickinson, a former trustee, has been a continuing source of support for many years.

Our colleagues on the SPI staff, past and present, have made major contributions to the design of the PIMS Program and have borne the primary responsibility for applying PIMS models to management problems. We should like to acknowledge, in particular, our debts to Mark Chussil, Donald Swire, Joel Rosenfeld, Robert Luchs, Donald F. Heany, Joseph Patten, Keith Roberts, John Guiniven, and Ruth G. Newman.

Much of the PIMS-based research has been carried out by academic investigators—a bibliography listing their publications is contained in Appendix C. Among the most important contributors have been Ralph G.M. Sultan, who helped to design the first phase of the program, and Ralph Biggadike. More recently, our academic research program has benefitted greatly from the guidance of our advisory council. Members of the council include Richard E. Caves (Harvard University), F.M. Scherer (Swarthmore College), George Day (University of Toronto), Lynn Phillips (Stanford University), and David Reibstein (University of Pennsylvania).

John McArthur, Dean of the Harvard Business School, kindly arranged Bob Buzzell's assignments to allow for time spent in writing. Thanks are also due to Dean John Rosenblum and Professor Paul Farris of the Colgate Darden Graduate School of Business, University of Virginia, for providing a quiet and friendly atmosphere for computer work and writing.

Finally, we are grateful to those who have helped us in organizing and preparing the manuscript for publication. Bob Wallace of The Free Press has encouraged us since the time the book was only a gleam in the eye. Bel Rustin at SPI, and Janis Forde and Susan Blackman at HBS, have patiently processed our words.

We appreciate the help and support of all these people and many others associated with The PIMS Program. None of them, however, should be held responsible for the errors and omissions of this volume.

SPECIAL AKNOWLEDGMENT

The basic ideas underlying both The PIMS Program and the strategic planning models at the General Electric company from which PIMS evolved were originally developed by Sidney Schoeffler. Without his creativity, original approaches to data analysis, and determination to gain acceptance for his ideas, very little of the work summarized in this volume could have been done. We, and everyone else associated with PIMS, are deeply indebted to Sid. From the outset he has been a never-ending source of business problems and research ideas. He has constantly challenged us to make the insights provided by the PIMS data base relevant to managers and accessible to the business community at large.

We hope that Sid will be pleased with this book. He bears no responsibility, however, for its shortcomings.

Cambridge, Massachusetts   Robert D. Buzzell
December 1986   Bradley T. Gale

Chapter 1 _____

Are There Any General Strategy Principles?

The central theme of this book is that we can relate business strategies to performance by studying past experience. Every manager, of course, learns from his or her own experience, from that of associates, and by studying competitors' actions. Besides learning from these direct sources, we believe that general relationships between strategy and performance can also be found by analyzing the experience of many companies across a wide variety of industries. This is the kind of research that we and our colleagues at the Strategic Planning Institute have been doing since The PIMS (Profit Impact of Market Strategy) Program was initiated in 1972. Since that time, more than 450 companies have contributed information to us, documenting the strategies and financial results of nearly 3,000 strategic business units (SBUs) for periods that range from 2 to 12 years. The data base available for study covers large and small companies, markets in North America, Europe, and elsewhere, and a wide variety of products and services, ranging from candy to heavy capital goods to financial services.

By exploring the actual experiences of this vast array of businesses, we believe that we and our co-workers have succeeded in showing important linkages between strategies and results in different market and competitive settings. In this book, we summarize the principal lessons that have been learned from the PIMS research, and from its application since the early 1970s to hundreds of real-life situations. We have also tried to integrate our PIMS-based work with the ideas and research findings of others, including such authorities as Peter Drucker and Michael Porter and the empirical investigations of the Federal Trade Commission's Line of Business research program.

We believe that the general principles of strategy outlined in this book should be included in the basic education of managers in free-enterprise economies. These principles do not provide formulas for resolving specific business issues, any more than the general principles of hydraulics or thermodynamics do for specific engineering projects. But they can provide a foundation for the situation-specific analysis that is always needed to arrive at good decisions. In this way, we believe that our explorations of general relationships between strategy and performance can contribute to greater effectiveness for individual firms and for the economy as a whole.

THE PIMS APPROACH

How can "strategy principles" be discovered? The approach we have used in the PIMS Program has been that of documenting the actual experiences of many businesses, operating in many different kinds of market and competitive settings. For each of these businesses we have collected three kinds of information:

- A description of the *market conditions* in which the business operates. These include such things as the distribution channels used by the SBU, the number of its customers, and their size, and rates of market growth and inflation.
- The business unit's *competitive position* in its marketplace. Measures of competitive position include market share, relative quality, prices and costs relative to competition, and degree of vertical integration relative to competition.
- Measures of the SBU's *financial and operating performance*, on an annual basis, over periods ranging from 2 to 12 years.

By analyzing these kinds of information for a sufficiently large number of business units, we can find common patterns in the relationships among them. To cite a simple example: if we compare businesses that typically sell to their customers in large average transaction amounts (over $1,000) with those that sell in smaller amounts, we find a substantial difference in average profitability. Businesses in the first group have an average pretax rate of return on investment (ROI) of about 21%, while the average ROI of those with smaller average transactions is 27%.

It is not enough, however, to simply observe a difference in the profitability of two groups of businesses. We must also ask whether the difference makes sense. Why should profitability be higher when sales are made in small amounts? In this instance, the reason is fairly obvious: when customers buy big-ticket products, or large quantities of products, they are likely to bargain more aggressively, and to shop around, because the potential savings are worth some effort. For small purchases, buyers are more likely to follow some kind of purchasing routine, such as sticking with the same supplier or selecting a known brand. (Compare your own last purchase of an automobile with your last purchase of batteries.) The impact of purchase amount and other aspects of customer buying patterns on performance are discussed in more detail in Chapter 4.

Our effort to discover and document strategy principles, then, involves both statistical analysis and the application of logic to find differences in business performance that are both significant and sensible. Sometimes the rationale for a principle is derived from economic theory: we investigated the linkage between market share and profitability, for example, because theory led us to expect that economies of scale would influence performance in most situations. In addition to formal economic theory, we have been guided by the judgments and beliefs of the many experienced managers who have participated in the design of The PIMS Program and the work that preceded it in the 1960s at the General Electric Company.

KEY DIFFERENCES BETWEEN PIMS AND PORTFOLIO PLANNING

Many business executives, management consultants, and academics in the field of strategic management view PIMS as a variant of portfolio planning. From this perspective, a PIMS-based appraisal of a business or collection of businesses is an alternative—or sometimes a supplement—to an evaluation in which businesses are classified according to their positions in a portfolio matrix or grid.

Portfolio classification systems come in a variety of shapes and sizes. The simplest one is the Growth-Share matrix popularized by the Boston Consulting Group in the early 1970s.[1] Others include the so-called General Electric/McKinsey Attractiveness–Position matrix and the Competitive Position–Life Cycle classification scheme developed by Arthur D. Little, Inc. While there are important differences among these and other portfolio systems, the same rationale underlies all of them. As summarized by Richard Bettis and William Hall, the basic idea of assigning businesses to portfolio categories is that:

> ". . . the position (or box) that a business occupies within the matrix should determine the strategic mission and *the general characteristics of the strategy for the business.*"[2]

In one form or another, portfolio planning methods are now widely used by corporations, especially by large and diversified ones, in the United States and other industrialized countries. According to a 1980 survey of large American companies by Phillipe Haspeslagh, more than half of them used portfolio planning systems.[3] Over the years, the process of discussing, using, and appraising the portfolio approach has generated a new vocabulary for managers, consultants, and business school students, one that features such now-familiar metaphors as "dogs," "cash cows," and "milking strategies."

The logic of the approach we and our associates have used in assembling and analyzing the PIMS data base is similar to that of the popular portfolio approaches in one basic and important respect. We all take as a common starting point the notion that reasonable financial objectives for a business, and at least some of the general characteristics of the strategy it should adopt, depend on (1) its strategic position, and (2) the characteristics of its marketplace.

There are, however, some vital differences between the PIMS approach and portfolio classification systems. For one thing, portfolio systems attempt to explain business performance in terms of just a few key factors. The Growth-Share matrix, as its name implies, assigns businesses to one of four groups based on only two characteristics: market growth rate and relative market share. All of the many other things that affect profitability are implicitly ignored. In contrast, the PIMS Program was designed, from its inception, to explore *many* possible dimensions of strategy and of the market environment that might influence performance. We have, for instance, shown that investment intensity, product or service quality (relative to that of competitors), labor productivity, and vertical integration—among other strategic factors—have powerful effects on business performance. None of these dimensions of strategy is included in the widely-used portfolio classification systems.

A second big difference between PIMS and portfolio planning systems is that we have assembled and used a *data base* to determine how strategies affect results under different circumstances. This data base includes many different kinds of businesses operating in a wide variety of industries and countries. Only by investigating varied types of situations, we believe, can we or anyone else arrive at meaningful conclusions about competitive strategy. What works in one situation may be disastrous in another. Put another way, all "dogs" should not be treated alike, and neither should all "cash cows."

THE REACTION AGAINST STRATEGIC PLANNING

Portfolio planning, and theoretical approaches to planning more generally, became faddish during the period from the early seventies up to the early eighties. Planning consultants and corporate planning staffs grew rapidly in number, size, and power. Perhaps inevitably, a reaction against this movement has taken place. As Kenneth Andrews put it in a 1984 article:

> As with all enthusiasms that have swept the management community, a back-lash has developed against strategic planning.[4]

The backlash cited by Andrews has led to wholesale reductions in planning staffs, changes in planning procedures, and shifts in the kinds of work done by the consultants who popularized the new view of strategy a decade earlier.[5] "Bashing" portfolio planning has become almost as much of a fad as the approach was in the first place.

Among the criticisms that have been levelled against formalized strategy analysis, one is of particular relevance here. Strategy consultants, it has been claimed, have misled managers by making recommendations that are based on excessively broad generalizations or "principles." Some commentators have gone so far as to suggest that there are no valid generalizations about strategy at all. Michael Lubatkin and Michael Pitts raised this issue in an article comparing what they termed the "policy perspective" with the "PIMS perspective." As they see it, the policy perspective assumes that " . . . no two businesses are exactly alike . . . there can [therefore] be few, if any, specific formulas for achieving competitive advantage.''[6] They go on to suggest that the ''PIMS Perspective'' involves a mechanistic application of formulas to complex management problems, with predictably unhappy consequences.

We should acknowledge that criticisms like these are, to some extent, reactions against the over-enthusiastic and oversimplified claims made by some advocates of PIMS and of other generalized approaches to strategy. When PIMS research results were first reported publicly in the mid–1970s,[7] the whole idea of generalizing about strategy was new. Inevitably, in this first wave of enthusiasm for theories of strategic management, ideas were oversimplified and excessive claims were made. The same cycle of overselling and unrealistic expectations, followed by disillusionment and debunking, occurred a generation earlier when quantitative methods (''operations research'') were first applied extensively to business problems.

Like those who have criticized PIMS and portfolio planning, we reject the notion that there are ''formulas'' for management decision-making or that ''easy wins'' can be had by applying general rules to specific problems. We hope we have avoided any appearance of such an oversimplified approach in this book. We do not claim to have discovered universal and precise ''laws of strategy,'' like those of physics. But, once again, we suggest that there are general relationships that can provide valuable guidance to managers. It is just as much an oversimplification to say that every situation is unique as it is to say that they all fall into a few general categories.

Our view, then, is that there *are* principles that can help managers understand and predict how strategic choices and market conditions will affect business performance. Some of these principles apply to virtually all kinds of businesses, while others apply only to specific types or under certain conditions. None of them constitutes a complete formula or prescription for any individual case because there are always situation-specific factors to consider in addition to the more general ones. The general principles must be calibrated to fit the distinctive features of a particular situation, and elements of the situation that are not covered by any general principle must also be taken into account.

STRATEGY PRINCIPLES: SOME EXAMPLES

To illustrate what we mean by strategy principles, and to give a preview of some of the topics that are explored in subsequent chapters, we summarize here a half-dozen of the most important linkages between strategy and performance.

1. *In the long run, the most important single factor affecting a business unit's performance is the quality of its products and services, relative to those of competitors.* A quality edge boosts performance in two ways:

- In the short run, superior quality yields increased profits via premium prices. As Frank Perdue, the well-known chicken grower, put it: "Customers will go out of their way to buy a superior product, and you can charge them a toll for the trip." Consistent with Perdue's theory, PIMS businesses that ranked in the top third on relative quality sold their products or services, on average, at prices 5–6% higher (relative to competition) than those in the bottom third.
- In the longer term, superior and/or improving relative quality is the most effective way for a business to grow. Quality leads to both market expansion and gains in market share. The resulting growth in volume means that a superior-quality competitor gains scale advantages over rivals. As a result, even when there are short-run costs connected with improving quality, over a period of time these costs are usually offset by scale economies. Evidence of this is the fact that, on average, businesses with superior quality products have costs about equal to those of their leading competitors. As long as their selling prices are not out of line, they continue to grow while still earning superior profit margins.

The linkages between relative quality and business performance are shown in Exhibit 1–1. As the exhibit suggests, businesses usually achieve quality advantages first by innovating in product/service design and later via product improvements. Investments in quality, when successful, lead to gains in volume that provide scale economies.

We should emphasize that the sequence depicted in Exhibit 1–1 represents what happens on average, as reflected in the PIMS data base. Not all efforts to improve quality pay off, and even when they do the added costs may exceed the benefits. In most cases, however, quality strategies do pay off.

While the importance of quality has come to be widely recognized by American and European executives in the 1980s, there has

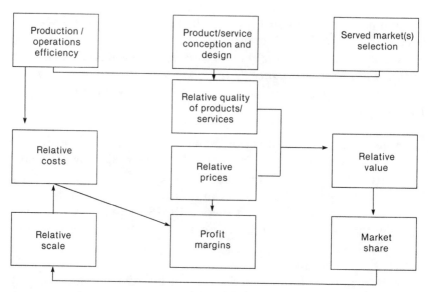

EXHIBIT 1-1
Primary Linkages Among Relative Quality, Market Share, and Profitability

been little real evidence to back up such claims as Philip Crosby's in the title of his best-selling book, *Quality Is Free*. The experience of the businesses in the PIMS data base do support Crosby's generalizations, and also show how quality contributes to growth as well as to profitability. These relationships are examined in greater detail in Chapter 6.

2. *Market share and profitability are strongly related.* As shown in Exhibit 1-2, business units with very large market shares—over 50% of their served markets—enjoy rates of return more than three times greater than small-share SBUs (those that serve under 10% of their markets).

The share-profitability relationship has been questioned by some observers who claim that it is largely spurious.[8] By this they mean that both a strong market position and high ROI are reflections of other factors, notably management skill or luck. It is true that part of the profit premium earned by large-share businesses can be explained in terms of factors that usually accompany a strong competitive position—especially superior relative quality. But when we take quality as well as some 20 other market and strategic factors into account, market share still has a strong positive impact on profitability. Its net effect is about 3 1/2 points of ROI for every 10 points of market share (See Chapter 5 for further discussion).

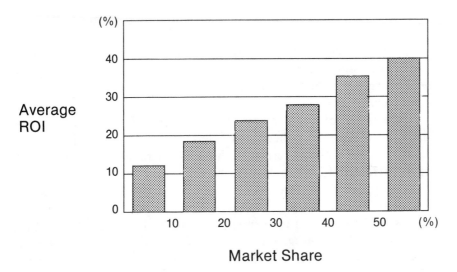

EXHIBIT 1-2
Market Share and ROI

NOTE: Based on 4-year averages of pretax, pre-interest ROI for 2,611 business units in the PIMS data base.

The primary reason for the market share–profitability linkage, apart from the connection with relative quality, is that large-share businesses benefit from scale economies. They simply have lower per-unit costs than their smaller competitors. These cost advantages are typically much smaller than those once claimed by over-enthusiastic proponents of "experience curve pricing strategies," but they are nevertheless substantial and are directly reflected in higher profit margins.

The fact that market share and profitability go together does not mean that every business can or should strive to increase its share! The costs attached to a share-building campaign may be prohibitive, especially if the primary means used is price-cutting. A vivid example of this was the kamikaze attack launched by Yamaha in the early 1980s on Honda, the world market leader in motorcycles. Yamaha's president, Hisao Koike, was determined to overtake Honda and tried to do so by cutting prices, introducing new models, and advertising heavily. The end result was a crushing burden of debt, massive lay-offs, and ultimately Koike's dismissal.

While the costs of gaining share may exceed the payoffs, this is not always the case. Indeed, most of the PIMS businesses that have improved their market-share positions also enjoyed rising profitability! We explore the subject of share-building strategies further in Chapter 9.

3. *High-investment intensity acts as a powerful drag on profitability.* Investment-intensive businesses are those that employ a great deal of capital per dollar of sales, per dollar of value added, or per employee.

Whichever of these measures is used, high investment intensity—in the form of either fixed assets or working capital—usually leads to lower rates of return. Exhibit 1–3 demonstrates the impact of this strategic factor, measured by the ratio of total investment to sales (adjusted for differences in plant capacity utilization). As investment intensity rises, pretax profit margins on sales change only modestly. Because the investment base is rising, ROI falls steadily and sharply. The average rate of return for the most capital-intensive businesses is less than half that earned by the low capital intensity SBUs.

The profit-depressing effect of high capital intensity is particularly important because:

- None of the widely-used portfolio planning systems recognizes the impact of investment intensity on profitability.
- The popular notion of re-industrializing American and Eu-

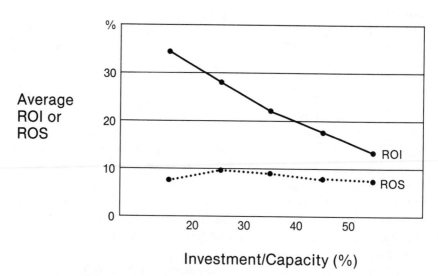

EXHIBIT 1–3
Investment Intensity and Profitability

ropean manufacturing industry involves massive new investments in plant and equipment. Leading companies in such industries as automobiles, steel, and machine tools are attempting to regain their competitiveness through mechanization. Will these efforts drive their rates of return down instead of up?

Managers, of course, do not pursue capital intensity for its own sake. They make decisions or adopt policies, however, that result in increased capital intensity. They add capacity, mechanize production processes, and liberalize credit terms or inventory limits, all in the hope of increasing sales or lowering costs. When these kinds of decisions lead to higher ratios of investment to sales, the explanation sometimes is inaccurate forecasting (anticipated sales gains don't materialize), and sometimes competitive retaliation. Whatever the mechanisms at work, however, the fact is that when capital intensity rises, ROI usually falls.

The fact that high capital intensity tends to depress profitability does not mean that managers should shun new capital investments. Even a large addition to a business unit's investment base need not affect capital intensity adversely, as long as sales and value added grow commensurately. Furthermore, it may be desirable to accept a reduction in the average rate of return on investment as long as the ROI on a particular incremental investment exceeds the applicable cost of capital.

For further discussion of the interplay between investment policy and performance, see Chapter 7.

4. *Many so-called "dog" and "question mark" businesses generate cash, while many "cash cows" are dry.* The guiding principle of the growth-share matrix approach to planning is that cash flows largely depend on market growth and competitive position (your share relative to that of your largest competitor). Thus, SBUs with dominant shares of static or declining markets should be cash generators, while those with small shares of growing markets should use much cash. The simplicity of this alleged principle makes it appealing as a foundation for planning. The problem is that it is often wrong.

Our analyses, and PIMS-based research by others, show that while market growth and relative share *are* linked to cash flows, many other factors also influence this dimension of performance.[9] As a result, forecasts of cash flow based solely on the growth-share matrix are often misleading. Some evidence on this point is shown in Exhibit

1–4: here, we show the percentages of businesses with various growth-share positions that were *net-cash generators*. (Net cash flow equals after-tax income, plus depreciation, plus or minus the net change in a unit's investment base.) More than half of the "question marks," and six out of ten "dogs," were cash generators! Conversely, more than one in four "star" businesses (those with top-ranking market shares in growing markets), and almost as high a proportion of "cash cows," were actually net cash users.

The reason for these deviations from normal cash flow performance is that growth and relative share are just two of a long list of factors that influence cash flows. In fact, cash flow is affected by essentially the same market and strategic factors that determine profitability. These factors are outlined in Chapter 3, and many of them are explored in greater detail in subsequent chapters.

5. *Vertical integration is a profitable strategy for some kinds of businesses, but not for others.* This "general principle" is one of many that reflects a contingent relationship between strategy and performance. Whether increased vertical integration helps or hurts depends on the situation, quite apart from the question of the cost of achieving it.

Exhibit 1–5 shows how ROI varies with vertical integration for SBUs with different market share positions. For small-share businesses, ROI is highest when the degree of vertical integration is low. But for businesses with average or above-average share positions,

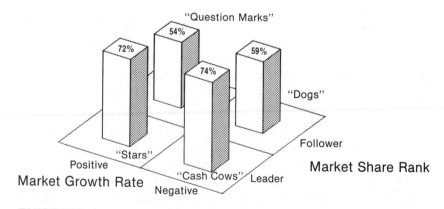

EXHIBIT 1–4
Percent of Businesses Generating Positive Cash Flows, by Growth-Share Matrix Position

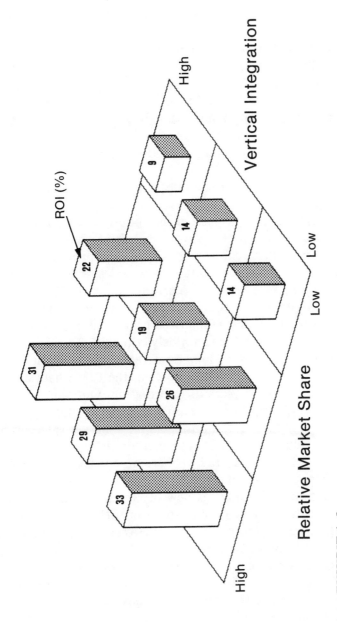

EXHIBIT 1-5
Vertical Integration, Market Position, and Profitability

ROI is highest when vertical integration is either low or high, and lowest in the middle!

The complex linkage between vertical integration and profitability reflects several things. For one, increased vertical integration usually leads to higher capital intensity. This poses major problems for small-share businesses because they may have difficulty in achieving a minimum efficient scale of operations at each of several vertically-linked stages. A small producer of electronic equipment, for example, cannot utilize a high enough volume of components to justify a captive source of microprocessors. Large-share businesses, like IBM and AT&T, can and do produce their own components profitably.

The pros and cons of vertical integration are explored further in Chapter 8.

6. *Most of the strategic factors that boost ROI also contribute to long-term value.* Much of our work with PIMS has been directed toward explaining differences in business unit profitability, measured either in terms of profit margins on sales or ROI. While we have used 4-year average profit figures to minimize the impact of annual ups and downs, we could still be (and have been) accused of aiding and abetting the over-emphasis on short-run results for which American managers have been so widely criticized. To avoid this, we have developed a measure of long-term value enhancement and applied it to the more than 600 businesses in the PIMS data base for which we have at least 7 years of information. Our value enhancement measure rates performance on the basis of discounted cash flows plus the net change in a business unit's market value, using a stock market valuation model. (The measure is explained in detail in Chapter 11.) Using this kind of measure enables us to give due credit to businesses that, in order to strengthen their strategic positions, invested in such things as new products or quality improvement, often at the expense of short-term profits.

To what extent is there a conflict between maximizing current profitability and building long-term value? Exhibit 1-6 shows how the two measures are related. For each business, we calculated average ROI over a 5-year planning horizon (using 2 earlier years as a base period). Then, we constructed an index of value enhancement that includes both discounted cash flows for 5 years and the (discounted) market value of the business at the end of the period. Our index is defined as the ratio of total value (DCF plus future market value) to an SBU's beginning market value.

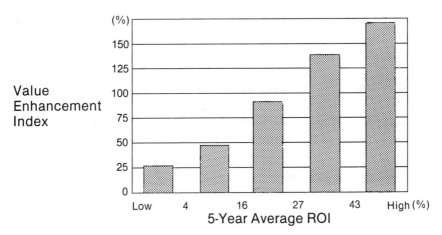

EXHIBIT 1-6
High ROI and Long-Term "Value Enhancement" Usually Go Together

NOTE: For an explanation of the Value Enhancement Index, see accompanying text. Based on data for 623 businesses for which at least 7 consecutive years of information was available.

As Exhibit 1-6 shows, businesses with high ROIs usually also performed well on the long-term value enhancement index. Consistent with this, more detailed analysis shows that most of the strategic and market factors that enhance ROI also tend to increase long-term value. Businesses with strong initial competitive positions, for example, generally scored well on long-term value. So did businesses with high employee productivity, and superior relative quality, and those with cost advantages relative to competitors.

There are some trade-offs between current profitability and long-term value enhancement. Not surprisingly, the most visible trade-offs have to do with levels of spending on marketing and R&D, and with capacity expansion. In each of these areas, the SBUs that performed best over the long term were more aggressive than similar businesses that scored lower on our value enhancement index. The differences between good and poor long-term performers are outlined in greater detail in Chapter 11.

OVERVIEW OF THE BOOK

The six strategy principles summarized in the preceding section illustrate the approach that we and our co-workers have followed in the research on which this book is based. The basic concepts are outlined in more detail in Chapter 2, where we define what we mean by strategy and by performance. The methods used to collect and analyze the PIMS data are discussed in Chapter 3, and additional technical details are provided in Appendices A and B.

The principal strategic factors that influence business performance are discussed in Chapters 4–12.

Chapter 4, "Picking Profitable Markets," shows how profitability is affected by market characteristics such as stage of the life cycle, growth rate, and inflation. Competitive position and relative product quality are explored in Chapters 5 and 6. In these chapters we show how businesses attain strong market positions and how some lose them, and we outline a systematic approach to quality measurement and improvement.

The influence of capital intensity on competition and profitability is discussed in Chapter 7, while Chapter 8 presents the pros and cons of vertical integration.

Strategic options for market leaders and followers are compared in Chapter 9. Chapter 10 shows how these options change as a market evolves over time.

Chapter 11 presents our version of a long-term value enhancement performance measure and shows how it is related to market conditions and strategic choices. In Chapter 12, we explore issues involved in formulating integrated strategies for clusters of related businesses.

Linking Strategies
to Performance

In Chapter 1 we summarized a few of the general strategy principles that have been documented by investigations of the PIMS data base. How can managers apply these general kinds of relationships to specific management problems? Consider two real-life situations:

- The Chief Executive of a large, diversified corporation based in Europe was considering a proposal to acquire a division of an American company. The acquisition involved a combination of the second and fourth-ranked businesses, on a worldwide basis, in a product category with a strong, aggressive market leader. The investment could only be justified if the profitability of the new, combined unit were substantially higher than that of the two existing operations. What was a reasonable profit objective for the post-acquisition business? The company's planners used the PIMS data base and models to simulate the performance of the combined business unit, and this analysis was a key piece of evidence in the final decision to go ahead.
- Corporate management in a leading health-care products company use PIMS to calibrate the plans submitted to them by product division general managers. Top managers review the actual performance of other businesses in the data base *most similar* to each of the company's divisions—their "look-

17

alikes.'' They report that this approach gives them a better feel for the realism of division forecasts.

These examples illustrate the kinds of questions to which systematic research on strategy can provide useful partial answers. In the first, the basic issue is: given the characteristics of a business and its market environment (real or hypothetical), what is a reasonable expectation for its performance? In the second example, the problem is one of estimating how proposed changes in strategy are likely to affect results. These are just two of the kinds of management situations in which PIMS-based analyses have proved to be useful. More generally, the PIMS data base can provide insights whenever managers need to estimate the results (performance) that can be expected from a given set of policies (strategy) in a given situation.

Up to this point, we have used the terms "strategy" and "performance" without defining them. In this chapter, we outline just what is included, and what isn't, in the PIMS concept of strategy. We also explain how we have measured performance.

What Is "Strategy?"

"Strategy" has been a very popular term since the mid–1970s. Strategic planning departments, strategy consultants, and books and seminars on strategy have all flourished. The word itself has been used to mean so many things that it has become virtually a synonym for "management." Thousands of words have been written about how strategy should be defined. To some, for example, a strategy includes a statement of objectives. Others hold that objectives are separate, and strategy is the means of attaining them.[1]

We shall avoid the temptation to join in the debate about the proper definition of strategy. (Indeed, we would have preferred not to use the term at all. This, however, would have led to some awkward terminology.) For purposes of this book, we use strategy to mean:

> The policies and key decisions adopted by management that have *major* impacts on financial performance. These policies and decisions usually involve significant resource commitments and are not easily reversible.

In a one-business manufacturing company, for example, strategic policies and decisions include, among others, those dealing with the product line, sourcing of products, the extent of factory mechanization, distribution channels employed, basic pricing approaches, and the extent of vertical integration. Each of these functional policies has, at least potentially, a significant impact on the firm's competitive position, on profit margins, and on capital requirements. Moreover, the various functional policies should be developed as parts of a consistent, coherent overall pattern.

In a diversified company that operates in several or many different businesses, there is a second level of strategic issues. Not only must corporate management be concerned with the functional policies of each business unit, but also with the issue of which business to emphasize, add, or drop. We can, therefore, distinguish between *business unit strategy* (how to compete in a given business) and *corporate strategy*, which involves questions of resource allocation *among* businesses as well as the design of a portfolio of SBUs that reinforce each other.

The organization structures of most large companies reflect the need for planning and performance measurement at both the business unit level and that of the corporation as a whole. Beginning in the 1920s, as documented by historian Alfred Chandler, companies like General Motors, Du Pont, and General Electric began adopting the product division form of organization.[2] The general manager of each product division in such a company is responsible for developing his or her own strategy (subject to general corporate policy limits) and each is held responsible for divisional performance.

More recently, as part of the move to strategic management in the 1970s, the traditional product division structures of many leading corporations have been modified. For purposes of strategy formulation, strategic business units (SBUs) have been defined in ways that may or may not match existing product division boundaries.[3] Usually, SBUs are subdivisions of traditional product divisions, which in large companies usually include several distinct product lines, types of customers, or geographic markets. For example, in the early 1970s the Norton Company adopted a new strategic planning system organized in terms of SBUs.[4] Within Norton's extensive abrasives operations, separate SBUs were defined for U.S. Coated Abrasives, U.S. Bonded Abrasives, European Coated Abrasives, and so on. As explained by Robert Cushman, Norton's chairman at the time, the idea was to do a better job of strategy formulation by doing it separately for units with very different competitive positions, market conditions, and profitability records. In addition, Norton's corporate management could allocate resources among the SBUs more effectively by comparing them in a common "portfolio" framework.

During the past 15 years many other companies have adopted strategic business units as their building blocks for planning. All of these systems are designed to facilitate the process of formulating strategies and, later, measuring results for business units that differ in terms of markets, competitors, production/operations systems, and other factors.

In this book, we focus mainly on linkages between strategy and performance at the business unit or SBU level. Most of the information in the PIMS data base is defined in terms of business units. Thus, much of what we have to say about strategy is concerned with policies or courses of action that might be pursued by managers responsible either for a business unit within a corporation or for a single-business company.

The experience documented in the PIMS data base is also relevant for corporate-level strategies. We can, for example, determine the relative profit potentials of many different business units in a corporate portfolio, based on their current competitive positions and anticipated future changes in such factors as market size, product quality, and new product introduction. This kind of assessment can clearly be useful in making decisions about resource allocation. Similarly, diagnosis of a business's inherent profit potential, based on PIMS experience, can provide guidance for decisions about acquisitions or divestitures. Examples of the application of PIMS to portfolio-level strategy assessment are given in Chapter 12.

MAJOR DIMENSIONS OF STRATEGY

We have defined strategy, at either the business level or the corporate level, as including all the policies and key decisions that significantly affect performance. Having done so, we acknowledge that in this book we do not cover everything that might fit into the definition. The concept underlying the PIMS Program, from its inception, was one of investigating as many dimensions of strategy as possible, based on two criteria: *general relevance* across industries, and *measurability*.

Because the companies participating in PIMS are drawn from many different industries, we have made no effort to explore strategy issues that are unique to a single industry. For example, the deregulation of the airline industry in the United States has created new options for carriers to choose the cities they serve. Whether and how to respond to these new possibilities has clearly been an important strategic question for the airlines, as demonstrated by Frontier Airlines' unfortunate experience in the mid-1980s. We have not investigated this or any of the many other industry-specific aspects of strategy. Instead, we have focussed on strategic "common denominators." The major strategy dimensions we have explored are listed in Exhibit 2-1.

Our treatment of strategy is also confined to dimensions that can be measured in reasonably clear terms. Thus, for example, we have explored how performance is related to a business unit's degree of vertical integration (see Chapter 8). While there is lively debate on just how vertical integration should be measured, there is general agreement that businesses do vary in terms of their degree of integration and that a decision to increase or reduce the extent of integration is usually an important one. At least in principle, then, vertical integration can be measured. In contrast, some other elements of strategies cannot readily be measured, or perhaps measured at all. There has been much discussion, for example, of the pervasive influence of corporate cultures on success or failure.[5] No doubt companies differ in terms of their cultures, and such differences unquestionably affect performance. But we know of no way to measure the key policies, management processes, or personality factors that shape corporate cultures. Consequently, we have made no effort to explore this area, or others that would be equally difficult to quantify or even classify.

EXHIBIT 2-1
Some Major Dimensions of Business Strategy

- Product/Service Policies
  - Quality of Products/Services
  - Relative Rate of New Product Introduction
- Pricing Policies
- Marketing Programs
  - Sales Force
  - Advertising
  - Sales Promotion
- Investment Strategy
  - Mechanization/Automation of Operations
  - Capacity Additions
  - Inventory Levels
- Work Force Productivity
- Vertical Integration
- Research & Development

COMPETITIVE POSITION

When start-up plans are developed for a new business, there is usually considerable room for choice about all of the dimensions of strategy shown in Exhibit 2-1. All of them are "up for grabs," at least within limits. The choices actually available are constrained by the technologies that are practical in a given kind of business, by capital or human resources available or, possibly, by overall corporate policy constraints.

In an established business, the range of strategic choice available to management is typically much more limited. The established business, unlike a new one, must tailor its strategy for the future to its current competitive position, which in turn reflects the results of past strategies.

In appraising a business unit's competitive position, management must consider where it stands, relative to its competitors, on all of the dimensions listed in Exhibit 2-1.

Each of the factors listed has a significant impact on performance. Moreover, they are all interrelated. For example, it is seldom possible to charge premium prices for inferior-quality products or services. Similarly, work force productivity is usually linked to mechanization, and the benefits of a program of productivity improvement must be weighed against the penalty of the increased investment required to achieve it.

A key dimension of competitive position, in addition to those already mentioned, is a business's market share. Market share can be measured either as a fraction of the overall market in which a business participates, or relative to one or a few leading competitors. Both concepts are important—they are indicators of a unit's size relative to rivals, of its competitive strength or weakness, and of its bargaining power vis-à-vis suppliers and customers.

Market share, as a measure of competitive position and as a strategic objective, plays a prominent role in all of the portfolio planning systems that so many U.S. and European corporations have adopted in recent years. In some popular discussions of strategic management, increasing market share is treated as if it were a strategy in and of itself. In our view, this usage is misleading. Achieving any particular level of market share, or simply building it up as much as possible, is not a strategy. These can certainly be, and often are, central objectives for a strategy. After the fact, the change in market share accomplished in a given time period is also an important measure of results.

Competitive position interacts with strategy in determining business performance in two important ways:

- First, the strategy options available to a business depend on its "going-in" position. A program of extensive product innovation along with a policy of premium pricing, that would produce outstanding results for a market leader, might make no sense for a small-share competitor.
- Second, performance in a given time period is heavily influenced by beginning competitive position as well as by current strategy moves. This implies that, in order to develop measures of how performance relates to strategy, we must disentangle the effects of beginning position and changes made during a given time period.

MATCHING STRATEGY TO THE MARKET

The influence of market and industry factors on business performance is widely recognized. When financial analysts evaluate a company's earnings prospects, for example, they routinely explore such topics as expected market growth, rates of inflation, and labor relations. All of these things, along with others that are more industry-specific, are known to affect the profitability of all businesses that participate in a market.

The connections between market/industry characteristics and profits have also been explored extensively by economists. Within the field of industrial organization, numerous studies have been made to determine how these situational factors affect firms' profits. These studies usually focus on average profit rates for entire industries, rather than for individual competitors, because until recently only industry-level data have been readily available to researchers. (Information provided by corporations' annual reports is not very useful for this kind of research because company financial data usually reflect results in a combination of several different markets and industries.)

The Federal Trade Commission's "Line of Business" (LB) research program, established in 1974, has collected financial data for subdivisions of several hundred large U.S.-based corporations. The objective of the LB Program, which was vigorously opposed by many of the companies it covered, was precisely that of investigating, in more detail than had previously been possible, how profitability is affected by industry/market characteristics such as growth, seller concentration, and competition from imports. By late 1985 numerous studies based on the LB Research Program had been published.[6] These studies demonstrate clearly that profitability is indeed systematically related to variations in market situations. In subsequent chapters we cite some of the findings of the LB Program and, where possible, compare them with the patterns revealed by PIMS-based research.

The market/industry factors that PIMS researchers have found to have the greatest influence on business performance are shown in Exhibit 2–2. As in the case of competitive position, these factors not only affect profitability and growth directly, but they also interact with competitive position and current strategy. A strategy that produces good results in a rapidly growing market, for instance, might be very inappropriate in a mature, slowly growing one.

MEASURING PERFORMANCE

Linking strategy to business performance obviously requires that we specify how to measure performance. The simple answer, implied by the phrase "bottom line," is that managers try to maximize profits. In line with common management practice, we use two measures of profitability here: profits as a percentage of sales (ROS) and profits as a percentage of investment (ROI). For some purposes we also use a business unit's net cash flow (cash generated minus cash used) as a supplementary performance measure. An explanation of how

---

EXHIBIT 2–2
Market/Industry Factors that Influence Performance

• Stage of Market Evolution and Growth Rate	• Supplier Concentration
• Selling Price Inflation	• Typical Customer Purchase Amount and Importance
• Degree of Product/Service Standardization	• Degree of Employee Unionization
	• Extent of Industry Exports and Imports

business-level ROS, ROI, and cash flow are defined in accounting terms is given in Chapter 3.

Return on investment, or ROI, is clearly superior to ROS as a measure of business performance because it relates results to the resources used in achieving them. Presumably for this reason, surveys of the practices of diversified companies have shown that the overwhelming majority use some variant of ROI in measuring divisional performance.[7] We have also used ROS both because it is a familiar index of profitability and because it sheds additional light on how strategies impact on results. As the widely used "DuPont Formula" shows, ROI depends on two key factors—profit margin (ROS) and investment turnover. Using both ROS and ROI allows us to distinguish between these two components.

However it is measured, the profitability of a business unit can vary enormously from year to year, either because of economic conditions or because of management tactics and accounting practices aimed at allowing managers to "make their numbers." For purposes of evaluating strategy options, these year-to-year fluctuations are irrelevant. The results of a strategic choice are usually apparent only over a period of several years, and the appropriate measure of its effects is, therefore, *average* profitability during a multi-year period. In most of what follows, we use measures of average ROS and ROI for 4-year periods as a basis for comparing alternative strategies.

Even when profitability is computed or estimated over a period of several years, however, it is not a complete measure of business performance. Strategies that maximize current profits—even when "current" is stretched to mean four years—may weaken or destroy a business's longer-term viability. During the 1980s, American management and investors have been widely criticized for overemphasizing short-term results at the expense of long-term competitive strength.[8] Presumably in response to such criticisms, many high-level corporate executives have adopted the position that their task is to maximize, or at least improve, "shareholder value" or "shareholder wealth." This is interpreted to mean a combination of current profitability and appreciation in common stock value, appropriately balanced in those cases where tradeoffs between the two arise.

It is certainly true that it takes several years to carry out many kinds of strategic change and for the results to become apparent. In light of this, an ideal measure of business performance would take into account both the short-term effects of a strategy and its eventual impact on the market value of shareholders' equity. Given enough time, it is easy enough to do this for a company as a whole, at least after the fact. The "shareholder wealth" created in a given time period is simply the stream of dividends received by the shareholders plus or minus the change in the market value of the stock. *Forecasting* the change in shareholder wealth that a company can be expected to create is, naturally, much more difficult. But at least it is possible to define clearly what needs to be forecast.

At the level of a business unit within a company, defining an appropriate measure of "value creation" is more difficult. Business units as such do not pay dividends, nor do they issue common stock and sell it in the open market. Nevertheless it is possible to apply the same logic to business units as to entire corporations in measuring past performance, or estimating future performance. This approach, termed "value-based planning," has been advocated in recent years by several consulting firms, and is now widely used in industry.

What value-based planning means, when applied to individual business units, is that the effects of a proposed strategy should be measured in terms of two components:

- The cash flows that it is expected to generate over a period of time. Because these cash flows occur over a period of several years, they must be discounted at appropriate rates.
- The change in the business unit's market value between the beginning and the end of the planning period. Since there is no actual market value for a business unit's equity, an imputed value must be estimated, using a valuation model derived from an analysis of the factors that appear to affect companies' stock prices.

Our method of estimating "value creation" for business units is explained in Chapter 11, where we show how some of the major dimensions of strategy are linked to long-term performance.

PERFORMANCE—COMPARED TO WHAT?

Regardless of how performance is defined, actual results must be judged in relation to some kind of standard. Three widely-used standards are a company's or business unit's own past experience, the performance of others in the same industry, and the cost of capital.

The logic of setting goals and assessing actual results on the basis of one's own past record is obvious. This leads to the near-universal format of "This Year vs. Last Year" in periodic internal accounting reports. It also leads to the widespread practice of basing management incentive compensation systems on improvements in earnings from year to year. But the weaknesses in the approach are obvious, too: for one, if past performance has been extremely poor, even a big improvement may not be any cause for rejoicing. Conversely, if past performance has for some reason been artificially high, it may be unrealistic to set goals based on matching or exceeding it. Thus, it is an intuitive notion that there is some kind of norm with which ROS, ROI, or any other measure should be compared.

One appealing kind of performance norm is the average experience of companies in one's own industry. The rationale for this, obviously, is that companies in the same industry use similar technologies, similar distribution methods, and so on. Consequently, what is outstanding performance in one industry may be just so-so, or even terrible, by the standards of another industry. For example, in 1984 Deere & Company earned 5.7% on shareholders' equity. Its major competitors in the agricultural equipment business—Allis Chalmers, International Harvester, and Massey-Ferguson—all reported losses, and the last two had negative equity positions.[9] In light of this, should Deere's 1984 performance be judged as excellent? It certainly would not have been in most other industries, given that the overall 1984 average ROE for large U.S. corporations was 13.4 percent.

There is one standard of financial performance that applies to all industries—the cost of capital. Even if a company's profitability is well above the average level of its industry, it is inadequate if it is lower than the cost it must pay for debt and equity capital resources. The concept of "shareholder value," mentioned earlier, is based on exactly this point. When a firm makes investments that yield returns below the cost of capital, the result is a *reduction* in shareholder value. Value is reduced via a decline in the market value of a company's stock, relative to its book value.

THE PIMS COMPETITIVE STRATEGY PARADIGM

In this chapter we have suggested that business performance depends on three major kinds of factors: the characteristics of the market in which a business competes, the business's competitive position in that marketplace, and the strategy it pursues. The linkages among these factors are summarized in Exhibit 2-3, in what we will call "The PIMS Competitive Strategy Paradigm." The arrows in the diagram are meant to indicate that each of the three classes of performance influences has a direct impact on results, and each interacts with the others. Thus, in the short term, strategy is constrained by competitive position and by market structure conditions. Over time, competitive position is shaped by past strategies and by performances, and each of these contributes to changes in market structure.

We do not claim that the PIMS Competitive Strategy Paradigm includes *everything* that affects business performance. Profitability, growth, and other dimensions of performance are also affected by such things as inventory valuation methods (e.g., FIFO vs. LIFO) and by conditions specific to a particular industry or company—such as regulatory changes, swings in currency exchange rates, or labor disputes. But the general, measurable factors included in Exhibit 2-3 *do* explain most of the variations in performance among business units, once year-to-year fluctuations are averaged out. (For a discussion of this point in statistical terms, see Chapter 3.)

The PIMS Competitive Strategy Paradigm incorporates ideas from several important research traditions and viewpoints:

- The notion that differences in market structure strongly influence profitability has been explored in depth by scholars in

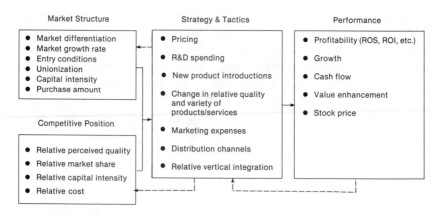

EXHIBIT 2-3
The PIMS Competitive Strategy Paradigm
NOTE: Unit of analysis = business unit and its served market.

industrial organization economics. As noted earlier, these economists traditionally have focused on explaining differences in the average profitability of industries rather than individual business units. But their studies nevertheless demonstrate the importance of such factors as market growth and barriers to entry.

- Authorities in the field of Business Policy, especially those at the Harvard Business School, have developed and refined the concept of competitive strategy, emphasizing the idea that what matters most is an enterprise's position and policies relative to those of competitors.
- Managers and planning specialists at the General Electric Company developed methods of measuring competitive position and performance that would allow comparisons among diverse product divisions. They also originated the concepts of a business unit and a served market, which are the basic building blocks of strategic analysis in PIMS and elsewhere.

Combining all of these ideas leads to a complex paradigm or model of competitive strategy. The "PIMS Principles" are, consequently, not simple ones. But, we believe, they capture the interactions of market structure, strategy, and performance more realistically than simplistic prescriptions could do.

Chapter 3 _____

Learning from Experience: The PIMS Approach

In their book *A Passion for Excellence*[1] Thomas Peters and Nancy Austin refer to PIMS as "the most extensive strategic information data base in the world." We can go one step further: PIMS is unique. It is the *only* strategic data base in the world that covers a wide variety of industries, products, and markets.

In this chapter we describe briefly the kinds of businesses that are included in the PIMS data base, and our measures of competitive position, strategy, market/industry conditions, and performance. We also give an overview of the principal linkages between strategic factors and performance, as a background for the in-depth discussion that is provided in later chapters of this book. A more detailed description of the data base is provided in Appendix A, while a more technical discussion of the statistical methods and results is contained in Appendix B.

BACKGROUND OF THE PIMS PROGRAM

The PIMS Program of research on "market strategy" began in 1972. Initially it took the form of an exploratory investigation, organized by the Marketing Science Institute, a research institute affiliated with the Harvard Business School. The success of the General Electric Company in using the approach for strategic planning helped persuade 36 other companies to join the program. They contributed information and financial support, and are our original group.

GE's internal efforts to analyze the company's own strategic experience commenced in the 1960s.[2] By the early 1970s this work, under the direction of Sidney Schoeffler, had produced a statistical model known as "PROM" (for Profit-Optimizing Model). GE's corporate management and staff used PROM as a means of testing the reasonableness of plans submitted by the general managers of operating units. While this system seemed to provide useful inputs to planning, some of GE's managers wondered if the strategy-performance relationships incorporated into the PROM model were valid only in the company's existing kinds of businesses. Hence the idea of "spinning off" the activity and inviting other companies to join in.

The PIMS Program was an instant success. Following the original pilot project, by late 1972 it had grown to include 57 companies and 620 business units.[3] In 1975 Schoeffler founded a separate organization, the Strategic Planning Institute (SPI), to carry out PIMS research and, later, to conduct educational programs and provide advisory services to the companies involved in the program. SPI was, and continues to be, a non-profit institute governed by representatives of its member companies. In the early 1980s, growing activity in Europe prompted SPI to establish a branch office in London and the formation of a Scandinavian joint venture, PIMS AB, with the Indevo consulting group.

Over the years more than 450 companies have participated in the PIMS program for varying periods of time. Some have been involved continuously from the outset, while others have found PIMS useful primarily as a vehicle for the kinds of major strategy reviews that are undertaken infrequently, usually in connection with a change in top management.

BUSINESS UNITS AND SERVED MARKETS

Two concepts are basic to the architecture of the PIMS data base: the *business unit* and its *served market*.

As noted in Chapter 2, an important dimension of all the so-called portfolio planning systems that have been widely adopted since the early 1970s is the use of planning units that are defined in terms of strategic needs and opportunities. These units, variously termed

Strategic Business Units, Strategic Business Segments, Product/Market Units, or Planning/Control Units, are typically subdivisions of the traditional product divisions that make up most large corporations. In the PIMS Program we adopted a definition essentially the same as that used by General Electric: A business unit, according to the PIMS definition, is a division, product line, or other profit center of a company that:

- produces and markets a well-defined set of related products and/or services;
- serves a clearly defined set of customers, in a reasonably self-contained geographic area; and
- competes with a well-defined set of competitors.

The reasoning behind this definition is that it represents the *smallest* subdivision of a company for which it would be sensible to develop a distinct, separate strategy. An example, mentioned in Chapter 2, is the Norton Company's treatment of coated abrasives and bonded abrasives as separate units.[4] Norton executives recognized that the two product lines were bought to a considerable extent by different customers and for different applications. Moreover, Norton's strongest competitor in coated abrasives, 3M, did not participate in the bonded market at all. Consequently, the strategic issues that were important for the two product lines differed, even though they were produced from the same raw materials and sold by the same field sales force. For similar reasons, Norton also treated its coated abrasives operations in the U.S. and Europe as two distinct business units.

When we say that each business unit in a company should have its own distinct, separate strategy, we do not mean to imply corporate anarchy. The strategies of related businesses should—indeed, must—be coordinated. If they are not, duplication of effort, inconsistent policies and parochialism can seriously damage a company's overall competitive effectiveness. According to some observers, in the early 1980s the 3M Company and Hewlett-Packard, both companies with long-standing traditions of decentralized management, suffered from lack of strategic coordination among some of their operating units.[5] Thus, it is perhaps more accurate to say that a business unit should have one distinct but *partial* strategy within a broader framework than it is to suggest complete strategic independence.

Closely related to the question of how to define a business unit is that of how to define its served market. With few exceptions, businesses don't offer literally every product or service that they conceivably could, or sell to all of the customers that they could. Instead, they limit their operations to some portion of a broader "total market." The concept of the served market is depicted in Exhibit 3–1.

The served market is a central concept in all of our analysis because:

- A business unit's *market share* is measured in relation to its served market.
- Market *growth rates* are measured or estimated for each unit's served market.
- The identity and market shares of leading *competitors* are determined by the scope of the served market.
- Assessments of the *relative quality* of a business unit's products and services are made in relation to competitors in the served market.

By defining competitive position and market characteristics in terms of served markets we are, in effect, asking the management of each business: "Where do you actually compete?" Where a business chooses to compete is a major strategic decision in itself—some would say it's the most important decision of all.

Adopting too narrow a market definition can make a business vulnerable. Many American companies, for example, have traditionally limited their operations—and their thinking—almost en-

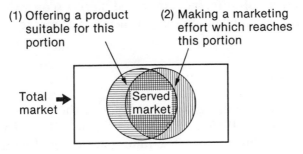

EXHIBIT 3–1
The "Served Market" Concept

tirely to the domestic U.S. market. This provincialism left open market opportunities in other countries and enabled Japanese and other producers to achieve competitive parity or superiority. By the mid-1980s most managers have come to recognize that many markets (such as cameras and pharmaceuticals) are inherently global. The relevant measure of market position in such cases is "share of worldwide sales" or perhaps "share of sales in industrialized countries."

Just as it may be misleading to define a served market too narrowly, it may also be wrong to define it too broadly. For example, according to some observers, in the early 1980s General Electric approached the factory automation business in an unrealistic and, eventually, painfully unsuccessful way. GE defined the business so as to include a wide variety of products and services, such as robots, computer-aided design (CAD) equipment, machine tools, and numerical controls, only some of which it manufactured. Conceiving all of these as parts of integrated automation systems, the business unit's management promoted them as such and even offered to guarantee the *overall* performance of the systems they installed. By late 1983, the business had run into serious problems. The factory automation group was disbanded in early 1985 and its head resigned a few months later; cumulative losses for the operation at the time were estimated at $120 million.[6] The failure of the program was no doubt due to a combination of factors. But it seems reasonable to attribute it, in part at least, to an excessively broad way of conceiving and defining the business and its market.

The PIMS data base includes some information on the ways in which SBUs' served markets have been defined. Specifically, each SBU reports whether its product line, types of customers, number of customers, and range of customer sizes were narrower, broader, or about the same as those of major competitors. Apart from these limited measures of differences in served market scope, we must accept the business units' definitions of their served markets as givens.

THE PIMS DATA BASE

The PIMS data base has grown steadily over the years since it was first set up. In mid-1986 it included data (for at least 4 years) for more than 2,600 businesses.[7] The time spans covered by this information range from the early 1970s up to the mid-1980s, including periods of both recession and expansion.

For each business unit, the financial data are compiled from accounting records; in some cases, allocations or other adjustments are required to derive estimates of costs or assets so that each unit can be treated as if it were separate from other components of its parent company. Measures or estimates of the size of a business unit's served market, its historical growth rate, competitors' sales, and other competitive data are supplied by the unit's general manager, marketing executives, and appropriate staff specialists.

Many different industries, products, markets, and geographic regions are represented in the PIMS data base. As shown in Exhibit 3-2, more than 90% of the business units are engaged in manufacturing. About a third of these produce consumer products, while 20% make capital goods and the remainder are suppliers of raw or semi-finished materials, components, or industrial/commercial supplies. Service and retail/wholesale distribution businesses account for less than 10% of the total, which nevertheless represents a reasonably large sample (about 200) of these types of businesses. Exhibit 3-3 shows the composition of the data base by geographic location. About two-thirds of the businesses market their products/services nationally in the United States and/or Canada, while 16% serve regional markets in North America. European businesses are also well represented, with about 200 each in the United Kingdom and other Western European countries.

Established businesses by industry category (1985)

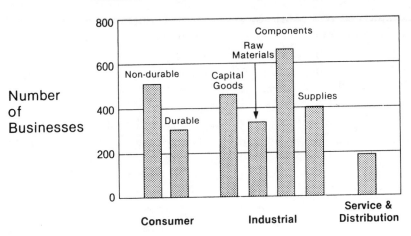

EXHIBIT 3-2
Distribution of the PIMS Data Base by Business Type

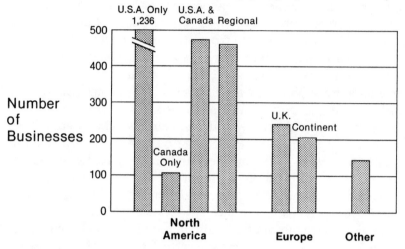

EXHIBIT 3-3
Distribution of the PIMS Data Base by Market Location

Additional information on the types of businesses represented in the data base is given in Appendix A.

MEASURES OF PERFORMANCE

As noted in Chapter 2, we use two conventional measures of a business unit's current profitability: net pre-tax operating profit as a per cent of sales (ROS) and as a per cent of investment (ROI). Exhibit 3-4 shows how these two measures of profitability are constructed and how they are related to other key financial concepts. The numbers in the exhibit are average values for the entire PIMS data base, all expressed as percentages of net sales.

Our definition of investment, as shown in the exhibit, is the book value of an SBU's assets minus its current liabilities. At the corporate level, this is equivalent to equity plus long-term debt—the "permanent capital" invested in the business. Net profit is calculated prior to taxes and interest charges. Thus, our measure of ROI represents an SBU's pretax rate of return on total investment, both debt and equity.

The businesses in the PIMS data base vary tremendously in terms of profitability. Pretax ROI, averaged over 4-year periods, ranges

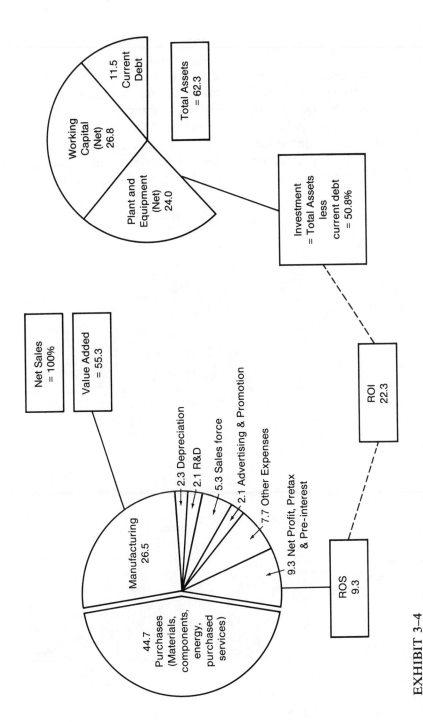

EXHIBIT 3–4
Basic Financial Components of Business Performance Measures
(Numbers Shown Are Averages for PIMS Data Base)

37

from -25% to $+80\%$, while ROS ranged from -25% to $+30\%$. These huge differences in performance reflect the equally big differences in competitive positions and market environments that exist even among SBUs in a given corporation. Exhibit 3–5 shows the distributions of ROI and ROS for the PIMS businesses.

An issue that arises in computing net profit at the business unit level is that of allocating expenses (and assets) that are shared by two or more units, such as corporate administrative expenses, central R&D expenses, and the costs of pooled sales forces or distribution

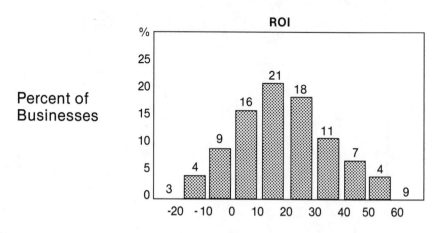

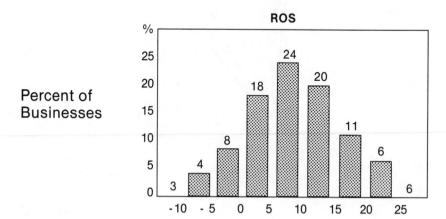

EXHIBIT 3–5
Distributions of ROI and ROS
(4-Year Averages)

facilities. Most companies allocate part or all of these kinds of costs to business units, but methods of allocation vary. Some critics of the FTC's Line of Business Program have claimed that differences in accounting procedures—including those used to allocate shared costs—make comparisons of profitability for subdivisions of companies meaningless.[8] The same accounting issues apply to PIMS data.

When we compare SBUs in terms of profitability, differences in companies' accounting systems undoubtedly do have some impact. We do not believe, however, that these *accounting* differences are so great as to distort our results significantly. For one thing, as shown in Exhibit 3-4, "other expenses" (which includes allocated costs) represent on average only 7.7% of sales. Our discussions with representatives of the companies that have supplied data to PIMS suggest that the bulk of the "other expense" figure represents costs at the SBU level, not allocated corporate costs. Moreover, there is no reason to suppose that differences in cost allocation practices are systematically related to the strategic factors we are exploring. For example, why should businesses with large market shares have lower allocated corporate expense charges than those with small market shares? As long as the methods used to allocate costs don't vary *systematically* with the profit influences we're studying, the fact that practices differ from company to company will not affect our conclusions.

A final point about accounting allocations: a study by William Long of the FTC's Line of Business data showed that using different methods to allocate joint costs had very little effect on overall patterns of profitability for the "lines of business" studied by the FTC.[9]

Our final measure of current performance is a business unit's net cash flow as a per cent of investment. Net cash flow is calculated by adding depreciation expense to after-tax profit and subtracting the change in the unit's total investment.

Both ROS and ROI are measures of current performance. As noted in Chapter 2, we use a different measure—Value Enhancement—to assess long-term performance. This approach is introduced in Chapter 11.

MEASURES OF COMPETITIVE POSITION AND STRATEGY

Economic theory and business experience suggest that performance depends on all of a business unit's policies and programs, not just those in one or two areas. Procter and Gamble may be best known for its prowess in marketing, for example, but the company's managers also recognize the importance of efficient manufacturing and pay careful attention to it. Similarly, in the 1980s some leading companies in the computer industry—best known for their technological capabilities—have discovered the need for effective marketing.[10] As these examples suggest, linking performance to strategy requires that we take into account as many dimensions of strategy as possible.

The primary measures of competitive position and strategy used in analyzing the PIMS businesses are listed in Exhibit 3-6. These measures correspond to the dimensions of strategy outlined in Exhibit 2-1.

Some of our measures of strategy are derived from an SBU's financial statements, as shown in Exhibit 3-4. For example, ratios of research & development and of marketing expenses to sales are used as indicators of an SBU's strategies regarding innovation and marketing. Ideally, we should compare what a business spends in each of these areas with the spending levels of its competitors. In fact, we attempted to do this but found that reliable estimates of competitive spending were generally not available.

Measures of several key strategic factors are based on management estimates or judgments about an SBU's position relative to its principal competitors. (As noted earlier, "principal competitors" are the largest that compete in the same served market.) In many instances, these judgmental assessments are based on hard data from industry association surveys or marketing research studies. For example, producers of food or personal care products would use data from commercial research firms such as A.C. Nielsen or SAMI to get measures of market size and market shares in a product category such as toothpaste. In other industries, no such commercial research data are available and most (or all) of the measures of an SBU's position relative to competition are, of necessity, estimates based on whatever partial information management has access to.

One key strategic factor, *relative quality,* deserves special comment. As shown in Exhibit 3-6, one of our measures of competitive position/strategy is an index of the quality of a business unit's products and services, relative to those of its principal competitors. The concept of this relative quality index is explained in the ruled insert. This particular PIMS strategy measure has been questioned by many, because it is a judgmental assessment and therefore subjective.

EXHIBIT 3-6
PIMS Measures of Major Competitive Position and Strategy Dimensions

Elements of Position	Position Measures	Change Measures
Competitive Standing	• SBU Market Share (MS) • SBU Market Share Rank	• Change in MS • Change in MS Ranking
Product/Service Policies	• Index of Quality, relative to leading competitors* • New Products/Services as a Percent of Sales, and relative to competitors	• Change in Quality Index • Change in New Product/Service %
Pricing	• Index of SBU Relative Prices (average of competitors = 100)	• Change in Relative Price Index
Marketing Programs	• Marketing Expense, % of Sales	• Change in Marketing/Sales
Investment Strategy	• Value of Plant & Equipment, relative to (1) sales, (2) value added, (3) employment • Newness of Plant & Equipment (net book value, % of gross book value) • Labor Productivity (Value Added per Employee) • Inventory, % of Sales	• Changes in Fixed Asset Ratios • Change in Newness • Change in Productivity • Change in Inventory/Sales
Vertical Integration	• Value Added, % of Sales (adjusted)** • Vertical Integration, relative to competitors (more/same/less)	• Change in Value Added/Sales • Change in Relative V.I.
Research & Development	• R&D Expense, % of Sales	• Change in R&D/Sales

*For an explanation of the quality index, see the ruled insert on page 42.
**For an explanation of the adjustment in value added, see Chapter 8 and Appendix A.

A Measure of Relative Quality

Each business unit in the PIMS data base has provided, on an annual basis, a measure of the Relative Quality of its products or services. The quality index can range from -100 to $+100$, and is intended to represent *customer* perceptions of product quality—including the quality of services, such as installation—*relative* to principal competitors.

The relative quality measure was originally obtained by asking managers and planning specialists to judge what percentage of their business unit's total sales consisted of products that were (1) superior to those of leading competitors, (2) equivalent, and (3) inferior. The index was then calculated as Per Cent Superior *minus* Per Cent Inferior. (In making these judgments, the respondents were asked to use all relevant marketing research and product test data.)

Since 1980, SPI has employed a more structured approach to collecting relative quality data. Respondents are now led through a "quality profiling" process in which they identify all the key non-price product and service attributes that count in the purchase decision. They are then asked to develop *importance weights* for the product and service attributes that add to 100. Finally, respondents are asked to rate their performance and the performance of leading competitors on a scale from 1 to 10 for each product and service attribute.

A high quality score is obtained by having performance ratings higher than competitors on attributes that are heavily weighted. Quality scores reported in exhibits in this book have been converted to percentiles. (For a more detailed discussion, see Chapter 6.)

There is no doubt that the PIMS measure of relative quality is a judgmental measure. But it is also clear that the quality of an SBU's products and services is an important element of strategy that has a substantial impact on profitability and growth. To omit quality from the exploration of strategy and performance would be far worse, in our view, than to use a subjective measure. Moreover, a study of the reliability of the PIMS quality index showed that it *is* a consistent indicator of this aspect of competitive position.[11]

Just what "quality" means to customers varies greatly among different kinds of products and services. For machine tools, important dimensions of quality might include such things as durability, impact on labor costs, and ease of maintenance. For a food product, important features would include taste, uniformity over time, and ease of preparation. Any strategy aimed at improving overall quality must be designed in terms of these kinds of specific quality dimensions. Recognizing this, SPI has since 1980 been assembling a supplementary Quality Data Base in which information is compiled for specific product and service attributes. Illustrations of how this more detailed approach to quality measurement can be used are given in Chapter 6.

Exhibit 3-6 lists only major dimensions of competitive position and strategy. By "major" dimensions, we mean those that have significant impacts on profitability for most types of businesses in most types of competitive environments. In subsequent chapters we'll discuss additional strategic factors that appear to affect performance only in certain kinds of situations.

MEASURES OF MARKET/INDUSTRY FACTORS

Regardless of the strategy that management may adopt for a business, its profitability will also depend to a considerable degree on the nature of its market/industry environment. A U.S.-based producer of steel or shoes, for instance, would be unlikely to achieve the same profitability as a pharmaceutical manufacturer, even if their strategies were identical in terms of the dimensions shown in Exhibit 3-6.

Some of the major market/industry factors that influence profitability are outlined in Exhibit 3-7. Under most circumstances, the managers of an individual business unit cannot control these factors. Overall market growth, inflation, the extent of import competition, and unionization are usually determined by external forces rather than by management choice. Similarly, supplier concentration, the importance of products to customers, and whether products are standardized or custom-produced are usually givens in a particular business arena. There are exceptions, of course. A business may have some choice about such matters as concentrating their purchases. To the extent that management *can* control the factors listed in Exhibit 3-7, they can be regarded as elements of strategy rather than environmental givens.

More detailed definitions of all of the strategic and environmental factors listed in Exhibits 3-6 and 3-7 are provided in Appendix A.

EXHIBIT 3-7
PIMS Measures of Major Market/Industry Influences
on Business Performance

Market/Industry Factors	Measures
Market Growth	• Average Rate of Change in Real Market Volume
Stage of Market Evolution	• Age of Product/Service Category • Life Cycle Stage
Inflation	• Average Rate of Change in Selling Prices
Unionization	• Percent of Employees Unionized
Import Competition	• Imports and Exports, Percent of Industry Sales
Suppliers	• Percent of Purchases from 3 Largest Suppliers
Product/Service Standardization	• Standardization vs. Customization of Products/Services
Importance of Products to Customers	• Typical Transaction Size • Purchases of Product Class, Percent of Customer's Total Purchases

RELATING PERFORMANCE TO STRATEGY AND MARKET FACTORS

The whole point of assembling a data base that contains measures
of performance, strategy, and market/industry conditions is to make
it possible to explore the relationships among all of these factors.
For this purpose we use standard statistical methods, primarily *multiple linear regression analysis,* to explain the variations in ROI and
ROS among businesses in the PIMS data base. This approach allows
us to estimate how *all* of the factors listed in Exhibits 3-6 and 3-7,
in combination, influence profitability.

Multiple regression and related statistical methods are powerful
tools. These methods were developed for just the kind of analysis
that we need to determine how each of many factors influence a
given end result. An analogy may be helpful on this point:

Physicians recognize that the likelihood of heart disease depends on many
things. Among the most important are heredity (family history of heart disease), blood pressure, frequency of exercise, weight, blood cholesterol level,
and smoking habits. To assess a given individual's situation, some doctors collect information on all of these factors and combine them in the form of a
"Risk Profile." This approach, it is believed, gives a more accurate picture
than just focussing on one or two disease-related factors. More important, it

provides a basis for designing a strategy that a patient can adopt to minimize the likelihood of heart disease.

The logic of the statistical method used in the Risk Profile approach to medical diagnosis and prescription is identical to what we employ here for strategic diagnosis and prescription. Not only is the logic the same, but so is the method of measuring the key relationships. To determine how cholesterol level is related to heart disease, for instance, medical researchers compile the records of thousands of individuals. Using this information, they can compare the incidence of heart disease among people with high, medium, and low cholesterol levels. By measuring other factors in addition to cholesterol, they can determine its *net* effect in relation to such other things as exercise and smoking habits.

Like the medical researchers, we use a cross-sectional approach. To determine how profitability is affected by market share, for instance, we compare ROS and ROI for businesses with large, average, and small market shares. To determine the *net* effect of market share in relation to the many other factors that influence profits, we use appropriate multi-variable statistical techniques.

The relationships between performance and strategic factors discussed in this book are based primarily on relatively simple regression methods. More complex methods have also been used, and with a few exceptions the results have confirmed the patterns described here. (Studies utilizing a variety of statistical approaches are listed in the Select Bibliography.)

MAJOR INFLUENCES ON PROFITABILITY: AN OVERVIEW

Having explained how we measure profitability, competitive position/strategy factors and market/industry conditions, we can now present an overview of how all of these factors are related. The impacts of the major competitive position and strategy dimensions on current ROI and ROS are summarized in Exhibit 3–8. Five factors stand out as important positive influences: market share, product/service quality, newness of plant and equipment, labor productivity, and vertical integration.

Factors that are negatively related to ROI and ROS include fixed capital intensity, inventory investment, the rate of new product introduction, and current levels of spending on marketing and R&D.

EXHIBIT 3-8
Competitive Position, Strategy, and Profitability:
an Overview of Major Relationships

| | Impact on | |
| | ROI | ROS |
Competitive Position/Strategy Factors	+ = Positive	− = Negative
Market Share	+	+
Relative Product/Service Quality	+	+
New Products, % of Sales	−	−
R&D Expense, % of Sales	−	−
Marketing Expense, % of Sales	−	−
Value Added, % of Sales[a]	+	+
Fixed Assets, % of Sales (at capacity)	−	−
Newness of Plant & Equipment	+	+
Labor Productivity	+	+
Inventories, % of Sales	−	−
Capacity Utilization Rate	+	+
FIFO Inventory Valuation	+	+

[a]Value added is adjusted to remove above-average or compensate for below-average net profits. For explanation, see Chapter 8 and Appendix A.

In Exhibit 3-8 we show how two other factors, capacity utilization and inventory valuation method, are related to profitability. Strictly speaking, these two are not components of "strategy." The use of the FIFO method of inventory valuation—versus LIFO or some other method—is a decision about accounting method that is based primarily on tax considerations. During periods of rising prices, SBUs that use FIFO valuation will report higher profits (and consequently pay higher taxes) than those using LIFO. It is not surprising, therefore, that Exhibit 3-8 shows higher reported profitability for businesses using FIFO. The exhibit also shows that profitability is positively related to an SBU's rate of capacity utilization. While capacity utilization is not in itself an element of strategy, it reflects the impacts of past strategic decisions about the amounts and the timing of additions to capacity. A proposed addition to capacity may in fact have both a negative impact (by making the business more fixed-capital intensive and lowering its utilization rate) and an offsetting positive impact (by making the plant newer and raising labor productivity).

Exhibit 3-9 completes our overview by showing the impacts on profitability of market and industry characteristics. Both ROI and

EXHIBIT 3-9
Market/Industry Influences on Profitability:
An Overview of Major Relationships

| | Impact on Profitability | |
| | ROI | ROS |
Market/Industry Profit Influences	+ = Positive	− = Negative
• Real Market Growth Rate (annual %)	+	+
• Stage of Market Evolution		
—Growth Stage	+	+
—Decline Stage	−	−
• Rate of Inflation in Selling Prices	+	+
• Concentration of Purchases with Few Suppliers	+	(+)[a]
• Typical Customer Purchase Amount		
—Small	+	+
—Large	−	−
• Importance of Product Purchase to Customer		
—Low	+	+
—High	−	−
• % of Employees Unionized	−	−
• Industry Exports	+	+
• Industry Imports	−	−
• Standardized Products (vs. Custom-Produced)	+	+

*Relationship not statistically significant. NOTE: For definitions, see Appendix A.

ROS are typically higher in rapidly growing markets; in industries that export more than is imported; when products are standardized (as opposed to custom-ordered); and when customers buy in relatively small quantities. ROI (but not ROS) is higher for businesses that concentrate their purchases with a few suppliers. Aspects of the market environment that tend to depress profitability are unionization of employees and large-quantity typical customer purchases.

Exhibits 3-8 and 3-9 show only the *directions* of effect for strategic and market/industry factors. In later chapters we explore how much effect each factor has on profitability.

ARE ALL BUSINESSES ALIKE?

Exhibits 3-8 and 3-9 are based on statistical analyses of all 2,600 businesses in the PIMS Data Base. By pooling all of these units together, we are in effect treating them as if the same relationships between strategy and profitability apply to all of them more or less equally. Given the diversity of the businesses, it is not surprising that there *are* some important differences, which we can identify by separately analyzing sub-groups within the data base.

One way to group SBUs is by basic business type, along the lines of Exhibit 3–2. Another is to break out businesses that operate in North America from those in other parts of the world. When we analyze these sub-groups separately, some differences do appear. Several of the more important are listed in Exhibits 3–10 and 3–11. Some of the factors that strongly affect profitability for industrial product business are not important in consumer goods markets, and vice versa (see Exhibit 3–10). For example, handling customized products is not a relevant consideration for consumer product marketers, presumably because very few of them pursue this strategy. Differences also show up in the profit impacts of market share and product/service quality, with the former being most important in consumer markets and the latter being most important in industrial and service/distribution business arenas. These differential effects no doubt reflect the greater rationality, and consequent emphasis on quality, of buyers in non-consumer markets.

EXHIBIT 3–10
Differences in Impacts of Key Profit Influences
by Types of Business

Profit Influences	Differences in Impact on ROI
Rate of Price Inflation	Not related to ROI for service & distribution businesses
Typical Customer Purchase Amount & Importance	Impact on ROI greatest for industrial product manufacturers
Exports vs. Imports	Effect on ROI significant only for industrial product manufacturers
Customized Products	Not a significant factor for consumer products
Market Share/Product Quality	Market share has greatest impact on ROI for consumer products; effect of quality is greatest for industrial products and service/distribution
New Products/R&D	Neither of these hurts ROI in service & distribution
Inventory, % of Sales	Not a significant factor in service/distribution
Plant Newness	Effect is significant only for consumer products

NOTE: Based on statistical analyses summarized in Exhibit B–4, Appendix B.

EXHIBIT 3-11
Differences in Impacts of Key Profit Influences
by Location of Served Market

Profit Influences	Differences in Impact on ROI
Rate of Price Inflation	No relationship with ROI outside North America
Typical Customer Purchase Amount & Importance	Effect on ROI significant in North America, not elsewhere
Exports vs. Imports	Effect on ROI outside North America is reversed
R&D	Not related to ROI outside North America
Plant Newness	Impact is greater outside North America
Employee Productivity	Weak relationship to ROI outside North America
FIFO Inventory Valuation	Not a significant factor outside North America

NOTE: Based on statistical analyses summarized in Exhibit B-5, Appendix B.

Just as consumer, industrial, and service/distribution businesses vary, so too do marketplaces located in different parts of the world (Exhibit 3-11). Some of the variations are due to differences in accounting practices: methods of inventory valuation have no connection with profitability for foreign businesses, nor does the rate of inflation. (Chapter 4 will explain how a high inflation rate increases *reported* profitability for U.S.-based businesses partly via its effect on inventory holding gains.) Also, variations in the level of industry exports and imports are not related to ROI for domestic businesses in the way that might be expected for foreign businesses. High levels of both exports and imports are much more common in Western European industries, where most of our non–North American businesses operate.

The type of business and geographic location are just two of many possible ways to subdivide business units into more homogeneous groups. Others that have been used in PIMS-based research include "generic strategy" groupings,[12] business unit age,[13] and the type of production technology employed.[14] Overall, research along these lines shows that the main profit influences—such as market share, relative quality, and capital intensity—affect almost all kinds of businesses in similar ways. There are, however, important differences, and we report many of them in subsequent chapters.

ARE INDUSTRIES DIFFERENT?

As mentioned in Chapter 2, most managers find it intuitively appealing to compare the performance of a company or business with others in the same industry. Economists, too, have emphasized differences among industries—partly because most of the information available from government sources deals with industry characteristics (such as seller concentration) and average industry profitability. After we have taken into account the factors listed in Exhibits 3-8 and 3-9, does a business unit's profitability still depend on the industry in which it participates? The answer seems to be "No and Yes."

More than half the businesses in the PIMS data base provided information on specific industry membership, based on the (American) Standard Industrial Classification system. For these businesses, we can determine whether average profitability is higher or lower than would be expected, based on the strategic factors shown in Exhibits 3-8 and 3-9. This analysis leads to two conclusions:

1. Most of the differences in profitability among industries are due to differences in such strategic factors as growth rate, unionization, and capital intensity.
2. After all of the strategic factors have been taken into account, businesses in several industries do have significantly higher or lower-than-expected rates of return on investment. Those with higher rates of return are Industrial Chemicals (SICs 2800–2869), Specialty Chemicals (2830–2899), Industrial Electrical Equipment (3600–3629) and Household Appliances (3630–3651). Industries with below-expected ROI are Flour & Grain Products (SICs 2040–2052), Paper & Paper Products (2600–2661), Machine Tools (3540–3549), and Communications and Office Equipment (3570–3662).

EXPLAINING DIFFERENCES IN PROFITABILITY

The statistical analyses of profitability that we and others have done using the PIMS data base have all been aimed at explaining why ROI and ROS vary from one business to another. If we knew literally all of the factors that influence profits, we could explain 100% of the variation depicted in Exhibit 3-5. How close can we get to this standard of perfection?

Using information for just the major profit influences listed in Exhibits 3-8 and 3-9, we explain about 40% of the differences in ROS and ROI among the PIMS businesses. A more complete statistical model used by SPI—the so-called "PAR" ROI model—explains over 70%. The main reason for this improvement in statistical results is that the more complete model includes a series of terms that show how the impacts of various factors change under different conditions. For example, it reflects the fact that the impact of a high level of vertical integration depends on the growth rate of the market in which a business participates. (See Appendix B for further explanation.)

For purposes of this book, we have chosen to use a simplified model of profitability that reflects only the most important determinants of business performance. However, many of the contingent relationships between strategy and results are discussed in subsequent chapters.

Chapter 4

Picking Profitable Markets

The starting point for a winning business strategy is to pick the "right" markets or industries in which to participate. Some kinds of competitive arenas have high inherent profit potential, while in others even the most diligent competitors earn only modest rates of return. A striking example of the latter, in the early 1980s, was the Caterpillar Tractor Company. Caterpillar was one of the handful of corporations singled out for highly effective management by Thomas Peters and Robert Waterman in their best-selling book, *In Search of Excellence*.[1] Yet Caterpillar lost huge amounts of money in the early 1980s, and the company's stock was selling at less than half its book value in late 1985.

If we accept Peters and Waterman's appraisal of the quality of Caterpillar's management, we must conclude that the construction equipment field was an inherently unprofitable one, at least in the years 1980–84. In contrast, some other industries have been consistently profitable for most participants. For example, in each of the years 1974–1977, financial data collected by the Federal Trade Commission's Line of Business program showed that Breakfast Cereals and Cookies and Crackers were among the top 10 (out of 273) industries in terms of operating profit as a percentage of assets.[2] There may well be some unprofitable individual competitors in these two industries, but the odds in favor of earning adequate profits are surely much better than they are, for example, in the Children's Outerwear industry, which was consistently ranked by the FTC studies among the 10 least profitable industries.

MARKET/INDUSTRY PROFIT INFLUENCES

What makes one competitive arena more profitable than another? In this chapter we show how certain characteristics of a market affect profitability, based on the experience of the businesses in the PIMS data base. Among the most important profit influences, as shown in Exhibit 3-8 (Chapter 3), are:

- The market's stage of evolution and its real (inflation-adjusted) *growth rate;*
- The *rate of inflation* in selling prices;
- The extent of *concentration among suppliers;*
- The *size of typical customer purchase amounts* and the *importance of the product or service* to the customer;
- The extent of *employee unionization;*
- The magnitude of *exports and imports* from and to an industry.

Except for exports and imports, which are measured at the industry level, all of these profit influences operate at the level of a business unit's served market, as defined in Chapter 3. Within some industries, a business may be able to find one or more segments, submarkets, or "niches" that are much more attractive than the rest of the industry. In other cases, all sectors of an industry may be subject to essentially the same basic forces and have similar levels of profitability.[3]

In this chapter, we discuss how each of the market forces listed above affects profitability. By designating these factors as market or industry characteristics, we are suggesting that usually they are not matters of strategic choice, at least not after the decision has been made to participate in a market in the first place. This assumption is not, however, always a valid one. Sometimes management can make choices, within a given market, about such things as concentration of purchases among suppliers or selling in large vs. small amounts to customers. Knowing how these factors affect profitability can, in such cases, given some guidance to the design of competitive strategy within a market as well as to decisions about entry, expansion, or withdrawal.

MARKET EVOLUTION AND GROWTH

One of the most widely-accepted ideas about strategic management is that the evolution of markets over time follows a common general pattern or "life cycle."[4] Markets in the early stages of their evolution display an erratic pattern of growth and instability in technology, market structure, and methods of competition. For those that survive this turbulent period, there follows a stage of rapid growth. Still later, markets mature and stabilize. Maturity may persist for many years, but ultimately almost all markets are fated to decline either because a new and superior technology emerges or because of changing customer needs.

The PIMS data base includes several measures related to the process of market evolution. These include:

- The *age* of the products or services sold by the businesses in the market, i.e., how long ago they were first developed.[5]
- The market's *life cycle stage*—Introduction, Growth, Maturity, or Decline—as perceived by a business unit's management.
- The market's *real growth rate,* excluding inflation in prices.

These three indicators of a market's stage of evolution *usually* go together in the way that would be expected: most "mature" markets are older, and have lower growth rates, than most "growth" markets. But there are some important exceptions to the general rules. Exhibit 4–1 shows how market age, life cycle stage, and real growth rate are interrelated. (The Introduction stage of the Life Cycle is omitted because very few of the PIMS businesses were so classified.) Note, for example, that of the markets designated as being in the "growth phase," over 30% actually had low or negative real growth rates. Conversely, of the "mature" markets, nearly 30% had real annual growth rates of 6% or more. Even among markets labelled as "declining," one fourth were growing at rates of at least 3%.

All of this suggests that markets evolve in different ways and at varying rates. The "life cycle" model is a useful general frame of

EXHIBIT 4-1
Measures of Market Evolution: Age, Life Cycle Stage,
and Real Growth Rates

Age of Product Category[a]	Distribution by Life Cycle Stage			Average Real Growth Rate
	Growth	*Mature*	*Decline*	
20 Years or More	9%	83%	8%	1.9%
10–20 Years	29	67	4	4.1
Less than 10 Years	46	52	2	8.1

Life Cycle Stage	Distribution by Growth Rate			Average Real Growth Rate
	Under 3%	*3–6%*	*Over 6%*	
Growth	31%	10%	59%	10.1%
Maturity	58	14	28	2.0
Decline	75	10	15	−1.7

[a]The age groupings are only approximate. The original data were reported in terms of time periods, e.g., "Before 1930," "1950–1954." The reporting dates range from 1973 up to 1981 (the first year of a 4-year period in each case.)

reference, but there are many departures from the typical sequence of stages and frequent cross-currents of more or less rapid growth within a given stage of development. (Life cycles are discussed in more detail in Chapter 10.)

To evaluate the impact of market evolution on profitability, we first consider the effects of market growth rate and then ask whether, given the growth rate, a market's life cycle stage makes any difference.

NOTE ON STATISTICAL METHODS

Exhibits 4–2 and 4–3 compare the performance of businesses operating in markets with different real growth rates. In this and subsequent chapters we present many other comparisons in the same basic form—that is, relating performance to one or two factors at a time. These exhibits do *not* take into account the effects of all the other profit influences listed in Chapter 3. Our statistical analyses *do,* however, consider all of the major profit influences simultaneously. We have, therefore, measured the *net* impact of each factor on profitability. These net impacts are shown in Appendix B.

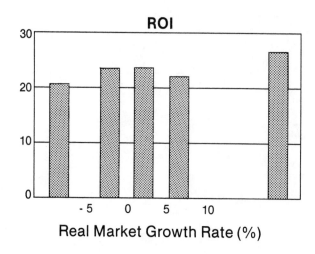

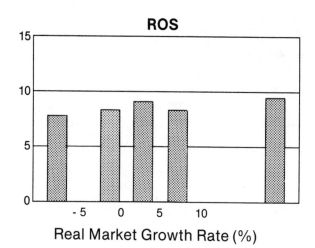

EXHIBIT 4–2

Real Market Growth and Profitability

NOTE: Bars representing businesses in the lowest and highest quintiles are shown at their average growth rate positions on the horizontal axis.

Exhibit 4–2 shows average ROI and ROS for businesses with varying real (inflation-adjusted) market growth rates. (In this and similar exhibits, the 2,600 PIMS business units are divided into several groups of roughly equal size. The ROI and ROS figures shown are the averages for each group, based on 4-year averages for each business unit. For an explanation of the statistical approach we have used, see the ruled insert on page 55.)

The impact of market growth on profitability is most apparent at the extremes. When the market is expanding rapidly—at a real annual rate of 10% or better—ROI is 4 points higher, on average, than it is in markets that are declining at rates of 5% or more. In between the two extremes, profitability shows little or no relationship to the growth rate.

How does rapid growth boost profitability? Exhibit 4-3 compares several key financial ratios for businesses in markets with varying growth rates.

These figures show that markets with high growth rates are characterized by:

- High gross margins
- High marketing costs (but not enough higher to offset the improved margins)
- Low rates of inflation, both for selling prices and for materials and wages. In rapidly-growing markets, prices typically rise at a rate *below* that of costs, creating a "cost-price squeeze."
- Rising productivity (Apparently this is usually more than enough to offset the differential between the rates of change in prices and costs.)
- A need to increase investments to keep pace with growth (In-

EXHIBIT 4-3
Real Market Growth and Key Financial Ratios

Averages	Real Annual Growth Rate				
	−5% or Lower	−5% to Zero	Zero to 5%	5 to 10%	Over 10%
Percent of Sales:					
Gross Margin	23.5%	25.6%	26.9%	25.7%	29.7%
Marketing Expense	8.1	9.5	9.4	8.8	10.1
Rate of Change in:					
Selling Prices	11.0%	9.5%	7.5%	6.9%	5.7%
Costs of Materials and Wages	10.4	9.5	8.5	8.7	8.3
Value Added per Employee	8.7	9.5	9.8	10.3	13.0
Investment	5.0	8.0	9.7	11.6	17.8
Cash Flow, % of Investment	6.0	4.9	3.5	2.4	−0.1
Number of Businesses	(413)	(446)	(582)	(365)	(508)

terestingly, the investment base tends to grow, although at a slower pace, even in declining markets!)

- Low or negative cash flow, even though ROI is rising. As predicted by the Growth-Share Matrix approach to planning, "Stars" and "Question Marks" in a company's portfolio are likely to use more cash than they generate.

The net effect of all of these differences is that profits are highest in fast-growing markets and lowest in declining ones. The same pattern has been found in research based on the FTC's Line of Business data.[6] The widespread belief that growth is good for performance, then, is strongly supported by the evidence. As we shall show in Chapter 10, growing markets may also call for different strategies than are appropriate for static or declining ones.

LIFE CYCLE STAGE

Once we have taken growth rate into account, does a market's life cycle stage affect profitability? Apparently there *are* some differences related to the life cycle, as shown in the following comparison:

	Real Growth Rate		
Life Cycle	Average ROI		
Stage	*Under 3%*	*3–6%*	*Over 6%*
Growth	22.8	24.4	24.3
Maturity	21.7	22.0	24.1
Decline	16.4	22.3	

These figures suggest that profitability tends to decline as a market evolves over time, not just because of diminished growth but also for other reasons as well. Several forces appear to lie behind this pattern. For one, product and service differentiation tend to diminish over time. In the early stages of market evolution, early entrants often have big quality advantages based on patents and proprietary technologies. Typically these advantages are eroded through a process of competitive imitation. Partly for this reason, competition shifts increasingly to price and rates of return fall. There is also a tendency, at least among manufacturing businesses, for capital intensity to increase as a market ages. (The relationship between capital intensity and profitability is explored in Chapter 7.)

INFLATION AND PROFITABILITY

The higher the rate of inflation in selling prices within a served market, the greater profits are likely to be for businesses participating in the market. As shown in Exhibit 4-4, ROI and ROS are both lowest in markets with low inflation rates.

When prices are increasing, of course, costs are also likely to be rising. The figures in Exhibit 4-4 suggest, however, that costs have a nasty tendency to go up even when prices don't! Only when the rate of inflation is over 10% does the rate of price increase exceed that in the costs of raw materials and components.

The impact of inflation on profitability is mitigated by the fact, mentioned earlier, that markets with low rates of inflation tend to grow (in real terms) more rapidly. When the offsetting effects of growth and inflation are combined, significant differences in profitability show up only at the extremes, i.e., very high and low rates, of either growth or inflation.

The influence of rapid inflation on profitability became a subject of widespread discussion and controversy in Western industrial

EXHIBIT 4-4
Inflation and Profitability

	Rate of Change in Selling Prices (Annual)				
	Under 3%	*3-6%*	*6-8%*	*8-12%*	*Over 12%*
Average ROI	20.2	23.4	21.6	23.8	23.0
Average ROS	8.7	9.3	8.3	9.8	9.7
Annual Rate of Change					
Selling Prices	0.1%	4.6%	6.9%	9.7%	17.5%
Materials Costs	4.5	6.2	7.8	10.2	16.6
Number of Businesses	(382)	(504)	(442)	(528)	(458)

countries in the mid-1970s, when "double-digit" inflation became commonplace for the first time in more than a generation. Of particular concern, it was recognized that depreciation charges—based on original acquisition costs—were insufficient to cover the rising replacement costs of fixed assets. Also, for companies using the traditional FIFO method for valuing inventories, reported profits include holding gains on inventories. (Among PIMS businesses using FIFO, ROI was 1.4 points higher, on average, than it was for businesses that employed other valuation methods.) For these reasons, among others, accountants and governmental agencies urged (and eventually required) corporations to compile and report profits on an "inflation-adjusted" basis in addition to the conventional figures.

Using the financial information in the PIMS data base, we can adjust each business unit's profits to eliminate differences due solely to inflation in selling prices. The adjustments are described in the ruled insert.[7]

Average *inflation-adjusted* ROI and ROS for businesses operating in markets with varying inflation rates were:

	Inflation-Adjusted	
Rate of Inflation	*Average ROI*	*Average ROS*
Less than 3%	11.4	5.8
3–6%	13.6	6.4
6–8%	10.8	5.6
8–12%	11.3	5.4
Over 12%	8.9	4.5
All Businesses	11.3	5.6

As these figures suggest, the impact of inflation on reported profitability is entirely due to the discrepancies in the monetary values used to calculate profits under conventional accounting methods. The implication is that managers should not look for any particular operating advantages in markets with high inflation rates. If anything, rapid increases in selling prices appear to depress profitability after the effects of inflation itself are removed.

Whether the positive effects of inflation on reported profits should be regarded as "artificial" is still a controversial question

Adjusting ROI for Inflation Effects

By historical standards the 1970s was a period of rapid inflation in the U.S. and Western Europe. With prices rising in some years at "double-digit" rates, managers and accountants paid increasing attention to the impact of inflation on traditional methods of measuring and reporting profitability. "Inflation-adjusted" figures have now become a standard feature of the annual reports of publicly-held corporations.

The profitability measures that we use for business units (ROS and ROI) are calculated in accordance with conventional accounting methods. They are, consequently, subject to the same kinds of distortions as the financial data reported by public companies. We can, however, make adjustments in the components of ROS and ROI to eliminate the effects of inflation. The adjustments are as follows:

1. The data base includes, for each business, an estimate of the ratio of *replacement* value to *book* value of Plant & Equipment. To calculate inflation-adjusted ROI, we replace the book value of P. & E. with the corresponding replacement value (less accumulated depreciation).
2. Reported annual depreciation expenses on Plant & Equipment are based on book values. To allow for the (almost invariably) higher replacement cost that should be covered by depreciation allowances, we make an appropriate adjustment in annual charges which reduces net profit.
3. The method of inventory valuation used by a business also affects reported profits. Businesses using FIFO tend to overstate profits by including "holding gains" on ending inventories. Those using LIFO, conversely, understate the value of the inventory component of investment. We adjust FIFO reported profits and LIFO investment figures, using the relationships between otherwise similar businesses in the data base that employed each valuation method.

When all of these adjustments are made, the average ROI falls from 22% (reported) to 11% (inflation-adjusted). The differences between reported and inflation-adjusted profitability are greatest for businesses with high fixed capital-to-sales ratios and for those with relatively old plant and equipment.

among accountants and financial analysts. But few if any management incentive compensation systems make a distinction between profits due to inflation and those that come from other sources. Perhaps they should.

SUPPLIER RELATIONSHIPS

Most managers would probably expect profits to be lower for businesses that deal with only a few suppliers than for those with many suppliers. Actually, our analysis shows that concentrating purchases *improves* profitability, at least up to a point. Our measure of supplier concentration is the percentage of each business unit's total purchases that are made from its 3 largest suppliers. This index ranges from a low of just 5% to a high of 100%, with an average of 35%. As Exhibit 4-5 shows, both ROI and ROS are highest when the supplier concentration index is between 25% and 50%.

The positive net effect of a moderate degree of purchase concentration suggests that the efficiency gains that can be achieved via this approach to procurement are usually big enough to offset the disadvantages that might be expected as a result of an inferior bargaining position. A frequently-cited example of the benefits of concentrating purchases is that of the Japanese automobile industry. In contrast with their American counterparts, the major Japanese auto makers have followed a policy of long-term, cooperative relationships with a relatively small number of parts suppliers rather than one of competitive bidding among many suppliers. This approach has been cited as one of the factors that makes the just-in-time manufacturing system possible.[8]

While concentrating purchases with a few suppliers may make sense, *competing* with suppliers usually does not. About 15% of

EXHIBIT 4-5
Supplier Concentration and Profitability

Percent of Purchases from 3 Largest Suppliers	ROI	ROS
Under 25	20.5	8.9
25–50	23.7	9.8
Over 50	22.8	8.9

PIMS businesses reported that one or more of their major suppliers competed with them via forward integration. The effects of this kind of competition are clear:

Averages	Competition with Suppliers	
	No	*Yes*
ROI	22.7	20.7
ROS	9.3	8.3
Gross Margin	26.7	24.8

Other things being equal, then, markets in which major producers of raw materials or components participate both as suppliers and finished-product sellers are less attractive areas for investment than they otherwise would be.

PURCHASE AMOUNT AND IMPORTANCE

Sales of some products and services usually involve large transaction amounts, either because the product has a high unit value or because it is bought in large quantities at a time. Markets in which transactions involve big sums of money tend to be less profitable than ones characterized by small purchase amounts. Differences in ROI and ROS related to transaction size are shown in Exhibit 4–6. When customers typically buy in amounts of $1,000 or less, ROI is 6½ points higher than at the other extreme, where purchases average more than $100,000. (These "typical purchase amounts" refer to the quantities involved in individual transactions, which in some cases cover forward buying contracts. Purchase amounts may or may not correspond to the amounts in which products are shipped or services provided.)

The profit-depressing impact of a large typical purchase amount is most pronounced for industrial products manufacturers. Among this group the difference in average ROI between the two extremes is about 9 points, while for consumer products and service/distribution businesses it is between 4 and 5 points.

Not only are profits lower when products or services are sold via high-value transactions, they are also lower when the product is "important" to the customer. Our measure of importance is quantita-

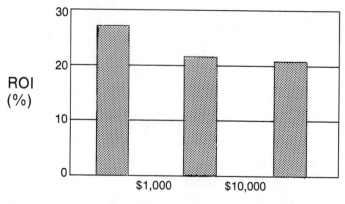

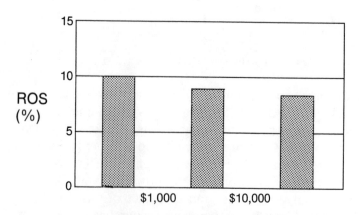

EXHIBIT 4-6
Profitability and Typical Purchase Amount

tive: the fraction of the customer's *total* annual purchases of all goods and services represented by the product category. For example, wheat represents a large fraction of a flour miller's purchases and steel is similarly an important purchase for a producer of household appliances, while purchases of office supplies are unimportant to both.

Products and services that are important to customers tend to be less profitable than other products and services, as shown in Exhibit 4-7.

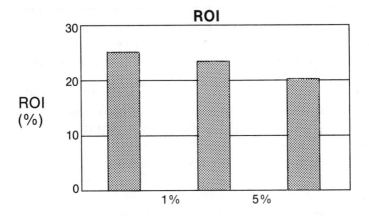

Typical Purchase Importance
(% of customer's total purchases)

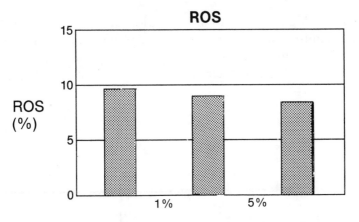

Typical Purchase Importance
(% of customer's total purchases)

EXHIBIT 4–7
Profitability and Purchase Importance

UNIONIZATION

In many cases, perhaps in most, management cannot control the extent to which employees are unionized—dealing with a union is part of the "price of admission" in numerous industries. There are many exceptions to this statement, of course. By locating in the Southern United States or in small towns, or by locating sources in Eastern

Europe or the Far East, some firms have gained significant labor cost advantages over their union-labor competitors. But frequently these choices are not viable, and participation in a particular market brings with it, as one of its basic economic conditions, the presence of an organized labor force.

How is profitability affected by unionization? Unions may create important benefits for their members, but they certainly do not generally help profitability. Exhibit 4–8 shows that the higher the percentage of unionization among a business unit's employees, the lower ROI and ROS tend to be. Both measures of profitability are highest in situations where unions are not present at all, and lowest when a majority of workers (over 60%) are union members. Beyond that point, further increases in unionization have little or no impact, probably because once union contracts cover a majority of employees, the key contract terms are usually extended to all hourly workers anyway.

Why do higher levels of unionization affect profits adversely? Two mechanisms seem to be at work: highly-unionized workers are less productive in terms of value added per person than are non-unionized workers, and their wage rates rise more rapidly. Exhibit

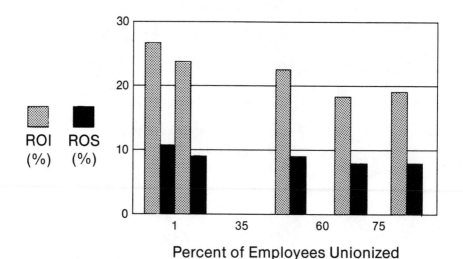

EXHIBIT 4–8
Unionization and Profitability

NOTE: Bars representing businesses in each group are shown at their average unionization values on the horizontal axis.

EXHIBIT 4-9
Unionization, Productivity, and Wage Rates

Percent of Employees Unionized	Value Added per Employee ($000)	Rate of Increase in Wage Rates
None	36.0	8.4%
1-35	40.5	8.8
35-60	42.0	8.7
60-75	36.1	8.9
Over 75	32.1	9.5

4-9 summarizes the evidence on both points. The productivity figures show that output per worker is actually highest when *some* employees (up to 60%) belong to unions. The relationship is complicated, however, by the fact that increasing levels of unionization are usually accompanied by greater mechanization, measured in terms of the value of plant and equipment per employee. (Unionization and mechanization are probably causes and effects of each other.) When we control for this interrelationship, the negative effect of a high level of unionization is even more clear-cut. Moreover, the impact of unionization is greatest in industries that are highly mechanized, such as chemical processing and automobile production. For businesses ranking in the top third on mechanization (Plant & Equipment of $25,000 or more per employee), the output per employee was almost 25% lower when unionization was high (over 65%) than it was when unionization was low (under 25%).

IMPORTS AND EXPORTS

From a conceptual standpoint, a served market is ideally a self-contained competitive arena. But in reality participants in most markets compete not only with each other but also with outsiders. One kind of inter-market competition which has increased in importance in the 1980s is that which takes place via imports and exports.

Imports and/or exports are dominant forces in some industries, such as copper refining and airframe manufacturing. But for most of the PIMS business in the seventies and early eighties, they were still of relatively minor importance. On average, exports accounted for slightly over 7% of industry sales, while imports represented just under 5% of (domestic) served market sales.

As might be expected, a high level of exports boosts profitability for industry participants, while import competition has an adverse effect. The same pattern was shown in studies based on the FTC's Line of Business data base.[9] For PIMS businesses, average rates of return for different combinations of exports and imports were:

	ROI		ROS	
Exports	*Imports under 5%*	*Imports over 5%*	*Imports under 5%*	*Imports over 5%*
Under 5%	20.3	22.0	8.0	9.0
Over 5%	26.6	22.0	11.6	9.0

For American and European companies, finding markets with good exporting prospects and little import competition is increasingly difficult, but if such markets can be found, the rewards can be handsome.

SUMMING UP: HOW MARKET FACTORS INFLUENCE PROFITABILITY

In this chapter we have shown how profits are affected by a series of market and industry factors that are usually outside management's control. When we look at all of these factors in combination, how much difference can they make? One way to show this is to compare rates of return (ROI) for businesses operating in markets that are favorably situated on all of the "attractiveness" dimensions with the returns that are typical for "unfavorable" market situations. Exhibit 4–10 summarizes the impacts on ROI of each market factor for three hypothetical businesses:

- *"Unattractive"*—A business operating in a market that ranks in the bottom (least favorable) fifth of the PIMS data base on each dimension.
- *"Attractive"*—A business whose market ranks in the top (most favorable) fifth of the data base.
- *"Average"*—A business with average scores on each market/industry factor

EXHIBIT 4-10
Combined Impact of Market/Industry Factors on Profitability

Factor	Unattractive Level	Unattractive Impact on ROI	Average Level	Average Impact on ROI	Attractive Level	Attractive Impact on ROI
Market Growth Rate	−4%	−1.2	+4%	0	+11%	+1.1
Inflation Rate	4	−1.0	8	0	12	+1.0
% Purchases from Top 3 Suppliers	17	−0.8	42	0	70	+0.8
% Unionization	75	−2.4	42	0	0	+2.9
Purchase Importance	5%+	−3.0	1-5%	0	< 1%	+1.8
Purchase Amount	$10K+	−4.0	$1-10K	0	< $1K	+5.2
Exports	0 }	−0.4	5 }	0	10 }	+0.7
Imports	6 }		3 }		0 }	
TOTAL OF IMPACTS		−12.6		0		+13.5
All Other Profit Influences		22.4		22.4		22.4
Expected ROI		9.8		22.4		35.9

All three hypothetical businesses are assumed to have identical, average characteristics in terms of all the other strategic factors that influence profitability. Thus, each is assumed to have average market share, average product quality, an average level of vertical integration, and so on. The differences among them are, therefore, due entirely to varying rates of growth, inflation, unionization, and other market or industry conditions. (The net effects of these conditions are estimated by our overall statistical model—for an explanation, see the ruled insert on page 55; for a technical discussion see Appendix B.)

The combined impact of all of the factors shown in Exhibit 4-10 is enormous. The prototype unattractive business has an expected ROI of only 10.6, while a business operating in an "attractive" market would be expected to earn 35.9 per cent on its investment. The biggest differences between the two arise from unionized vs. non-union work forces and from selling important, big-ticket products vs. unimportant, small-ticket ones.

The point of this illustration is that picking the right kinds of markets and products can make a very big difference. So, too, can the proper choice of competitive strategy within a given market, a topic to which we now turn.

Chapter 5 _____

Market Position
and Profitability*

Having discussed the importance of picking the right markets in Chapter 4, we turn to the task of diagnosing how your profitability is related to the competitive position you attain in the markets you've decided to serve. Large market share is both a reward for providing better value to the customer and a means of realizing lower costs. Under most circumstances, enterprises that have achieved a large share of the markets they serve are considerably more profitable than their smaller-share rivals. This connection between market share and profitability has been recognized by corporate executives and consultants, and it is clearly demonstrated in the results of our research over the last fifteen years.

Yet, despite all the published evidence, even well-known experts on business strategy have offered the business community widely diverging, often shifting and conflicting, interpretations about the link between market position and profitability.

Granted that high rates of return usually accompany large market share. But the mere knowledge that large share and high returns go together isn't enough for planning purposes. You need answers to these questions:

---

*Portions of this chapter are based on our working paper, "Does Market Share Still Matter?" (Strategic Planning Institute, 1986).

- How much do profit margins differ between small-share and large-share businesses?
- Why is high market share profitable?
- Why do strategy consultants and academics disagree on their interpretations of the share/profitability relationship? Do the differences matter?
- Can the share/profitability relationship be quantified? Can it be calibrated to take into account specific business situations?
- What does the relationship imply for formulating strategy?

In this chapter we shall attempt to answer these questions by presenting evidence on the nature, importance, and implications of the links between market position and profit performance.

MEASURES OF MARKET POSITION

We use several measures of market position—absolute market share, market-share rank, and relative market share. Each measure captures a particular nuance of market position, but their similarities far outweigh their differences.

Absolute market share compares a business unit's sales to the sales of its served market. The served market's boundaries must realistically reflect customers' feelings about which companies, products, and services actually compete head-to-head in the marketplace (see Chapter 3).

Since businesses compete in many different kinds of served markets, an absolute market share of 15 may represent the market leader in a fragmented market or the number 4 competitor in a concentrated market. In light of this, we use market-share rank to make comparisons across the many served markets in the data base. Even in situations where the size of the served market (and therefore absolute market shares) cannot be determined accurately, managers typically have a good feel for the market-share *rank* of each competitor. For purposes of comparing a portfolio of businesses that compete in many different served markets, market-share rank is the simplest measure to use. But, a market-share rank of number 1 may represent a dominant leader with seventy percent of the market, or a first-among-equals position.

Two widely used measures of *relative* market share, which contrast a business's absolute share to the structure of its market, refine the concept of share rank. Share relative to the *single* largest competitor has been used by the Boston Consulting Group in their attempts to relate the "experience curve" to competitive advantage. Share relative to *three* largest competitors has been shown by our research to be the most useful measure of relative share for calibrating competitive advantage.[1] We have applied all of these measures in this chapter to diagnose the relationship between market position and profitability and to compare our interpretation of the relationship with the views of other authors.

Market Position and Profitability

There is no doubt that market share and return on investment are strongly related (Exhibit 5-1). On average, market leaders earn rates of return that are three times greater than businesses with a market-share rank of fifth or worse.

We can put these typical performance levels in perspective by comparing them to a pretax profit "hurdle rate" of 20%. We find that, on average, businesses ranked number one in market share beat

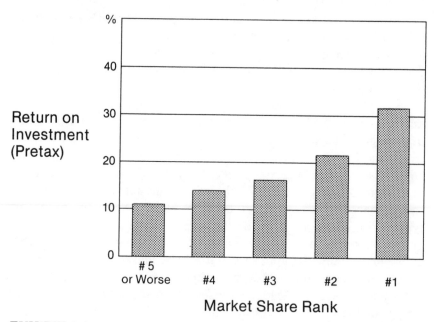

EXHIBIT 5-1
ROI Increases with Market Share Rank

this hurdle by 10 percentage points, but businesses ranked fifth or worse fall short by 10 percentage points.

The PIMS data base is the world's most extensive and detailed source of information on the share/profitability relationship, but additional evidence helps to confirm its existence. For instance, companies enjoying strong competitive positions in their primary product markets tend to be highly profitable. Consider, for example, such major companies as IBM, Gillette, Kellogg, and Coca-Cola, as well as smaller, more specialized corporations like Dr. Scholl (foot care products), Dexter (specialty chemicals and materials), and Sonoco Products (industrial packaging). Research on the Federal Trade Commission's line-of-business data base also supports the share/profitability relationship.[2] The FTC's analysis of results for some 3000 lines of businesses in 258 manufacturing industry categories in 1975 indicates a significant positive relationship between pretax return on sales and absolute market share.

WHY IS MARKET SHARE PROFITABLE?

The data demonstrate that market leaders and small-market-share businesses have very different ROIs (Exhibit 5-1). This evidence that the relationship exists, does not, however, tell us *why* there is a link between market share and profitability. There are at least four possible reasons:

- Economies of scale
- Risk aversion by customers
- Market power
- A common underlying factor

The most obvious rationale for the high rate of return enjoyed by large-share businesses is that they have achieved economies of scale in procurement, manufacturing, marketing, R&D, and other cost components. A business with a 40% share of its served market is simply twice as big as one with 20% of the same market, and it can attain, to a much greater degree, more efficient methods of operation within a particular type of technology. The effects of economies of scale represent the primary direct causal mechanism that links share to profitability. Related to scale economies is the so-called "experience curve" phenomenon widely publicized by the Boston

Consulting Group (BCG). Interpretation of the experience curve will be discussed in a later section of this chapter.

If a business has achieved (or is expected to achieve) the leading market-share position, risk-averse buyers may favor its products because they don't want to take the chances sometimes associated with buying from a smaller-share competitor. The customer preference comes as a direct consequence of share: a person placing an order with a dominant supplier feels he/she won't be challenged to defend that decision. IBM enjoys this kind of advantage in many of its business units. Many household consumers have the same kind of confidence in Kodak film, Gillette razor blades, and Bayer aspirin.

Many economists, especially in the antitrust field, believe that economies of scale have relatively little importance in most industries. These economists argue that if large-scale businesses earn higher profits than their smaller competitors, it is a result of their greater market power: their size permits them to bargain more effectively, "administer" prices, and, in the end, realize significantly higher prices for a particular product.[3]

The simplest of all explanations for the share/profitability relationship suggests that both share and ROI reflect a common underlying factor, for example, the quality of management. Good managers (including, perhaps, lucky ones!) succeed in achieving large shares of their respective markets; they are also skillful in controlling costs, getting maximum productivity from employees, and so on. Moreover, once a business achieves a leadership position—possibly by developing a new field—it is much easier for it to retain its lead than for others to catch up. (For further discussion of this point, see Chapter 9.)

These varied explanations of why the share/profitability relationship exists are not mutually exclusive. To some degree, a large-share business may benefit from all four kinds of relative advantages. It is important, however, to understand how much of the increased profitability that accompanies large market share comes from each of these or other sources.

Dissecting the Relationship

Analyzing the PIMS data base sheds light on the driving forces behind the strong relationship between market share and ROI. The data base allows us to observe real-life relationships between share and financial and operating ratios (Exhibit 5-2) and between share and

EXHIBIT 5-2
How Market Leaders Differ from Small-Share Businesses

Financial and Operating Ratios	Market Share Rank (%)				
	#5 or worse	*#4*	*#3*	*#2*	*#1*
Capital Structure:					
Investment/Sales	54.9	51.4	52.5	52.1	46.3
Receivables/Sales	15.3	14.8	14.7	14.7	14.7
Inventory/Sales	22.3	20.6	20.5	19.6	18.5
Operating Ratios:					
Pretax Profit/Sales	4.5	5.5	7.1	9.1	12.7
Purchases/Sales	51.3	48.9	45.8	43.4	41.8
Manufacturing/Sales	24.5	26.5	26.8	26.8	26.0
Marketing/Sales	9.2	9.3	9.5	9.5	8.9
R&D/Sales	1.9	1.8	1.9	2.3	2.1
Capacity Utilization	73.1	73.7	75.8	75.7	77.1

measures of relative prices and relative quality (Exhibit 5-3). As you examine these figures, remember that the PIMS sample of businesses includes a wide variety of products and industries. Consequently, when we compare businesses with market-share rank of five or worse, say, with those having the number one share position, we are *not* observing difference in costs and profits within a single industry. Each subgroup contains a diversity of industries, types of products, kinds of customers, and so on.

The data reveal important differences between large-share businesses and those with smaller shares. ROI depends, of course, on both the rate of net profit on sales and the amount of investment required to support a given volume of sales. Differences in ROI can result from differences in return on sales, investment to sales, or both.

EXHIBIT 5-3
Market Leaders Have Higher Perceived Quality and Command Higher Prices

	Market Share Rank				
	#5 or worse	*#4*	*#3*	*#2*	*#1*
Relative Quality (Percentile)	43	45	47	51	69
Relative Price (%)	103.0	103.2	103.4	103.8	105.7
Number of Businesses	301	240	347	549	877

The data show that the major reason for the share/profitability relationship is the dramatic difference in pretax profit margins on sales (Exhibit 5-2). Market leaders average a return on sales of 12.7%, while businesses with market-share ranks of five or worse earn only 4.5%. In the PIMS sample, the average return on sales exhibits a strong, smooth, upward trend as market share increases. By contrast, the ratio of investment to sales declines only slightly with increased market share.

Market Position and Relative Cost

Why do profit margins on sales increase with market share? The PIMS and BCG strategic paradigms take two very different approaches to understanding and calibrating the effect of market position on profit margins. The PIMS approach observes operating expense ratios, relative quality, and capital intensity in different market positions, and quantifies their effect on profit margins. The BCG "experience curve" approach uses data on how unit costs and cumulative volume have moved together *over time* to infer what the cost ratios are among competitors at any given point in time. Those cost ratios are then translated into profit differences.

The PIMS and BCG approaches agree on the *direction* of the share/profitability relationship. But, to assess alternative market-share strategies, executives need to quantify the *magnitude* of the profit benefit normally associated with capturing a larger share of the market served. How much will our profitability go up after scoring a 10-point gain in market share? If our market share is twice that of a competitor, will our net profit margin on sales probably be two percentage points higher or ten percentage points higher than theirs?

Back in the heyday of the experience curve, cost reduction was touted as the primary reason for pursuing a share-building strategy. As explained in a 1973 Boston Consulting Group publication, "The growth-share matrix is directly derived from the experience curve. The experience curve is the means of measuring probable cost differentials. A difference (i.e., a ratio) in market share of 2 to 1 should produce about 20 percent or more differential in pretax cost on value added."[4]

How important are economies of scale (relative *current* output) and "experience" (relative *cumulative* output) in explaining the share-profitability relationship? We can shed some light on this issue by comparing the actual experiences of the PIMS data base businesses with the cost and profit differentials implied by the experience curve approach. In the early 1970s, as just quoted, BCG claimed that a 2-to-1 market share advantage should produce a 20% (or greater) advantage in "cost of value added." By this they presumably meant all *internal* costs, as opposed to the costs of purchased materials and services. Later on (in 1978) BCG revised their earlier estimates, stating that the cost advantage associated with a 2 to 1 share ratio is only about half (10% instead of 20%) of what would be expected based on the experience curve.[5]

We can use the BCG estimates of share-related cost differentials to derive expected differences in profit margins. For this purpose, suppose that the base case is a business with a relative share (i.e., relative to the largest competitor) of 1.0. Based on average PIMS results, this base case business would have the following cost structure:

Selling Price	100%
Purchases	44
Internal Costs	46
Pretax Profit	10

Using the more widely disseminated 20% differential in internal costs that is supposed to be associated with a doubling of market share, we can calculate the internal costs of businesses that are larger or smaller than the base case:

	Share Relative to Largest Competitor				
Percent of Sales	*0.25×*	*0.5×*	*1.0×*	*2.0×*	*4.0×*
Internal Costs	72	57	46	37	29
Purchases	44	44	44	44	44
Total Costs	116	101	90	81	73
Implied Profit Margin	−16	−1	10	19	27
PIMS Actual Average Profit Margin	6	8	10	12	14

Over the range of relative shares shown, the experience curve approach to calibrating competitive advantage implies a difference of 43 points (+27 versus −16) of pretax profit margin per 4 doublings of relative share. By this approach one would expect a business that is half as big as its leading competitor to earn a profit margin that is 11 points less! (The "modified experience curve" approach implies 5 points per doubling.) But the actual experience of the PIMS businesses with the indicated relative share positions shows only a 2-point difference in pretax profit margins. As some critics have suspected, the experience curve approach leads to exaggerated estimates of the effects of relative scale and experience.

Why are the share-related cost differentials so much smaller than the proponents of the experience curve claimed? There are, we believe, two primary explanations for this:

- Relative *current* market shares are often not accurate measures of relative *long-term* experience. If market positions have shifted over time, a business with a 2-to-1 current share advantage may have a much smaller advantage in cumulative output.
- Rather than the effects of "learning," many of the declines in costs over time that occur as cumulative volume builds are the result of scale increases and technological advances, often made by people outside the industry. These cost declines are not proprietary but available to *all* competitors who can use the new technology or gain in size. And even where learning or internally developed technology result in lower costs, what is learned can be transferred to competitors by equipment suppliers, departing employees, and competitive intelligence.

The share-profitability relationship *is* due in part to cost differences that reflect economies of scale and, perhaps, differences in experiences. But these cost differences are usually much smaller than what was claimed by overenthusiastic advocates of so-called experience curve pricing strategies.

Because the PIMS data base and BCG's Growth-Share classification scheme both indicate a strong positive relationship between market share and profitability, many executives apparently believe that the action implications of the two are the same. This is not necessarily so. As the data show, the experience curve approach to calculating probable cost differentials dramatically underestimates the viability of smaller-share businesses. We agree with the assumptions of the Growth-Share portfolio system about the *direction* of the impact of market share, but not about its *magnitude*. The difference is an important one, especially in situations where the key issue is whether one should stay in a particular business, or how much a gain in market share is worth.

Because it can take into account the important differences among competitors, the PIMS data base is a useful tool for calibrating the cost and margin differentials normally associated with differences in market share (and other key drivers of profitability) not only in general, as shown above, but also in an individual business's specific competitive environment, as we shall see.

Decline of the Experience Curve

Although Bruce Henderson's views of how to calibrate competitive advantage shifted dramatically during the 1970s, he never really understood the PIMS approach. According to *Forbes,*

> "To Henderson, PIMS merely confirms much of what he knew all along from a combination of intuition and experience."[6]

In 1979, Michael Porter wrote a column in The *Wall Street Journal* pointing out the limitations of the experience curve as a device for formulating strategy.[7] By 1981, Walter Kiechel III, was writing about "The Decline of the Experience Curve" in a *Fortune* series that examined some of the major concepts being used to formulate corporate strategy at that time. According to Kiechel,

> "The news for the 1980s isn't that the experience curve has been proved wrong. Indeed, its logic has been refined, its implications plumbed for new ideas such as shared costs and the life cycle of technologies. What's happening now, though, is that the curve is being consigned to a much reduced place in the firmament of strategic concepts. With it is going a good bit of the importance originally attached to market share."[8]

Since the differences between SPI/PIMS and BCG still had not been clearly stated at that time, the PIMS baby (a multi-market data base useful as a tool for calibrating competitive advantage and for strategy analysis) was thrown out with the BCG bath water, the mis-named "experience" curve.

In retrospect, it is ironic that BCG, the pioneering firm, and Bruce Henderson, its founder, who made a major contribution by bringing economic analysis and strategy formulation to the consulting business, turned out to be using a tool that was better suited "to project normal or potential cost declines of a given competitor" than it was for measuring competitive advantage.[9]

Other Factors Affect Relative Costs

Based on early (and even later) interpretations of the experience
curve, one would never have expected Japanese companies to crack
the North American market in autos or steel. Clearly General Motors, Ford, and U.S. Steel were cumulative volume leaders in the
1970s. Yet they have been forced to surrender a great deal of market
share to Japanese companies who had less cumulative volume. Why
didn't "experience" save the U.S. auto and steel industries from
Japanese competitors?

First, as we have just discussed, the competitive effects of cumulative volume were misunderstood and overstated. And while
market share has been and is still important, its measurement must
be refined to capture effective share in a global context.

Relative cost is driven by other factors as well as market share:

- Relative effectiveness in statistical process control,
- Relative productivity,
- International comparative advantage (relative costs of wages,
  materials, energy and capital), and
- Inventory and logistics costs associated with the proliferation
  of models and of options.

The globalization of competition over the last decade has increased the importance of these factors, relative to cumulative output, as determinants of relative costs. Unfortunately for the U.S.,
Japanese companies seem to have the edge over Detroit and Pittsburgh on many of these cost drivers.

International comparative advantage has played a major role in
the capital intensive auto and steel industries. Relative to the U.S.,
Japan has lower costs of capital and labor. Relative to Japan, the
U.S. has lower costs of energy and materials. The difference in relative capital and energy costs is the main reason why the Japanese
have had great success in exporting steel but little success in aluminum, which is energy intensive.

Market Position, Quality and Prices

Perhaps the key reason why Japan is currently so successful in automobiles is that customer-perceived quality often outweighs price

(cost) in the customer's purchase decision. The cumulative volume framework remains silent on relative customer-perceived quality and could not have helped to predict this quality effect.

By contrast, the PIMS framework explicitly charts the key steps through which perceived quality drives business performance. A study by Phillips, Chang, and Buzzell traced the linkages from superior relative quality to higher relative prices, market-share gain, lower relative costs, and higher profitability (Exhibit 5-4).[10] Their results showed that the PIMS measures of relative quality and other strategy variables are highly reliable indicators of the concepts represented. They concluded that relative quality does play a causal role in influencing business performance.

Quality is extremely important to market leaders. Looking back at Exhibits 5-2 and 5-3, the data do not always show smooth, continuous relationships between market share and the various components of quality, price, cost, and investment. Indeed, it appears that one pattern operates as share rank moves from 5 or worse to number 2, but a somewhat different pattern applies to market leaders. In particular, there are substantial differences in relative *quality* (and also in relative *prices*) between market leaders and followers (Exhibit 5-3). Market leaders not only command higher prices but also maintain their leadership position by offering products and services that are superior relative to those offered by their competitors.

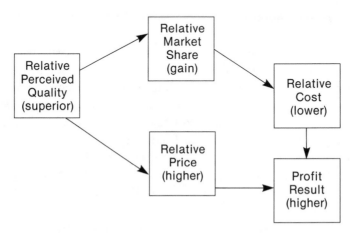

EXHIBIT 5-4
Winning with Superior Perceived Quality

Here is how Tom Peters summarized this subject in his best-selling book, *A Passion For Excellence:*

> The PIMS paradigm is diametrically opposite to the experience curve from a cause-and-effect standpoint: It says, First achieve a "relative perceived product-quality" edge over your competitors. If you do so, you will gain share. By gaining share (via relatively higher perceived product quality) you can, indeed, then take advantage of economies of scale as appropriate, and achieve low-cost distinction.
>
> The difference is radical. By the PIMS logic, you start from quality and achieve low cost as a result. According to the traditional experience curve approach, you buy your way in with low prices, achieve low cost, and may or may not have acceptable service and quality. If you don't have them, then you're constantly vulnerable to any higher-quality attacker who comes your way; the edge you scrambled so hard for is not likely to be sustainable. We call the distinction "earning your way in" (via quality and service) versus "buying your way in" (via heavy discounting). Only the former, it would appear, is sustainable.[11]

In the experiences of PIMS businesses, attaining a superior quality position does not seem to involve many of the strategic trade-offs, such as higher relative direct costs or marketing expenditures, that business analysts often attribute to quality strategies. Superior quality does, however, support higher prices. In the next chapter we will expand on the importance of measuring and tracking customer-perceived relative quality and differentiation, and linking them to business performance.

Procurement Economies

In our discussion of market position and relative costs, we focused on economies of scale in value-added costs and assumed there were no procurement economies. If we had built procurement economies into the analysis, the "experience" curve's expected profit margin differentials per doubling of relative share (which were already way too large) would have been even further off the mark.

Are there economies of scale in purchased costs of materials and energy? We believe that the answer is yes, but the empirical test is not as straightforward as you might think, even with the PIMS data base at hand.

It is difficult to get a clear look at purchased cost economies (or at manufacturing economies, for that matter) because large-share businesses tend to be more vertically integrated than small-share businesses. They tend to carry out more stages of the value adding chain that results in their final sales dollar. They do more "make" and less "buy," and this clouds our ability to examine economies of scale by looking at expense ratios to sales as a function of market share. Having said this, let's examine how expense ratios to sales are related to market share, and interpret the results with care.

For small-share businesses—those ranked number five or worse—purchases represent 53% of sales, compared with only 42% for market leaders (Exhibit 5-2). The decline in the purchases-to-sales ratio is quite a bit less, however, if we control for the level of vertical integration.

While the vertical integration explanation of the decline in purchases to sales is probably valid for some of the businesses in the sample, we believe that the decline in costs of purchased materials usually also reflects economies of scale in buying and, perhaps, bargaining power in dealing with suppliers. Economies of scale in procurement arise from lower costs of manufacturing, marketing, and distributing when suppliers sell in large quantities (see Chapter 8). For really large-scale buyers, custom-designed components and special formulations of materials that are purchased on long-term contracts may offer very large economies.

The shift toward "make" versus "buy" as market share increases also clouds our view of economies of scale in manufacturing. If there were no economies of scale in manufacturing, greater vertical integration ought to result in a higher level of manufacturing or operational costs.[12] But the data show little or no connection between manufacturing expense as a percentage of sales, and market share (Exhibit 5-2), probably because the rise in cost associated with the increase in vertical integration is offset by economies of scale.

Efficient Use of Investment

While the bulk of the ROI difference between market leaders and those ranked 5 or worse is due to differences in return on sales, some twenty percent of the ROI difference is due to differences in investment intensity. On average, market leaders support their higher margins with more efficient use of investment than do followers.

If there were no scale-related economies in inventories, receivables, or fixed capital, the vertical integration phenomenon would cause us to expect investment to sales to *increase* with market share.

But the investment-to-sales ratio actually *declines* slightly with increased market share (Exhibit 5-2). If we control for vertical integration, the decline in investment to sales is even more pronounced. Market leaders clearly benefit from economies of scale in inventories. The data show, too, that capacity utilization is slightly greater for large-share businesses.

CAN SMALL-SHARE BUSINESSES PROSPER?

The fact that market share and profitability generally go hand in hand (as shown in Exhibit 5-1) led some consultants and corporate executives to adopt the extreme position that small-share businesses *cannot* be profitable. Reacting to this, several investigators have demonstrated that *some* small-share competitors can and do earn very attractive returns. Two articles in the *Harvard Business Review* have reported these studies:

> Richard Hamermesh, M. J. Anderson, and J. E. Harris analyzed the performance of companies whose results are published in the annual *Forbes* magazine financial surveys. They found "numerous successful low-share businesses" and discussed three examples of this phenomenon in some detail. One of these, Burroughs, was praised for focusing on selected segments of the computer market. As a result, the company's profits grew during the early 1970s at a rate faster than IBM's despite a huge disadvantage in *overall* market share.[13]

> Carolyn Woo and Arnold Cooper examined the performance of low-share businesses in the PIMS data base. They identified 40 low-share businesses that enjoyed pretax ROI's of 20% or more and compared their strategies with those of "ineffective" low-share businesses. Among other things, the successful low-share businesses were found to be characterized by high relative quality, narrow product lines, and low total costs.[14]

As these two studies show, small-share businesses can indeed be profitable. This is hardly surprising in light of the fact, noted earlier, that share is just one of approximately two dozen key profit influences that have been documented in PIMS-based research—and that other profit determinants, such as "corporate culture," also play important roles. A small-share business that is favorably positioned on most other key strategic dimensions *should* earn satisfactory profits. PIMS research shows, for example, the average ROI of small-share businesses whose products or services ranked in the top third in terms of relative quality was 18%. If a business in this group also benefited from low investment intensity, high labor productivity, and

rapid market growth, its expected rate of return could easily be 25%
or better. But it should be emphasized that *most* small-share businesses don't fit this description. Of the 641 businesses in the PIMS
data base with shares of 10% or less, only about one in four achieved
an ROI of 20% or more. In contrast, three-fourths of the businesses
with shares of 40% or more had rates of return over 20%. It is useful
to recognize and understand the exceptions to the general rule—but
it is also important to remember that they *are* exceptions.

Is It Better To Be Small Than "Stuck In The Middle?"

The examples of profitable small-share businesses cited by Hamermesh et al. and by Woo and Cooper don't contradict the general
rule that share and profitability usually go together. A stronger dis-
sent, however, has been expressed by Michael Porter in his best-
selling book, *Competitive Strategy*. Porter suggests that while there
may be a positive share-profitability relationship in "some" industries, in others the relationship is inverse and in still others it is U-
shaped, i.e., high on both ends and low in the middle. Citing the
automobile and electric motor industries as examples of the U-shaped
pattern, he warns of the dangers of being "stuck in the middle."[15]
The clear implication is that in such industries, it is better to have a
small share than to be, say, the second or third-ranked competitor.
In the industries where the relationship is inverse, it would even be
better to be a small-share competitor than to be the market leader!

Can Porter's views be reconciled with the positive share-profitability relationship shown in Exhibit 5-1? We should note, first, that
there is an important conceptual difference between Porter's concept
of share and ours. He defines "share" as a business unit's sales in
relation to a broadly-defined industry such as computers or automobiles. (Hamermesh et al. followed the same approach, defining
the Burroughs Corporation's market share as its fraction of total
computer industry shipments.) In contrast, all of our market-share
figures are measured in relation to each business unit's *served market*. The served market is defined as that part or segment of an industry (in terms of products, kinds of customers, and geographic
areas) in which a business actually competes. For most businesses,
the market defined in this way is considerably smaller than the overall industry in which it participates. For example, one of the successful small-share competitors cited by Porter is Mercedes-Benz.

This highly-profitable firm has a very small share of total worldwide automobile sales. But, applying our concept of its relevant served market, Mercedes-Benz has a *large* share of the luxury car market. Put another way, we don't believe that Mercedes-Benz really competes with Honda, Toyota, or Volkswagen, and only to a very limited extent with General Motors. Its sales relative to these much larger producers is not, therefore, a meaningful measure of Mercedes-Benz's competitive position.

By defining market share in relation to a business unit's actual served market, we do *not* mean to encourage executives to limit their attention only to current customers, products, and geographic markets. Competitors operating in neighboring markets often can enter a market and overcome even the strongest incumbent, especially when capabilities developed in one sector are easily transferred to another. For example, Briggs & Stratton Corporation has long dominated the U.S. market for small engines of the types used in lawn mowers and garden tractors. Beginning in 1984, Honda began an aggressive campaign to promote its line of lawn and garden equipment in the U.S., utilizing its experience in manufacturing engines for motorcycles.[16] If Briggs & Stratton had been oblivious to the possibility of Honda's entry into its served market (which they were not), they could have been highly vulnerable. Thus, having a large share of a particular served market is not a guarantee of invulnerability to competition. But, we believe, a business unit's share of its served market is nevertheless a better measure of its *current* competitive position than its share of a broad and heterogeneous industry.

There is a more fundamental flaw in Porter's notion of a U-shaped relationship between share and profitability. By suggesting that small-share businesses typically earn high rates of return, he implies that this performance is *caused* by having a small share. In fact, the examples he cites illustrate how successful product differentiation can *offset* the disadvantages of a low share. As Exhibit 5-5 demonstrates, high quality can indeed yield high profits, even for small-share competitors—but it yields even bigger returns for those with strong market positions, and the latter is a much more common combination. A PIMS-based study by Lynn Phillips, Dae Chang, and Robert Buzzell showed that in the majority of cases superior quality, large share, *and* low costs relative to competition go together.[17] This contradicts the idea that so-called "generic strategies" aimed at low cost are incompatible with those based on product differentiation.

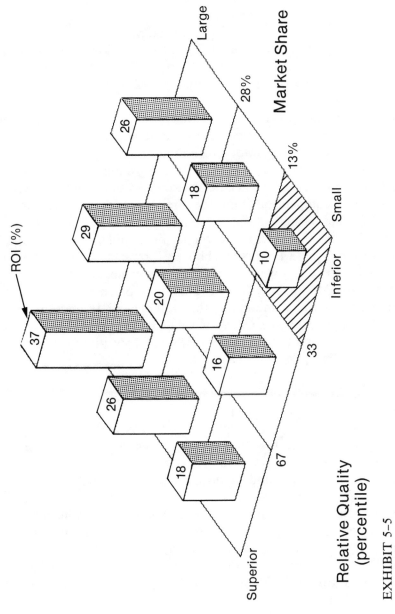

ROI (%)

Relative Quality
(percentile)

Market Share

EXHIBIT 5–5
A Business That Is "Caught in the Corner" Is in an Extremely Poor Strategic Position

87

Even if market share *is* defined and measured in relation to industries rather than served markets, the available evidence shows that share is generally positively related to profitability. If the relationship really varied from positive to negative to U-shaped, we would expect the *average* of a broad sample of industries to show a very weak connection, if any, between share and profit performance. But this is not the case: in the Federal Trade Commission's Line of Business research program, the profitability of business segments was related to a variety of factors including each segment's "share of industry sales." The results showed a strong, *positive* relationship between share and profits.[18] This is hardly what we would expect if there were an appreciable number of industries characterized by U-shaped or down-sloping share-profitability relationships.

An analogy may help to put the seeming anomaly of successful small-share businesses into perspective. In 1985 a nationally-televised "slam dunk" competition featured some of the most talented players in the National Basketball Association. Almost all of the contestants were at least 6'8" tall. But the winner, incredibly, was 5'5" Spud Webb of the Atlanta Hawks! Webb's performance certainly showed that small people can win at a big person's game. But no one, presumably, would conclude from it that small players are usually or even often better at slamdunking than tall players. In the same way, we find the occasional success of small-share competitors unconvincing as the basis for any general argument for preferring a weak market position.

OTHER VIEWS OF CAUSE AND EFFECT

While our purpose in this chapter is to focus on the strategic interpretations of the share/profitability relationship, we will briefly discuss the market power and random process interpretations.

Some economists believe concentrated market structures facilitate "oligopolistic coordination," a rather friendly, nonaggressive kind of competition, resulting in lower output, higher prices, and thereby higher rates of return than are typical in "competitive" markets. Therefore, they expect to see a direct relation between "industry concentration" (the combined market share of the top four companies) and profitability.

The PIMS business unit data base provides a straightforward approach to comparing the relative power of market share and concentration in explaining differences in profitability. The result: market share shows a far more dramatic effect on ROI than concentration when they are looked at together (Exhibit 5-6). Concentration actually does little to explain the structure-profit relationship. Our findings are supported by research on the Federal Trade Commission's line-of-business (LOB) data base. When analyzed in the LOB data base, share has a strong positive relation to profitability, but concentration has a weak negative relation to profitability.

We conclude that even though market share and concentration usually go together, it is the share that matters, not the concentration.[19] Put another way, the market power interpretation of the share/profitability relationship doesn't have much empirical support.

Is the share/profitability relationship all a matter of luck? Many academic technicians are attracted to a random-process interpretation of the share/profitability relationship. They reason, for example, that if many small-share competitors start out on equal terms, the lucky ones will probably gain both share and profitability. They focus their attention on change in share and change in profitability, rather than on how share differences affect profit differences in more stable market environments. Often they forget that many served markets are created by a pioneer rather than by a horde of small-share competitors awaiting the start of a random process. The pioneer starts with 100 percent share and subsequently faces challenges from early followers and late entrants.

We don't dispute that the assumptions of random process are logically sufficient to explain a dynamic share/profitability relationship. Indeed, one can find examples of businesses that (by skill or luck) were in the right place at the right time and gained in both share and profitability. But the random process view is not very interesting from a strategy perspective. If random events cause the share/profitability relationship, the action implication is to "be lucky." That advice is easy to understand, but hard to implement. Still, it is useful to know to what extent the observed share/profitability relationship is due to economies of scale versus random events.

In 1977 Caves, Gale, and Porter demonstrated that the random-process hypothesis is probably not the primary explanation for the observed relationship.[20] Here we will present a simplified update of one of their tests.

If the share/profitability relationship is due mostly to luck, it would show up more strongly in unstable markets where shares are

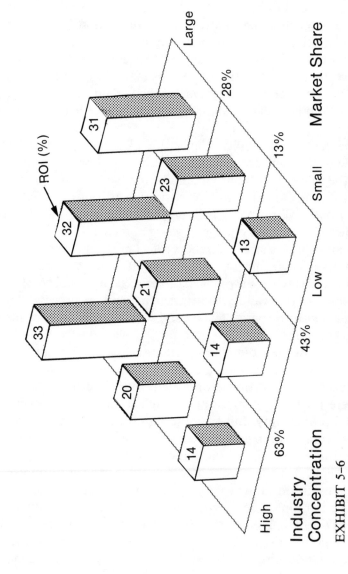

ROI (%)

Industry
Concentration

Market Share

EXHIBIT 5-6
Which Determines Profitability—Industry Concentration or Market Share?

shifting dramatically. Changing shares suggest that investment decisions by competing suppliers carry a great deal of risk. And the very fact that market shares are changing indicates that investments that succeed are capable of increasing a business's market share as well as its profit rate.

If the share/profitability relationship is stronger in markets where shares are stable, however, it is difficult to credit this result to the random-process view that luck causes share and profit to move together.

The evidence? The share/profitability relation turns out to be stronger where shares are stable as Caves, Gale, and Porter found in their 1977 study. In stable markets, market leaders on average reap 25 percentage points more ROI than small-share businesses. In markets where shares are unstable, the ROI difference is significantly less—only 17 percentage points. These results contradict the random process interpretation of the share/profitability relationship. We conclude, therefore, that the random process hypothesis not only offers little help from a strategy perspective, but also doesn't explain much of the relationship between profitability and market share.

The whole question of "spurious" versus "causal" relationships between share and profit performance is, we believe, a red herring. Market share *in itself* doesn't "cause" anything. How can it? A business unit's market share is nothing more than a measurement. It reflects two kinds of forces, however, that *do* cause high or low profits: (1) relative scale and/or experience-based cost advantages or disadvantages and (2) relative success or lack of it in designing, producing, and marketing products that meet the needs of the customers in a particular served market. In this chapter we have shown that both factors are important—large-share businesses *do* typically have lower costs, and they also typically have product quality advantages that translate into bigger profit margins.

Our interpretation of how the share-profitability relationship typically works is summarized in these key steps:

- Superior relative quality is achieved by a combination of skillful product or service design and proper selection of market(s) to serve,
- Providing superior quality enables a successful business to charge premium prices (within reason, of course) *and* to gain market share,
- By gaining share, the business attains scale and/or experience-

based cost advantages over its competitors (As noted earlier, these kinds of cost advantages are *not* generally incompatible with successful differentiation.),

- Higher profitability follows as a result of premium prices, costs equal to or lower than those of competitors, and advantages in procurement and utilization of invested capital, as noted earlier.

If this is a valid picture of the typical linkage between share and profitability, then the key "causal" factors operating are scale and quality. Market share is, in effect, a convenient kind of shorthand that reflects some combination of these underlying profit influences.

Change in Profit versus Level of Profit

In a recent study, "Is Market Share All That It's Cracked Up to Be?" Robert Jacobson and David Aaker suggest that the observed correlation between share and profitability might be due to a third factor (perhaps luck) rather than a direct effect of market share on ROI.[21] But then, to control for such third factors, they included past profitability as a factor to explain current profitability. In effect they related *change* in ROI to the *level* of market share.

Since large-share businesses do not continuously increase their ROI differential over small-share businesses we would expect the correlation between change in ROI and the level of market share to be essentially zero . . . which it is. This finding doesn't mean that ROI is not related to market share. It merely means that *change*-in-ROI is not related to market share and that the ROI differential between large-share and small-share businesses is reasonably stable over time.[22]

How then, *should* one control for third factors? By including in the ROI model any key profit influences that are related to both share and profitability. One such third factor is relative quality, which is positively related to both ROI and share.

When we relate ROI to market share *and* relative quality, we find a 4.7 point ROI differential per 10.0 points of market share. This is a better measure of the direct causal effect of market share on ROI than the 5.3 point differential observed when quality is left out of the ROI model.

The general profit differential of 4.7 points of ROI per 10.0

points of market share is merely an average. Customized profit differentials (among a business and its key competitors or between a business's current and planned market-share position) can be calibrated much more accurately for an individual business. This customization procedure takes into account the business's R&D and marketing cost versus manufacturing cost mix, its investment intensity, its share instability, and other business-unit specific characteristics.

Since share accounts for about 14 percent of the dispersion in ROI among businesses, we need to take more factors into account, even if they are not correlated with share. SPI's Par ROI model controls for many factors in addition to relative share and relative quality. These other drivers of profitability include capacity utilization, real market growth, purchase amount by immediate customer, investment intensity, and productivity (see Chapter 3).

SUMMARIZING THE DIFFERENT VIEWS

Exhibit 5-7 contrasts the ROI/share relationships depicted by Henderson, Porter, and Jacobson and Aaker, and compares them to the empirical relationships summarized by Buzzell and Gale. Relative to the actual experience of businesses in the marketplace:

1. Henderson overstates the relationship between ROI and share.
2. Jacobsen and Aaker understate the relationship between ROI and share.
3. Porter is stuck in the middle. He confuses the separate effects of market share and perceived quality on ROI.

Reductio ad Absurdum

While no analogy is perfect, the relationship between height and weight can take us a long way toward understanding these different interpretations of the ROI/share relationship and it may provide some comic relief. How would the Henderson, Porter, and Jacobson and Aaker approaches come out if applied to the relationship between weight and height rather than profitability and share? Speculation has resulted in the relationships shown in Exhibit 5-8.

Applying the PIMS approach, we find that weight is positively

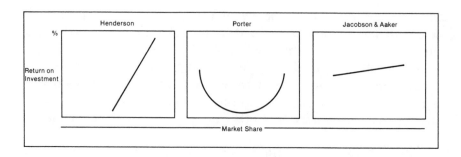

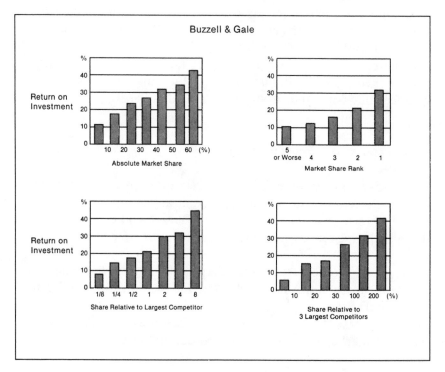

EXHIBIT 5-7
Interpreting the Relationship Between ROI and Market Share

related to height—about three pounds per inch. This general differential can be calibrated to reflect a person's sex and body frame.

When Henderson thought that the ROS differential per doubling
of relative market share was 11 points (5 times greater than it actually
is) he wrote a perspective on "The Rule of Three or Four." He rea-
soned that if smaller-share competitors were at a tremendous dis-

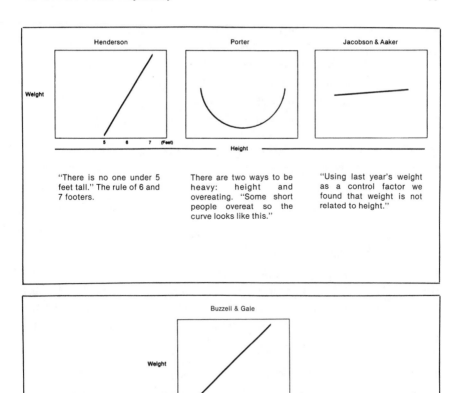

EXHIBIT 5-8
Reductio ad Absurdum: Speculations About Interpreting the Relationship Between Weight and Height

advantage, there would only be room for a handful of suppliers to any served market.

Suppose Henderson had similarly misgauged the weight/height relationship by a factor of 5. Observing from empirical data that the average six footer weighs about 180 pounds and believing that the weight differential was 15 pounds per inch, he might have concluded that "There Is No One Under Five Feet Tall."

Here's how Michael Porter's reasoning might be applied to the weight/height relationship. There are at least two ways to be heavy: height and overeating. Some short people overeat so the curve looks U-shaped. But what about the short people that don't overeat and the medium-height people who do overeat?

Applying Jacobson and Aaker's methodology, it is a good idea to control for factors other than height which might cause the observed weight/height relationship. Using last year's weight as a control factor we would be studying *change* in weight versus *level* of height and we would find that "weight is not strongly related to height."

WHEN IS MARKET SHARE MOST IMPORTANT?

Given that market leaders have a large relative market share and thus the profitability that goes with it, it is natural to question whether the share and profitability relationship shifts from industry to industry. What kinds of businesses will find market share most critical to their success? What industries need to think most carefully about share position?

Our analyses of the PIMS data base clearly demonstrate a strong general relationship between ROI and market share. But while these general findings are interesting, more specific analyses are necessary if you wish to reposition your business so that it will outperform its competitors. The importance of share does vary considerably from one type of industry or market situation to another. We have already seen that share is more important in stable markets than it is in unstable markets. Two other interesting variations focus on the functional components of value added and the degree of investment intensity.

R&D and Marketing versus Manufacturing

High-tech industries are characterized by heavy doses of R&D and marketing. Others carry out most of their value adding activities in the manufacturing function. Is market share more important in high-tech or smokestack industries?

People who follow the experience curve explanation of the share/ profitability relationship invariably answer that share is most important in manufacturing-intensive industries. By contrast, those who believe that economies of scale are the main reason behind the share/ profitability relationship feel that share matters more in industries where fixed costs are large relative to variable costs.

We used the ratio of R&D and marketing costs relative to manufacturing costs, to split the PIMS data base into two groups. For R&D and marketing intensive businesses the ROI of the average market leader is 26 percentage points greater than the ROI of the average small-share business (Exhibit 5-9). For manufacturing-intensive businesses the corresponding ROI differential is only 12 points. So, we conclude that market share is more important in high-tech industries.

Why? Compared to manufacturing costs, R&D and marketing costs tend to be relatively fixed. In most markets you need a certain amount of expenditure on innovation and marketing to remain a viable competitor. R&D and marketing activities are thus more subject to scale effects than are manufacturing costs.

Initially one might, therefore, expect R&D and marketing costs to decline as we move from small-share businesses to large-share businesses. But, we find that R&D-to-sales and marketing-to-sales ratios are about the same for large-share and small-share businesses (Exhibit 5-2). There are two reasons why we don't observe a decline. First, as noted earlier, large-share businesses are more vertically integrated (they "make" rather than "buy"). Second, and related, since R&D and marketing costs are more subject to scale effects, market leaders often pursue competitive strategies of developing product and service superiority and of introducing new products that are R&D and marketing intensive. This strategy makes it difficult for small-share competitors to keep pace. The vertical integration and innovation activities that tend to increase the R&D and marketing-to-sales ratios of large-share businesses are offset by economies of scale in marketing and R&D. This yields the flat pattern of average cost ratios we have observed (Exhibit 5-2).

Heavy versus Light Investment Intensity

Market leadership has a greater payoff in industries that are not very investment intensive. For businesses with low investment to sales the ROI of the average market leader soars 25 percentage points above the ROI of the average small-share business. For investment intensive businesses the corresponding ROI differential is only 11 points.

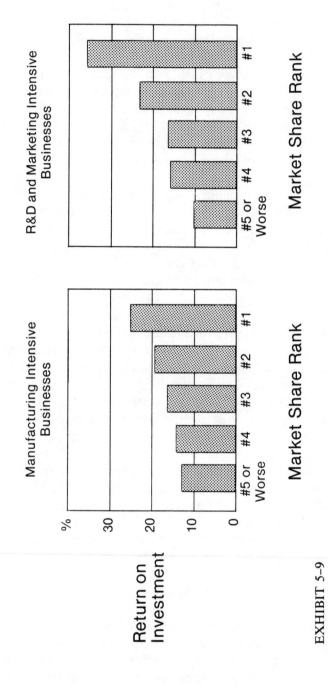

EXHIBIT 5-9
Market Share Is More Important in High-Tech or Marketing-Intensive Industries

Why? Market share helps return on sales (ROS) via economies of scale that reduce unit costs. Since

$$ROI = ROS \times (Sales/Investment),$$

the ROS differential between share leaders and followers is greatly leveraged in industries where investment-to-sales is very low.

In investment-intensive industries, on average, only the market leaders come close to earning a 20% pre-tax ROI . . . and even they fall a little short (Exhibit 5–10). By contrast, in low-investment situations all but the smallest-share competitors average returns well above 20%, and even the smallest-share competitors come close.

In addition to these industry differences (high-tech versus low-tech, investment-intensity light versus heavy) we have noted previously that the positive effect of absolute market share on ROI diminishes as market share gets larger because the drops in unit costs don't come as fast when market share is already large.

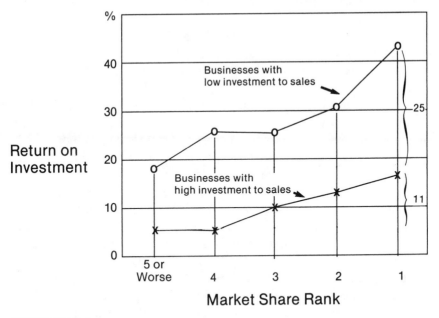

EXHIBIT 5–10
Market Leadership Pays Off Most in Industries That Are Not
Investment Intensive

MARKET SHARE AND COMPETITIVE STRATEGY

The importance of market share has, no doubt, been exaggerated by some commentators, especially those who linked the advantages of a large share to experience-based cost differentials. But the available evidence from PIMS and other sources clearly shows that share and profitability are strongly related. The relationship has been confirmed repeatedly, in analyses of the actual experiences of businesses in different kinds of industries, different time periods, and various parts of the world. Market share is not the only key to profitability, but it is certainly one of the most important. In light of this, how should market share be treated in the process of developing and evaluating competitive stretegies?

First, the pursuit of market share is not in itself a strategy. It is often an important strategic objective; but it is much easier to state such a goal than it is to determine how it can be attained. In this chapter we have emphasized the importance of relative quality, both as a means of staking out a strong market position and, later, of maintaining or improving one. Other important weapons in competing for market share include product innovation and spending levels for sales forces and advertising and sales promotion. All of these play a role: the special appeal of quality is that, in many cases, it offers a means of building share without incurring any short-term penalty.

When a business doesn't have a significant quality advantage over its rivals, adopting a share-building strategy can be very costly. We have already cited an example of this in Chapter 1—Yamaha's disastrous effort in the early 1980s to overtake Honda as the leader in motorcycle production. Yamaha's president, Hisao Koike, adopted the slogan "Take the Lead" and pursued an aggressive program of new model introductions. By April 1983 the company was heavily in debt to finance its inventories and more than 2,000 workers had been laid off. Koike was removed as president and the "kamikaze attack" was called off.

Efforts to wrest market share away from a well-established leader are unlikely to pay off unless the leader is complacent or distracted by other problems. Considerable attention has therefore been given to the question of alternative strategies for market followers. Several of the critics of the share-profitability relationship have cited the successes of small competitors who focused their efforts on particular market segments or niches. There is no doubt that this kind of market focusing is an important strategic option for many enterprises, especially those that have no possibilities of becoming leaders in more broadly-defined industries. It is for this reason that we, in the PIMS research program, have so strongly emphasized the idea of carefully defining and selecting a business unit's *served market*. Making the proper choices of products or services to offer, types of customers to serve, and geographic areas in which to operate are among the most important decisions that managers make.

Defining the served market is not, however, something that managers can control completely. Who competes with whom is an issue that is also affected by what other companies do and, ultimately, by the underlying economics of an industry. Consider, for example, the three examples of successful small-share competitors cited by Hamermesh et al. in 1978: the Burroughs Corporation (computers), Crown Cork & Seal (metal containers), and Union Camp (paper). All three had outstanding records of growth and profitability in the early 1970s. A decade later, the picture had changed considerably. During the years 1981–85, Crown Cork & Seal's average return on equity (ROE) was 11.3%; it ranked 12th among 13 companies in the packaging industry. Union Camp, with an ROE of 14.8%, placed near the middle of the rankings in the paper industry. Burroughs' ROE had declined to 7.1% (23rd out of 24 computer manufacturers) and the company was attempting to acquire Sperry in an effort to create a viable competitor to IBM in the large-computer business.

These illustrations suggest that what constitutes a distinct sub-market within an industry at one time may not be so distinct at a later time. A particular product variation or customer group may, for example, simply have been neglected by larger competitors, leaving it available to a smaller rival despite the latter's inherently inferior cost position or technology. Serving such a niche may be highly profitable for some years, but eventually it is likely to become much less so. The moral would appear to be: either take steps to accentuate the differences between a sub-market and the overall market (for instance, through product development) or be prepared to move on to another one.

Many of the criticisms of the market-share profitability relationship stem from the perception that it was being used, a decade ago, as a basis for overly simplistic strategic formulas. This is unfortunate; the share-profitability relationship is a fact of life that should be recognized and understood. It does not, in itself, provide any general prescriptions for management, but it does yield insights into the likely consequences of strategic choices.

The strategic implications of the market-share/profitability relationship do vary according to the circumstances of the individual business. But there is no doubt that the relationship can be translated into dynamic strategies for all companies trying to set market share goals. The PIMS data base is often used to calibrate the cost of growing against the benefits of growing, with some precision, for specific business situations and then translate this knowledge into action plans.

One example of a company pursuing strategic objectives that are consistent with the concepts and findings of this chapter is General Electric under the leadership of John F. Welch, Jr. He has said that

" . . . Our strategic aim is to evolve into a company that's either number one or number two in its arenas . . . "[23]

Major steps in this evolution include the disposition of Utah Mining and the acquisition of RCA and some financial service companies. GE is shifting its portfolio away from investment-intensive arenas toward high-tech and service arenas. Welch is attempting to become number one or number two in situations where being number one or number two matters most.

Once market position is established, market leaders and followers typically need to pursue different strategies. Coming up with these different strategies is the subject of Chapter 9.

Chapter 6 ———————————————

Quality Is King

The 1960s and 1970s brought a dawning realization that market share is key to a company's growth and profitability. The 1980s have shown just as clearly that one factor above all others—quality—drives market share. And when superior quality and large market share are both present, profitability is virtually guaranteed. But relative *perceived* quality is not identical to the traditional concept of "conformance" quality. It demands an entirely new perspective—one that calls for viewing quality externally, from the customer's perspective, rather than internally, from a quality-assurance point of view.

A company uninstructed in the importance of relative perceived quality might struggle to emulate the Japanese by achieving low scrap rates and zero defects measured against prescribed product specifications. In such a company the quality specialist normally would be a production manager. But many a perfectly manufactured new product has failed in its marketplace for strategic reasons. In this chapter, therefore, we will come to grips with quality as a strategic concept and explore how to manage it effectively.

Measuring Relative Perceived Quality

In order to study how relative perceived quality is related to your business's performance, you need to be able to measure it. During the past ten years SPI member companies and staff have evolved a "quality profiling" process that managers use for assessing the quality of their product/service offerings relative to competitors, formulating blueprint plans to improve relative quality, and estimating the payoffs. The method used to derive measures of relative quality is outlined in the set-off material, "Assessing Relative Quality." All of the quality scores shown in this chapter and elsewhere in this book are expressed as *percentiles*. Thus, for example, a business whose relative quality assessment ranked in the bottom fifth of the PIMS data base is represented by a percentile rating between zero and 20.

QUALITY AND BUSINESS PERFORMANCE

The PIMS strategy framework traces the different ways by which perceived quality and conformance quality drive business performance. Key linkages from superior relative quality to higher profitability and faster growth are spelled out in Exhibit 6-1.

There are two basic ways to beat your competitors. One is to achieve superior perceived quality by developing a set of product specifications and service standards that more closely meet customer needs than competitors. The other is to achieve superior conformance quality by being more effective than your competitors in conforming to the appropriate product specifications and service standards. These ways of winning are not mutually exclusive, so you should try to outperform your competitors on both perceived quality and conformance quality.

Most books on quality focus on either conformance quality or perceived quality, but not on both. A refreshing new exception is *The Chain of Quality* by John Groocock.[2] He not only covers both concepts of quality, but also presents evidence based on TRW businesses that support the PIMS findings on how superior perceived quality goes with profitability.

Achieving superior *perceived* quality gives your business three options—all of them good. First, you can charge a higher price for your superior quality offering and let the premium fall right to the bottom line. Second, you can charge a higher price and invest the premium in R&D and in new products to ensure your perceived quality and market share for the future.

ASSESSING RELATIVE QUALITY

The method used by SPI since 1980 to assess the relative perceived quality of a business unit's products and services involves the following steps:

1. A meeting is held, in which a multi-functional team of managers and staff specialists identify the non-price product or service attributes that affect customer buying decisions. For an office equipment product, these might include durability, maintenance costs, flexibility, credit terms, and appearance.
2. The team is then asked to assign "importance weights" for each attribute representing their relative importance as influences on customer purchase decisions. These relative importance weights sum to 100. (For markets in which there are important segments with *different* importance weights, separate weights are assigned to each segment.)
3. Finally, the management team rates their business unit's product line, and those of leading competitors, on each of the performance dimensions identified in Step 1. From these attribute-by-attribute ratings, each weighted by its respective importance weight, an overall relative quality score is constructed.

In many cases, the judgmental ratings assigned by the management team are tested (and, when appropriate, modified) by collecting ratings from customers via surveys.

Our approach to assessing relative quality is similar to the "multi-attribute" methods used in marketing research.[1] These research methods are, however, employed primarily for evaluating or comparing *individual products* (actual or prospective), while our scores apply to a business unit's entire product *line*.

Third, you can offer the customer better value by charging the *same* price as competitors, but for your superior product/service offering. This will allow you to build for the future by gaining market share. The gain in share means volume growth, rising capacity utilization and, ultimately, capacity expansion allowing you to introduce new equipment that embodies the latest cost-saving technology.

Achieving superior *conformance* quality yields two key benefits. First, it means a lower cost of quality than that of competitors, and thereby a lower overall cost. Second, conformance quality is often

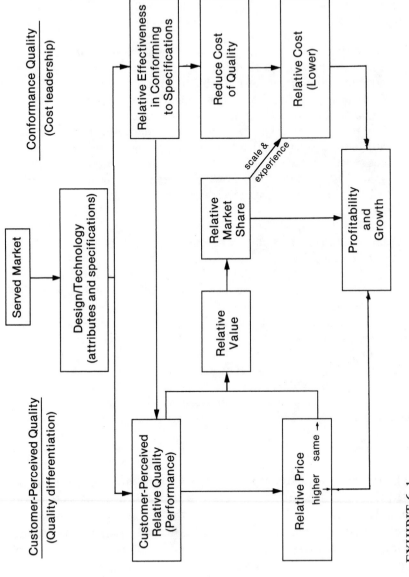

EXHIBIT 6–1
How Quality Drives Profitability and Growth

106

one of the key attributes that count in the purchase decision. So, achieving superior conformance quality yields both lower cost and superior perceived quality—a double benefit.

Now that the conceptual linkages between quality and business performance are clear, what does the evidence based on the experiences of PIMS businesses show? How much does superior perceived quality affect business performance?

QUALITY AND PROFITABILITY

There is no doubt that relative perceived quality and profitability are strongly related (Exhibit 6-2). Whether the profit measure is return on sales or return on investment, businesses with a superior product/service offering clearly outperform those with inferior quality. Several key benefits accrue to businesses that offer superior perceived quality:

- Stronger customer loyalty;
- More repeat purchases;
- Less vulnerability to price wars;

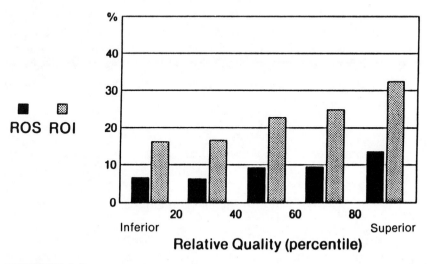

EXHIBIT 6-2
Relative Quality Boosts Rates of Return

- Ability to command higher relative price without affecting share;
- Lower marketing costs; and
- Share improvements.

Is the greater profitability of superior quality businesses associated with higher relative prices or lower direct costs? Since relative perceived quality and market share are correlated, we need to examine their joint effects on profitability, price, and cost to sort out the answer.

Together, relative market share and relative quality exert a strong positive influence on a business's profitability. Businesses that have both larger share and better quality than their leading competitors earn ROIs that are dramatically higher than those of businesses with small share and inferior quality (Exhibit 6-3).

Although quality and share are correlated, each has a strong separate relationship to profitability. Again, is the greater profitability linked to lower costs or higher prices?

The PIMS data show that *quality affects relative price;* but, separate from quality, share has little effect on price (Exhibit 6-4).

Conversely, *share affects relative direct cost;* but perceived quality has little effect on cost (Exhibit 6-5). Why is there no direct correlation between relative perceived quality and relative direct cost? Some elements of quality are free: savings on scrap, rework, and on complaint response can exceed the costs of preventing defects. This tends to drive down unit costs. But we are not using an internal measure of conformance quality here. We are focusing on relative perceived quality, and many product and service attributes are enhanced by spending more money:

Taste:	better and more ingredients
Appearance:	better and more packaging, paint, plating, finishing, etc.
Strength:	more and better grades of materials
Better support:	more, higher paid engineers

The net effect seems to be that as we move from inferior to superior quality positions, the reductions in costs associated with scrap and reprocessing are offset by the increased costs of improving product or service performance on key attributes that count in the purchase decision.

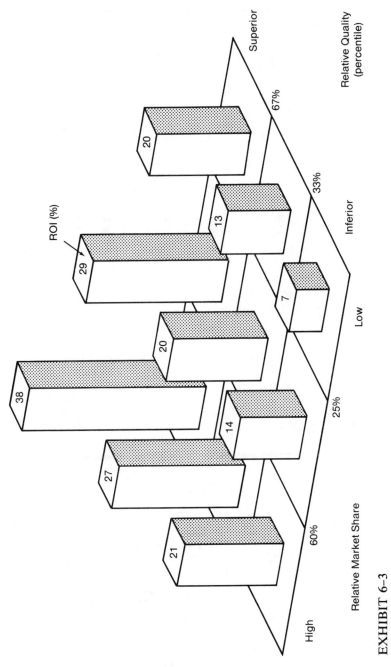

EXHIBIT 6-3
Quality and Share Both Drive Profitability

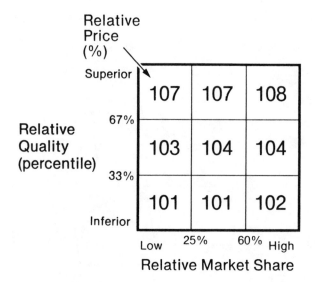

EXHIBIT 6–4
Quality Affects Price: Separate from Quality, Share
Has Little Effect on Price

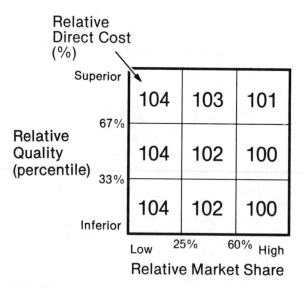

EXHIBIT 6–5
Share Affects Costs; Quality Has Little Effect on
Cost

The greater profitability of businesses with superior perceived quality is typically linked to their ability to realize higher prices while achieving comparable direct costs.

QUALITY AND GROWTH

Quality is related not only to profitability, but also to growth, the other key dimension of business performance, through the impact of quality on perceived value.

Value is the relationship between quality and price. A customer who gets superior quality at a low price gets better value; a customer who gets inferior quality at a high price obviously gets worse value. But who determines what counts as good or poor quality, high or low price? In a competitive context the customer's behavior is crucial: who he buys from, and at what price, determines who wins or loses in any competitive market. Therefore quality is whatever the customer says it is, and the quality of a particular product or service is whatever the customer *perceives* it to be. How does a customer decide whether a particular offering represents superior or inferior quality, or a high or low price? He makes that assessment on the basis of comparison: is this offering (product and services) better or worse than those of competitors? At how much higher or lower a price?

IBM, for example, holds a strong position in personal computers, despite (a) coming relatively late to the market; (b) going through unfamiliar distribution channels; and (c) offering machines whose technical specifications were often less impressive than those of machines selling at *lower* prices. How can this be? Recent research on corporate buyers showed that one of the most important criteria for selecting a PC supplier was confidence that the supplier would still be around in 10 years' time.[3] A dominant aspect of customer-perceived quality—and a determinant of who wins in PCs—has only a distant relationship to R&D and processing power. This should be a sobering thought to hundreds of hopeful start-ups focusing on technical wizardry.

So it is the *perceived relative value* of the total package of products and services that influences customer behavior, and thus competitive success.

In most markets, there are three value positions and five product/service positions that a supplier may adopt. A business may offer average value by offering comparable quality at a comparable price, by offering superior quality but charging a premium for it, or by discounting for inferior quality. These three forms of average value correspond to three common product/service offerings: average, premium and economy, respectively. When relative perceived quality and price are out of balance, a competitor adopts either a better value position (superior quality at the same or lower price), or a worse value position (inferior quality at the same or higher price). These five generic positions of a product/service offering are located on a value map in Exhibit 6-6.

It is important to bear in mind that, given this definition, relative value can change for any one of three reasons: you change what you are doing; customers' needs or preferences change; or competitors change what they are doing. The first type of change requires both an understanding of the product and service attributes that count in the purchase decision, and knowledge of how the customer views your performance. The second should be the focus of careful, and frequent, quality-directed field research. The third is seldom the focus of anything: the notion that quality and value depend on what competitors are doing is alien to most managers. Yet it is the essence of the competitive aspect of value, and it is an area where businesses frequently get into competitive difficulty.

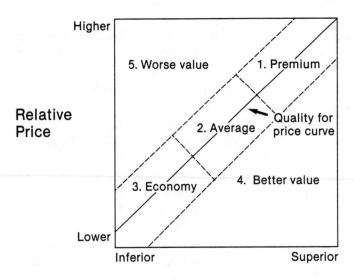

EXHIBIT 6-6
Value Map: Five Generic Product/Service Positions

To understand better the way that quality and value drive profitability and growth, let's examine the five generic offering positions on a value map. A value map is typically used to plot your line of business and those of your key competitors on a two-dimensional price-versus-quality chart.

The interaction of customers and suppliers in the marketplace tends to align products along a "comparable quality-for-price curve" so that each competing product/service offering provides the same value. Most businesses fall along the diagonal line that stretches from the economy end to the premium position. But, there are also quite a few businesses that, by accident or design, wind up in an unusual position—either no price premium for superior quality or charging a premium for inferior quality.

Offerings positioned along the quality-for-price curve give the customer roughly comparable value (for price) and they tend to hold their share.

Businesses that offer average value at the premium end of the market show the highest rate of profitability, on average. The surprising fact is that better-value businesses (superior quality, but no price premium) are nearly as profitable. What is lost in price (no premium), they make up in lower costs, stemming from their strong tendency to gain market share and the lower marketing costs that are incurred when one sells superior quality at a less than premium price. They achieve the same rate of return on investment, and do so on a growing investment base. In money terms, profits grow dramatically.

But a market-share war is a zero-sum game: one competitor increases share only if another competitor loses it. And by the definition of value (*relative* quality and price), one competitor can have better value only if another has worse value. It is the worse-value businesses that, despite heavy marketing expenditures, still lose share and consequently show disastrously low rates of profitability.

Many companies make only a half-hearted effort to understand how the customer sizes them up relative to competitors. They concentrate only on price (despite the fact that price is often the same across competitors) and never get to the real non-price cues and attributes that count in the purchase decision.

Theodore Levitt has said that you can differentiate just about anything.[4] But, if you think of your product/service offering as a commodity, that's what it will be—a commodity.

In many industrial businesses you hear the following line of reasoning. "Ours is a cost-driven business. Quality may be critical in markets like heart pacemakers and automobiles, but we have industry standards that have to be met or we don't sell anything. Once we've met those standards, though, customers buy only on price. So we can't afford to invest in quality, because we can't get it back in price."

This kind of competitive attitude, frequently met in industry, effectively extends "commodity" competition far beyond its perhaps proper place on the London Metal Exchange and the Chicago Board of Trade. By assuming that customers care only about price, competitors doom themselves to an endless spiral of cost-cutting and price-cutting. Yet there is evidence to suggest that quality may be a more powerful and dangerous competitive weapon even in price-sensitive markets where the basic product is standardized. The key to this apparent paradox lies in the effect of relative value on customer behavior.

In some situations there does tend to be a market price that all competitors charge. In these "commodity" markets, since all competitors charge the same average price, there are no premium or economy product positions. Therefore, a competitor who gains a sustainable relative perceived quality advantage (perhaps in service rather than product attributes) automatically adopts a better-value position. These businesses tend to gain market share. At the same time, other competitors will necessarily be pushed into worse-value positions and consequently lose share. Since volume (and the cost advantage that goes with it) is usually critical in "commodity" markets, the impact of perceived quality on these share changes is especially significant.

We have seen that businesses that achieve a superior quality position tend to gain market share. The superior quality and larger market share tend to boost profitability.

Improving quality also sets off a chain reaction. Rising perceived relative quality not only leads to market share gain, but also to rising capacity utilization, better turnover on investment, higher employee productivity and lower marketing expense per dollar of sales.

ACHIEVING QUALITY LEADERSHIP

If relative quality is so important, how do the winners achieve a quality advantage? Many quality leaders achieve their superior quality positions by anticipating what customers need and by being the first to offer it to the marketplace. Among the PIMS businesses, superior-quality competitors were usually pioneers rather than early followers or late entrants. PIMS businesses that are able to protect their innovation with a product patent also tend to score better on perceived quality. This is especially true of industrial businesses.

But better performance on product attributes is not the only way to win. By our definition, relative perceived quality covers all the non-price attributes that count in the purchase decision. Businesses frequently achieve a superior overall quality position by developing a better *image* than competitors or providing better *customer services* than competitors.

The PIMS data base also shows that businesses that offer a broader product line, and businesses that serve a greater variety of customers than competitors, also score better on perceived quality. We believe this indicates that these businesses have done a better job of understanding the different needs of customer segments within the served market and have also done a better job of differentiating their product/service offering to meet these differing segment needs.

Finally, we also found that vertically integrated businesses offer superior quality on average. By controlling several stages in the production process, these integrated businesses seem to be able to orchestrate the various technologies and operations necessary to meet customers' needs more effectively than competitors. (For further discussion on vertical integration, see Chapter 8.)

In summary, some quality leaders achieved their advantage by pioneering and protecting their position with a product patent. Others focused on relative image or service as the way to win. Some seemed to do a better job of diagnosing the needs of different customer segments. Others focused on superior coordination of various technologies and value adding operations. There are many ways to attain a quality edge.

WHY QUALITY ADVANTAGES ERODE

Achieving quality leadership is one thing. Maintaining it is another. Evidence from the PIMS data base and individual case examples yield several reasons why businesses allow quality advantages to decline. The first, and perhaps most obvious, is that product differences often diminish as a market matures (see Chapter 10). Over time, imitating competitors chip away at the uniqueness originally enjoyed by a pioneer.

Related to market maturity, complacency can also cause quality to erode. The experience of businesses in the PIMS data base indicates that failure to modernize plant can damage relative quality.

Beyond the PIMS data base, case examples also indicate how businesses have allowed quality to decline. A highly visible example is Schlitz beer. Excessive cost-cutting and misjudgement of customer preferences led to quality problems for Schlitz.

In the early 1970s, Schlitz reduced brewery labor per barrel, switched to low-cost materials (corn syrup, hop pellets) and shortened the brewing cycle by 50%. In the short term, this seemed to pay off. In 1973 Schlitz had a higher return on sales and a higher return on equity than Anheuser-Busch.

Forbes commented in 1974,

> "Does it pay to build quality into a product if most customers don't care?. . . . Schlitz seems to have a more successful answer (than Anheuser-Busch)."[5]

Long-term, however, results were different. Schlitz's volume declined 40% from 1976 to 1980. Its market position fell from #2 to #7. And its stock price collapsed from $69 (1974) to $5 (1981). Why?

Schlitz focused on cost cutting and misjudged consumer preferences. "Flaky" beer output in 1976 meant that 10 million bottles of beer had to be destroyed. New management reformulated the product in 1978, but Schlitz has not been able to regain its former market position. This case illustrates how cost-cutting blinders can cause a company to misunderstand customer preferences and suffer a dramatic erosion in market competitiveness.

A STRATEGIC VIEW OF QUALITY

The need for a revolution in thinking about quality is underlined by what most American and European companies presently mean when they refer to quality. Rather than focusing on customer preferences, management tends to evaluate the quality of its products from an *internal* perspective: does the product conform to predetermined specifications? Without denying the importance of quality assurance, managers also need to understand that potential customers often have little or no appreciation of how closely the product matches its specifications. Instead, customers see the offering as it arrives in its marketplace and they measure it relative to competing products.

Among the reasons that a quality-assurance perspective it far too narrow are the following:

Flawed Specifications

It's all well and good to conform to specifications, but what if the specs are wrong? Many a new product has been introduced, and perfectly manufactured, only to fail in the marketplace. The design team may have missed the importance assigned to a given function by the customer, over-designed the product, or failed to respond to evolving customer needs and preferences.

In the restaurant business, Howard Johnson's seems to have missed the increasing weight that many consumers place on quick turnaround. While fast food chains have flourished, Howard Johnson's has floundered by adhering to flawed service standards.

Quality Degradation en Route

The long arm of most quality assurance programs reaches only as far as the factory gate. Much can happen to degrade a product on its way to the customer. The launch of one confectionery product failed miserably because the product spent too long in the distribution system. Irate customers are not pacified when told "It was O.K. when we shipped it."

Competitive Influence

The inside quality assurance person seldom sees the competition but rather works against his/her given specifications. The customer, in contrast, is constantly comparing your product with the competition's. If your competitor suddenly shows superior performance, you can find yourself desperately cutting price to stay alive.

Service Counts

Of course, service is the name of the game in a service business. But, manufactured goods also come with service. Many computer manufacturers painfully learned this lesson in recent years, and many "technically" superior computers have been or will be driven from the market because of a lack of customer service and software.

A study conducted by a task force at General Electric clearly documents the need to focus on the customer rather than on the product alone.[6] Surveying customer attitudes towards various GE product lines, the researchers determined that businesses with poor quality images relative to competitors were managed by executives who did the following:

- Downgraded the customer's viewpoint;
- Made high quality synonymous with tight tolerance;
- Tied quality objectives to manufacturing flow;
- Expressed quality objectives as a number of defects per unit and
- Formalized quality control systems only for the manufacturing function.

By contrast, managers of the GE product-line businesses that were praised by customers did the following:

- Emphasized *real* rather than imagined customer expectations;
- Identified customers' real needs through market research;
- Used customer-based quality performance measures; and
- Formulated quality control systems for *all* functions, not just manufacturing.

With so much evidence indicating that relative perceived quality counts, why do so many companies refrain from using customer-based measures? Perhaps they are inhibited from broadening their perspective because quality conformance gurus like Crosby, Deming, Feigenbaum, and Juran have focused so much attention on the internal, operations view of quality. Perhaps companies find that it is easier to quantify defects per 1,000 units than it is to understand and measure a wide range of customer needs and preferences. Lack of relevant experience may also make it difficult for some companies to analyze quality in the broader customer context and to understand how to make relative perceived quality pay off.

Yet, to compete effectively, American and European managers must begin to see, understand, and react to the external half of the quality picture. John F. Welch, Jr., Chairman and Chief Executive Officer of the General Electric Company, recognizes this need. He feels that

> "Quality is our best assurance of customer allegiance, our strongest defense against foreign competition and the *only* path to sustained growth and earnings." (emphasis added)[7]

Jack Welch is well known for his statement that GE will be number 1 or 2 in the markets that they chose to serve. But, many people don't realize that Welch embraces perceived quality as the way to achieve market leadership. To Welch, the difference between being externally or internally focused is crucial. Making sure that his managers understand the difference is an obvious passion. He urges them to not just make their products cheaper, but to make them better. Commenting on the absolutely devastating way in which the Japanese had managed to decode U.S. marketing during the seventies—from cars to fishing gear, from copiers to textile machinery, from video cassette recorders to motorcycles, Welch noted that

> "Their focus on ends, not means, led them, forced them, to do a better job of figuring out what society was valuing, how people were living, what customers really wanted."[8]

With hindsight, the success of Japanese companies is understandable. At the time it seemed incredible that a foreign country, with such a different culture and language, could crack the riddle of the U.S. market so much better than some U.S. companies could. The Japanese used American dealers and distributors. They did not invent new ways to sell. But they had embraced marketing as the primary tactic to win success for their products.

EXAMPLES OF QUALITY PROFILING

Stories of marketing success don't all emanate from Japan. The chicken business has undergone a revolution in the U.S., thanks to the remarkable success of Frank Perdue. Let's use the PIMS quality profiling process to trace his steps.

Before Frank Perdue took over the chicken business from his father it was the quintessential commodity business. Chickens had as strong a claim to commodity status as pork bellies or crude oil.

The performance of each competitor was the same on each product and service attribute (Exhibit 6-7). This placed Perdue and his representative competitor at the 50th percentile on relative quality, neither ahead nor behind. With no differences in performance on product and service attributes, the customer bought basically on price.

After Frank Perdue took over the chicken business, he pulled ahead on almost every non-price attribute that counts in the purchase decision. His research showed that customers in his served market prefer their chickens plump and yellow. Careful breeding and the judicious use of feed additives enabled Frank to produce meatier, yellower chickens than competitors. His actions also produced a higher, more consistent meat-to-bone ratio.

To prevent wet pinfeathers from slipping past the torching process that's supposed to burn them off, he purchased a turbine engine to blow-dry his chickens just before they reach the torching station. This didn't get him to zero defects, but it did mean that fewer pinfeathers wound up in supermarkets or in family dining rooms. Notice that this particular investment in capital equipment did not expand capacity and it did not take out labor costs. It just improved the perceived quality of Perdue's chickens! Most capital appropriation requests have difficulty quantifying the justification for expenditures to improve perceived quality.

To make sure that the customer perceived and remembered his quality improvements, Perdue utilized catchy slogans in audacious media advertising: "It takes a tough man to make a tender chicken"; "Buy Perdue chickens—you get an extra bite in every breast." (Would *you* have spent millions trying to differentiate chickens?) Perdue developed a favorable difference, he made sure that it was perceived, and as a result he gets a substantial premium for what certainly *had been* a commodity. As Perdue himself says, "Customers will go out of their way to buy a superior product, and you can charge them a toll for the trip." Is your product, with all its potential associated services, really harder to differentiate than a dead chicken?

Since Perdue created performance differences on non-price attributes, consumers focus more on these differences, in effect placing more weight on product and service attributes (namely, quality) and less on price. In our hypothetical example, Frank Perdue piled up a strong quality score (90th percentile) by pulling well ahead of his competitors on attributes that became more heavily weighted (brand

EXHIBIT 6-7
Chicken Business: Customer's Purchase Decision

	Before Frank				After Frank			
		Customer Rating				Customer Rating		
Key Purchase Criteria	Rel. Wt.	Perdue's Dad	Others	Rating Diff.	Rel. Wt.	Frank Perdue	Others	Rating Diff.
Product								
Yellow Bird	5	7	7	0	10	8.1	7.2	+0.9
Meat-to-bone	10	6	6	0	20	9.0	7.3	+1.7
No pinfeathers	15	5	5	0	20	9.2	6.5	+2.7
Fresh	15	7	7	0	15	8.0	8.0	0.0
Service								
Availability	55	8	8	0	10	8.0	8.0	0.0
Brand image	0	6	6	0	25	9.3	6.5	+2.8
	100				100			

Weight on quality vs. price			
Before Frank		*After Frank*	
Quality	10	Quality	70
Price	90	Price	30
	100		100

122   THE PIMS PRINCIPLES

image, no pinfeathers, meat-to-bone) as Perdue created a difference. This enabled him to achieve quality and share leadership in the market he has chosen to serve, the eastern seaboard of the U.S.

QUALITY AND DIFFERENTIATION

By profiling how customers make purchase decisions, we can determine which attributès count and see how customers rate each attribute for each competitor. This information can be used not only to see how customers assess relative quality, but also to depict market differentiation.

Whereas relative quality measures your position relative to competitors (your competitive advantage) market differentiation measures the degree to which *all* competitors differ from one another across a market (a gauge of market attractiveness).

To illustrate how to measure market differentiation, we will examine two different sets of data on how customers make the purchase decision in heavy-duty trucks (Exhibit 6-8). In the no differ-

EXHIBIT 6-8
Heavy-Duty Trucks
Customer's purchase decision

• *No differentiation*

Attribute	Weight	Performance Rating			
		Navistar	*Paccar*	*Volvo*	*Mack*
Durability	35	7	7	7	7
Fuel economy	25	8	8	8	8
Living features	20	6	6	6	6
Ride	20	9	9	9	9

• *Substantial differentiation*

Attribute	Weight	*Navistar*	*Paccar*	*Volvo*	*Mack*
Durability	35	7	7	8	9
Fuel economy	30	9	8	7	7
Living features	20	6	9	7	6
Ride	15	5	7	8	6

Hypothetical examples.

entiation case, although the customer ratings vary from one attribute to another, they do not vary among competitors. While customers perceive that all competitors, in an absolute sense, do better on "ride comfort" than on "living features," customers do not see a relative difference among competitors on any attribute.

These data represent an example of a market with no differentiation in non-price attributes. The market differentiation score is zero because performance ratings are identical across all competitors.[9]

In the second and more interesting example, the performance ratings are not identical across all competitors. Based on these hypothetical data, Mack Trucks (bull-dog tough) outperform the competition on durability. Navistar wins on fuel economy; Paccar does the best job of providing living features in the cab, and Volvo has the edge in ride comfort. The market is quite differentiated.

Market differentiation and market segmentation are closely related. The essence of market segmentation is to divide the served market into customer groups such that customers within a group place roughly the same weight on each attribute, but different customer groups emphasize different attributes. Focusing on our heavy-duty truck example, we find at least three key segments in the served market: (1) construction, (2) fleets, and (3) owner operators. It is likely that the construction segment will emphasize durability, the fleet segment will emphasize fuel economy, and the owner operators will emphasize living features and ride comfort. If this is the case, our performance ratings suggest that Mack Trucks will do well in the construction segment, Navistar will be strong in the fleet segment, and Paccar will win the owner-operator segment.

In contrast to the chicken example where Perdue was ahead (and his competitor behind) on almost every attribute, each heavy-duty truck company has chosen to distinguish itself on an attribute that is different from the one chosen by its competitors. In general, if only one segment of the served market weights a company's chosen attribute heavily, that company wins that segment and becomes a niche business or brand. If most segments of the served market weight a company's chosen attribute heavily, that company achieves relative quality leadership across the served market and becomes the market leader or "power brand."

You achieve uniqueness on an attribute when you have a feature that competitors don't. Their performance score is zero, but yours may be 8 or 9. If several competitors in a market each have their own unique attribute, the market differentiation score will be very high and each competitor will tend to dominate the segment that places a great deal of weight on its unique attribute.

How Quality and Differentiation Drive Performance

The joint effect of relative quality and market differentiation on profitability yields a rather remarkable pattern. Businesses with the lowest returns compete in markets where there is no differentiation and therefore no relative quality advantages or disadvantages (bottom middle, Exhibit 6-9).[10]

The market differentiation measure keeps track of performance differences among competing suppliers on key product and service attributes. In markets where performance does differ among competitors, a winning business will achieve a perceived quality advan-

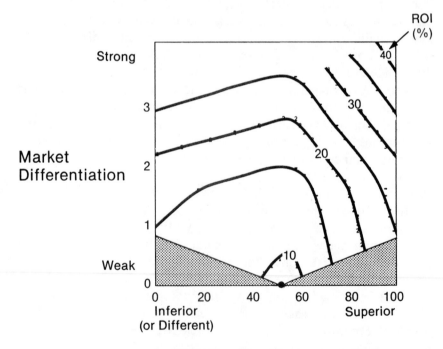

EXHIBIT 6-9
How Differentiation and Quality Drive Profitability
Source: SPI's Quality/Differentiation Data Base.

tage while others (losers and nichers) will wind up with low quality scores.

Losers receive low quality scores in *all* segments of the served market, which places them on the left side of the differentiation map (Exhibit 6–9).

A niche business typically is designed to be well received by a single segment of the served market but not by the other segments. Therefore its relative quality score may be superior for its segment, but inferior in the other segments. Calculating a niche business's relative quality across *all* segments of the served market, the minuses outweigh the pluses yielding a low quality score, which also places niche businesses on the left side of the differentiation map in an inferior (perhaps "different" is a better adjective) overall quality position. But, since their market differentiation tends to be substantial, nichers wind up in the *upper* left zone of the differentiation map where businesses typically earn a decent return on investment.

Market leaders or power brands attain that position because they tend to be well received by *most* segments of the served market. A superior quality position in a strongly differentiated market places a business in the upper right zone of a differentiation map where businesses normally earn very high rates of return.

Relative quality is also dramatically related to the odds of being the market leader. Businesses on the superior-quality side of the differentiation map have a very good chance of being ranked number one in market share, especially if they are in strongly differentiated markets.

Diagnosing Quality Problems and Opportunities

In this chapter we've described several new concepts and research insights that companies have found useful in diagnosing their quality problems and opportunities. Quality profiling, by segment, gives you a feel for what attributes count in the purchase decision, how the customer rates you versus leading competitors on each attribute and how customer needs differ by segment. The value map shows how you stand versus competitors in relative price, relative quality, and relative value. It tells whether you are likely to gain share or are vulnerable to share loss. The differentiation map clearly distinguishes power brands and nichers from commodity positions, and indicates the expected profit results of each.

Regardless of where you wind up, going through the quality pro-filing process and related diagnoses will give you a much better un-derstanding of how to improve your position.

STRATEGIES FOR QUALITY IMPROVEMENT

There are three generic ways to improve performance ratings: (1) catch up, (2) pull ahead and (3) leapfrog. Once you know how the customer makes the purchase decision for your offering, the most natural tendency is to try to catch up on those attributes where you are behind.

A catch-up move is good because it increases your quality score and thereby reduces your competitive disadvantage. However, a catch-up move is bad because it also reduces market attractiveness by reducing market differentiation.

By contrast, a pull-ahead move (or a series of pull-ahead moves in the case of Frank Perdue) increases both your competitive advantage and the market's attractiveness. A pull-ahead move is a double win. That's why higher profitability is reached so quickly as you move away from the commodity position (bottom middle) on the differentiation map toward the superior quality, strongly differentiated zone (Exhibit 6–9).

Therefore, once you know attributes, weights, and customer ratings for your business, resist the temptation to focus all your resources on catch-up moves. If you can find a way to make a sustainable pull-ahead move you're likely to get a much bigger profit and share-gain bang for your quality-improvement dollar. Search for an unmet need, an attribute where no one is really satisfying the customer, and see if there's a way to make a sustainable pull-ahead move. Pulling ahead is tougher than merely imitating competitors, but it's well worth the effort.

In his book, *Competitive Advantage,* Mike Porter uses the word differentiation to represent the superior side of relative perceived quality. While he mentions the concept of industry or market differentiation, most of his examples describe what we call a pull-ahead move. You create a competitive relative quality advantage and improve market differentiation at the same time. This sets the stage for commanding a premium price.

We believe that it is useful to break this differentiation move into its relative perceived quality and market differentiation components.

By using a differentiation map you can track the three things that happen when you make a pull-ahead move.

1. Your relative quality goes up;
2. Your competitor's relative quality goes down; and
3. Market differentiation increases.

By tracing the pull-ahead move through the various segments of the served market you can anticipate which customer groups and competitors will be most affected and most likely to respond. And you can also analyze how a competitor's pull-ahead, catch-up or leapfrog move would affect your relative quality and the degree of market differentiation in your served market.

LEAPFROGGING: JAPANESE VERSUS U.S. AUTOMOBILES

If poor relative performance on a particular attribute is hurting you in all segments of the served market, try to design a leapfrog move that will not only negate your competitive disadvantage, but also create a sustainable competitive advantage and maintain differentiation in your market.

This is what the Japanese have done in the compact-car market. Fuel economy and low cost provided the initial wedge for Japanese auto makers to penetrate the North American market. But in the early 1970s the Japanese had a reputation for making tinny rust-buckets. They needed to leapfrog Detroit in dimensions other than fuel economy and low cost in order to move up from the economy position and to expand their sales and profits.

Toyota's advertising tag line for the 1970s was "You asked for it.—You've got it.—Toyota." (You got a small, fuel-efficient car that met your basic transportation needs.) By leapfrogging Detroit on several key attributes, Japanese companies rolled further up the quality-for-price curve or shifted into better value positions. Toyota's tag line for the 1980s is "Who could ask for anything more?"

While the Japanese were leapfrogging in design quality, Detroit was trying to catch up in conformance quality. During the early 1980s Detroit claimed that although they had made tremendous advances in improving quality, American consumers did not perceive this progress.[11]

To see how the Japanese were positioned relative to Detroit, let's apply our quality profiling technique to the compact-car market. Our purpose in doing this is not to reannounce that Detroit is having difficulty competing with the Japanese in some served markets. Rather, the case shows that even rough data on perceived quality can be used to diagnose how the customer makes the purchase decision, and to formulate blueprints for improving relative perceived quality.

While Japanese auto makers have not yet cracked the medium-sized car market in North America, they appear to dominate the lower price end of the compact-car market. To calibrate this dominance, we analyzed seven American models and four Japanese models that had been rated as head-to-head competitors in several issues of *Consumer Reports*.[12]

The models were:

American	Japanese
Olds Firenza	Toyota Camry
Chevy Cavalier	Nissan Stanza
Mercury Topaz	Mazda 626
Ford LTD	Honda Accord
Plymouth Reliant	
Chevy Citation II	
Cutlass Supreme	

The difference between performance ratings on the American and Japanese models came out so great and the differences within each country's models were so small, we decided to show composite performance ratings in Exhibit 6–10.

The Japanese composite has a clear performance advantage on fuel economy, shifting, handling precision, braking, front seating, controls, and displays, and a dramatic advantage on predicted repair. The American composite has a minor advantage in climate control. Based on product attributes only, the Japanese models cluster around the 70th percentile while the American models cluster around the 30th percentile. After we make adjustments for the larger discounts from sticker prices and better performance on availability and convenience, American models are somewhat more competitive (Exhibit 6–11).

The striking finding is the dramatic difference in relative perceived quality between the Japanese cluster of models and the American cluster of models. Our findings are similar to those of David Garvin in his study of *conformance* quality in the air conditioner

EXHIBIT 6-10
Composite Performance Ratings for Compact Cars: U.S. versus Japan

Key Purchase Criteria		Weight[1] (%)	Ratings[2]		
			U.S.		Japan
Product Attributes					
Engine & Transmission	Fuel economy	10	5.0	<	7.0
	Engine driveability	5	8.4		8.5
	Shifting	5	6.1	<	9.0
	Acceleration	5	5.9		7.1
Handling & Braking	Accident avoidance	5	5.9		7.5
	Handling precision	5	5.0	<	8.5
	Braking	5	5.3	<	8.5
Comfort	Ride	4	5.0		5.0
	Noise	4	5.3		5.0
	Driving position	4	6.7		8.0
	Front seating	4	5.9	<	8.0
	Rear seating	4	3.3		4.0
	Climate control	4	9.0	>	8.0
Convenience	Controls	3	5.6	<	8,0
	Displays	3	6.4	<	9.0
	Servicing ease	3	6.7		6.5
	Predicted repair	7	2.7	<	8.5
Service Attributes					
	Availability	10	9.0	>	6.0
	Convenient service	10	9.0	>	6.5

[1]Rough estimates of weights by SPI staff.
[2]Ratings on product attributes from *Consumer Reports.*

industry. He found that while there were differences among Japanese manufacturers and among American manufacturers, the real difference was the very low level of in-plant failure rates for all Japanese manufacturers as compared to all American companies.[13]

This quality profiling of compact cars indicates that, although Detroit had made great progress in absolute quality improvement, their relative quality in this served market still lagged behind the Japanese. Relative quality is a dynamic concept and the competitor is always trying to improve as well.

In order to win on perceived quality you need to have more refined data than your competitors (know more about evolving cus-

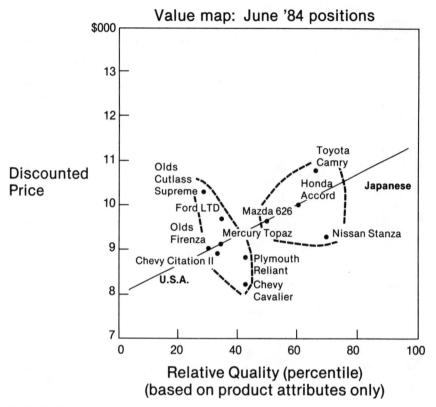

EXHIBIT 6-11
Price Discounts and Imports Quotas Make U.S. Models More Competitive

tomer needs by segment and more about changing competitive performance) and you need to *use* this information from quality-directed research in a strategic framework.

As of this writing, Jaguar has achieved a dramatic turnaround by focusing on both perceived quality and conformance quality. By contrast, General Motors is still losing share.[14]

We believe that part of General Motors' problem stems from a production orientation. General Motors' Chairman, Roger B. Smith, has said

> "I think mainly what happened in the U.S. was that (auto makers) took their eye off of the quality to get the volume."[15]

The problem with this view, of course, is that the volume that goes out the plant door with poor design or conformance quality winds up as inventory on your dealers' lots once competitors with better quality enter the market. Drastic price discounting is then required to move the inventory.

To catch up in conformance quality, General Motors has invested millions of dollars and is a part owner of Phil Crosby's conformance quality college. This has helped GM achieve a shift in focus from volume to conformance. Unfortunately, Phil Crosby is the one conformance quality specialist who denies that the concept of relative perceived quality is useful or even exists.[16] The shift in focus from production to product and then to the marketplace is most difficult and painful for many companies.

A Specific Case: Estimating the Payoff from Quality Improvement

Robert Luchs, who heads up SPI's London office, spotlighted the case of a company where a technical breakthrough had dramatically improved competitive position. This was a chemical business that had come up with a new process that increased the potency of its product and also reduced costs. Management was delighted, but at the same time felt worried. How could they make sure that the expected benefits from this quality improvement would be achieved? They needed to "reality-test" their plans and to revise them accordingly. Under Luch's supervision, the company was able to do just that, by learning from the experiences of "strategic look-alikes," businesses in the data base that were not necessarily chemical businesses, but that had a similar strategic profile.

For this chemical business, look-alikes with the following similar characteristics were studied:

- Competitive positions (relative quality, relative price, market share, and relative share)
- Market, customer, and product characteristics, (market growth rate, number of customers, purchase frequency and amount, and channels of distribution)
- Cost and product structures, (vertical integration, capital intensity, working capital, productivity, type of production process, rate of capacity utilization)

Once the look-alikes for the chemical company were located, two sub-sets were identified—one group that gained more than the normal amount of market share, and one that gained less than what might be expected (Exhibit 6–12). The latter group—relative to the former—were "market-share losers" because they tended to maintain their share when a gain was expected. The first step was to analyze the significant differences in the actions taken and results achieved by winners and losers. When that was accomplished, it was possible to reality-test the company's plan against the experiences of both groups and refine it accordingly.

In the case of this company, business units in the same strategic position gained market share, and share winners did exceptionally well. They also improved profitability (Exhibit 6–13). The share winners' better ability to improve profits was due to growth in volume. Their volume growth led to a significant improvement in capacity utilization and contributed to productivity improvement. Their investment intensity dropped dramatically, in terms of both fixed assets and working capital. And all these improvements helped them to improve their relative cost position.

And the key question: *How did the winners achieve their share/ volume growth?* They did so by not only maintaining but improving their high relative quality. By contrast, share losers had allowed their quality leadership position to erode.

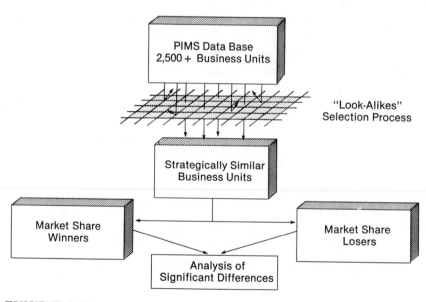

EXHIBIT 6–12
Look-Alike Analysis

EXHIBIT 6-13

Reality-Testing Our Plan Against the Experience of Winning and Losing Look-Alike Businesses

		Look-alikes	
	Plan	*Winners*	*Losers*
Market share, change p.a.	+0.5	+1.6	0
Relative market share, change p.a.	+1.0	+2.9	0
ROI, change p.a.	+3.0	+8.7	+1.9
Real sales growth, p.a.	+5	+20	+3
Change in capacity utilization, p.a.	+3	+5	+2
Change in value added per employee	+4	+10	+2
Fixed assets/sales, change p.a.	−3	−5	−3
Working capital/sales, change p.a.	−1	−4	−2

As an interesting contrast, we might summarize some other differences between the winners and losers.

There was no significant difference between them in regard to relative price. But both were significantly higher than the chemical company's plan. The winners did offer superior *service* to immediate customers, and continued to upgrade it. By contrast, the chemical business plan and the market-share losers had only average customer service and made no improvements.

In contrast to the losers, the winners had a high level of innovation. Twenty-seven percent of their sales came from new products that were introduced within the past three years, as contrasted with only 6% for the losers and 10% in our plan. The winners supported their on-going innovation with heavy R&D expenditures (7% of sales in contrast to 3% for the losers and 4% in our plan). At this point, the chemical company plan was beginning to look a lot like the losers.

On average there were no significant differences between the winners and losers on marketing expenses, but both spent more than the chemical company planned for (12% of sales for winners versus 10% for losers, and only 8% in the plan). The winners spent particularly heavily at the beginning (15% of sales) and, relative to market growth, continued to be aggressive. But, thanks to share growth, these marketing outlays fell as a percent of sales.

To sum up, in contrast to the winners, the chemical company, like the losers, was not planning for enough expenditures to exploit fully and expand its existing competitive advantage. Management therefore revised their plan and began to:

- Spend more on R&D and new products;
- Spend more on marketing;
- Focus more on customer service; and
- Realize a higher relative price

The company's share and profitability improvement were dramatic.

SUMMARY

We've shown that relative perceived quality is crucial to competitive success. Perceived quality can be measured, related to business performance, improved, and monitored over time. But still, most companies don't have good measures of relative perceived quality. Worse yet, many don't even grasp the idea that the concept of relative perceived quality (service as well as product) is useful or that it can be readily measured.

Many middle managers fear that an attempt to measure perceived quality will lead to finger pointing and attempts to assign blame rather than insights on how to leapfrog or pull ahead of competitors. The market research that is done focuses on new product/ concept identification, pricing, market segmentation, advertising and distribution rather than at measuring relative perceived quality. Only a few companies really carry out quality-directed measurement in a strategic context. And only a fraction of these have a top management culture that understands and uses the insights about the marketplace. These very few companies pay attention to detail and take action rather than letting what the market is trying to tell them just slip through bureaucratic cracks. Companies that are managed by consensus communicate across functions better and find it easier to concentrate on both perceived quality and conformance quality.

Capital Intensity Can Upset the Applecart

In Chapters 5 and 6 we saw how your business's financial performance is driven by the competitive position that it attains in the markets that you've chosen to serve. Profitability also depends, of course, on the effectiveness of your operations—how much output you produce per dollar of investment or per worker employed.

Capital intensive businesses employ a great deal of invested capital to generate each dollar of sales. The heavy capital burden they shoulder tends to drag down their profitability. High labor productivity can offset some of this drag, but for most businesses, productivity doesn't improve enough to pay for the heavier investment. Although there is a great deal of evidence to document the troubles caused by capital intensity, many executives continue to feel a sense of discomfort, and even surprise, when confronted with this finding. Intuitively they feel it ought to be otherwise.

Since many people in the business community find it difficult to believe that capital intensity so frequently upsets the applecart of profitability, we need to take a hard look at the factors that cause the low rates of return that usually accrue to capital-intensive businesses.

- What is capital intensity and how can it be measured?
- How is capital intensity related to productivity and profitability?

- Why does capital intensity depress profitability?
- Why do businesses become capital intensive?
- When do capital investments pay off and how can the capital allocation process be improved?

In this chapter we shall attempt to shed some light on these questions by presenting evidence on the nature, importance, and implications of capital intensity's links to productivity and profitability.

WHAT IS CAPITAL INTENSITY?

Most executives think of capital intensity as the amount of capital invested relative to the flow of output produced. The simplest measure is the ratio of investment to sales. Investment is measured as the net book value (historical purchased price minus accumulated depreciation) of plant and equipment, plus net working capital, plus other assets net of amortization. This is equivalent to total assets minus current liabilities. In other words, the money that the business uses to operate.

While the investment to sales ratio is a commonly used indicator, several other measures of the degree and type of capital intensity can yield additional insights on its relationship to profitability. Some companies are capital intensive because they use a great deal of plant and equipment (fixed assets) relative to the sales revenues generated. By contrast, other companies are capital intensive because they use a great deal of working capital to support their flow of sales. Still other companies are both fixed-capital and working-capital intensive. Exhibit 7–1 shows examples of some companies that are capital intensive and some that are not.[1]

Fixed-capital intensity can be measured as the ratio of net plant and equipment to sales. But, since the age of plant and equipment (and therefore the extent to which they have been depreciated) differs from one business to the next, fixed-capital intensity is measured more accurately as the *gross* book value of plant and equipment per dollar of sales.[2]

If we were to analyze ROI versus fixed-capital intensity for a single year, the observed relationship would be affected by business cycle and product-life cycle differences among businesses which affect ratios to sales via capacity utilization. Since we are interested in how profit performance is related to longer-term structural differ-

Fixed Capital Intensive	**Intensive in Both Fixed and Working Capital**
Average ROE = 8%	Average ROE = 4%

<table>
<tr><td colspan="2"></td><td colspan="2"></td></tr>
</table>

		Fixed Capital Intensive		**Intensive in Both Fixed and Working Capital**	
		Average ROE = 8%		Average ROE = 4%	
		Airlines	ROE	Mining	ROE
		Delta	6.6	Callahan	4.1
		Northwest	5.2	Homestake	6.7
		United	4.7	Newmont	2.8
		Energy			
	High	Eastern Gas & Fuel	7.6	Chemicals	
		Occidental Petroleum	9.1	Monsanto	9.1
		Sun Company	11.3	NL Industries	2.2
		Tenneco	11.3	Penwalt	8.4
		Texas Eastern	11.6		
		Paper			
		International Paper	5.8		
		Mead	5.0		
		Scott	9.7		
		Telecommunications			
		AT&T	10.1		
		GTE	12.1		
Fixed	63%	United Telecom	12.1		
Capital					
to Sales	35%				
		Not Capital Intensive		**Working Capital Intensive**	
		Average ROE = 14%		Average ROE = 10%	
		Retail Food Chains	ROE	Apparel	ROE
		Kroger Co.	14.6	Hartmarx Corp.	13.2
		Lucky Stores	17.0	Manhattan Indust.	7.1
		Safeway Stores	13.0	Phillips Van Heusen	10.6
		Stop & Shop Cos.	15.7	Book Publishing	
	Low	Supermarkets General	17.9	Harper & Row	9.2
		Other Retailers		Houghton Mifflin	12.7
		Longs Drug Stores Inc.	15.5	Electronics	
		Southland Corp.	14.1	Conrac Corp.	11.6
		Toys "R" Us Inc.	19.8	North American Phillips	10.7
		Walgreen Co.	19.3	Zenith	5.1
		Aerospace and Defense		Shoes	
		McDonnell Douglas	12.7	Interco Inc.	10.5
		Raytheon	18.0	Stride Rite	13.0

Low   7%   18%   High

Working Capital / Sales

EXHIBIT 7-1

Capital Intensity and Aftertax Profitability for Selected Companies

NOTE: The data are four-year averages taken from the Compustat data base, 1982–1985.

ences among businesses rather than in how performance is related to the business cycle or product life cycle, PIMS uses two controls for differences in capacity utilization. First, PIMS researchers study four-year averages of performance versus structure (investment to sales, working capital to sales, plant and equipment to sales). This reduces business cycle effects that have powerful impacts on year-to-year changes in profits. Second, to control for extended periods of high versus low capacity utilization, PIMS also measures fixed-capital intensity as the amount of plant and equipment employed relative to what sales revenues would have been if the business were operating at 100 percent of standard capacity (this measure was used in Chapter 3). This adjustment reduces differences that are due to start-up (or short-run) versus on-going operations.

In addition to looking at the ratio of capital to output, managers sometimes think of capital intensity as the mix of capital versus labor inputs to the operating process. This different concept of capital intensity can be measured as the amount of investment per worker or per dollar of labor cost.

CAPITAL INTENSITY AND PROFITABILITY

To understand capital intensity and its implications for business strategy, we need to examine how the various measures of capital intensity are linked to profitability.

There is no doubt that investment to sales and return on investment are negatively related.[3] Looking across businesses in the PIMS data base, ROI declines in a dramatic, systematic pattern as investment to sales increases (Exhibit 7-2). Businesses with investment to sales ratios of 20% or less earn rates of return that are dramatically greater than businesses with investment to sales of 80% or more. Eighty percent of the businesses in the PIMS data base have a four-year average investment to sales ratio between 20% and 80% (Exhibit 7-3). In this range, ROI drops from about 30% to 10% as capital intensity increases.

By contrast, the relationship between return on sales and investment to sales looks weak. The pattern is flat at first but drops off at high levels of investment to sales (back to Exhibit 7-2). For the low range of capital intensity, the findings do not appear to be startling. As we move from ten cents to sixty cents of investment per dollar of sales, businesses on average earn a pretax return of a little less than ten percent.

But isn't there more here than meets the eye? Shouldn't the margin on sales be increasing as capital intensity increases? Of course, it should—if capital-intensive businesses are to earn a normal return on their investment. But the fact is, return on sales declines with increased investment.

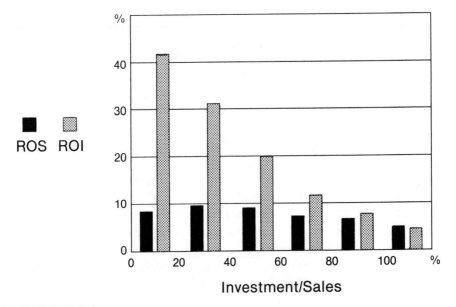

EXHIBIT 7–2
Capital Intensity Hurts Profitability

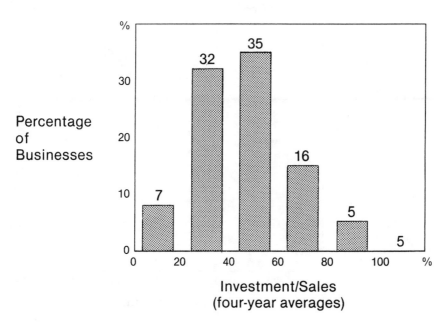

EXHIBIT 7–3
Capital Intensity Differs Dramatically Among Business Units

Moreover, when we compare the actual return on sales *realized* at one level of investment to sales, not with the return on sales at other levels of capital intensity, but with the return on sales *required* to earn an ROI of 20%, the pattern is striking (Exhibit 7–4). The most capital-intensive businesses earn only one-third of the margin required to beat a pretax ROI hurdle of 20%. By contrast, businesses with investment to sales of about 20% earn margins that are more than double the margin required for an ROI of 20%.

Other methods of looking at the effect of capital intensity on profit margins yield the same finding. For instance, when high inflation in the 1980s drove up the cost of capital, many companies adopted a capital charge on assets for their operating units. These financial charges were designed to transmit to the óperating units the need for (1) better margins in capital intensive situations or (2) reductions in capital intensity. We can use a similar technique and calculate a "residual income" to sales versus capital intensity. When

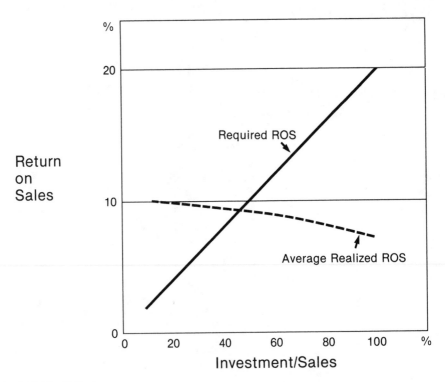

EXHIBIT 7–4
What Margin on Sales Is Required to Earn a ROI of 20%?

we calculate residual income as the pretax operating income less a financial charge of 10 percent of the investment used in the business, we again find that as capital intensity increases the pattern is sharply negative (Exhibit 7–5). Other rates of financial charge produce different slopes, but the same basic negative pattern.

Our analysis of profit margins and capital intensity are corroborated by findings from the FTC and Compustat data bases (Exhibit 7–6). In these three data bases the entities being analyzed and compared differ, but the findings are similar.

- The PIMS data base contains "business units" defined from a strategic/marketing perspective that reflects how competition occurs in the marketplace.
- The FTC's "lines of business" are defined from a manufacturing perspective; lines of business that use common materials and processes are aggregated to make up "industries." (For a comparison of the PIMS and LB data bases, see Appendix A.)
- The Compustat data base contains information on "companies," which are, of course, aggregations of operating units.

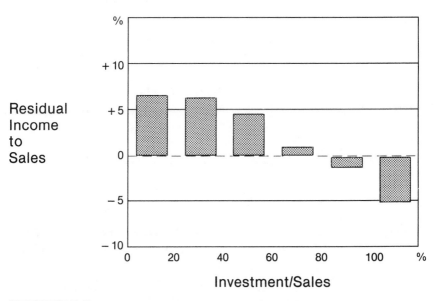

EXHIBIT 7–5
Return on Sales After Financial Charge versus Capital Intensity

NOTE: Residual income is calculated as the pretax operating income less a financial charge of 10% of the investment used in the business.

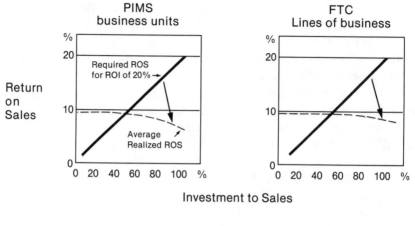

Investment to Sales

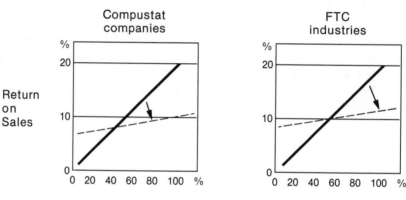

Investment to Sales

EXHIBIT 7-6
Return on Sales versus Capital Intensity: Three Data Bases, PIMS, FTC, Compustat

NOTE: Dashes represent lines of best fit to actual data.

The pattern of actual return on sales relative to that required to earn a pretax ROI of 20% is the same in all the data bases. Capital-intensive operations earn margins that are too low to beat an ROI hurdle of 20%. Operations that are low in capital intensity earn margins that allow them to easily beat the ROI hurdle.

Although the basic message is the same in each data base, there are some interesting differences in the patterns of realized ROS if we use a flat 10% return on *sales* as a reference point for all businesses, despite their differences in capital intensity. We will explain these differences in the next section where we discuss why capital intensity hurts profitability.

The Compustat data base can also be used to study the effects of capital intensity on leverage (the mix of debt and equity used to fund the investment) and return on equity, as well as return on investment. Capital-intensive companies do earn lower rates of return on investment (Exhibit 7-7), but they are also usually more leveraged. A bigger portion of their investment is funded by debt and a smaller portion by equity than is the case for companies that are not capital intensive.

You might surmise that capital-intensive operations are able to earn returns on equity that are comparable to companies with low capital intensity because of their greater leverage. Unfortunately for capital-intensive companies, this is not the case. Despite their greater leverage, capital-intensive companies (investment to sales greater than

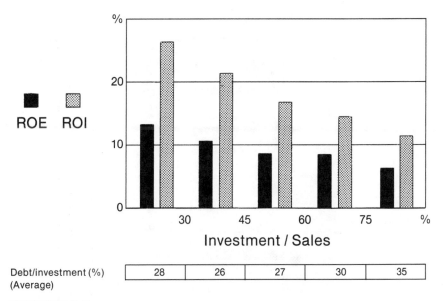

EXHIBIT 7-7
Capital Intensity Hurts Corporate Profitability

SOURCE: Compustat data base, 1982–1985. Aftertax return on equity and pretax return on investment.

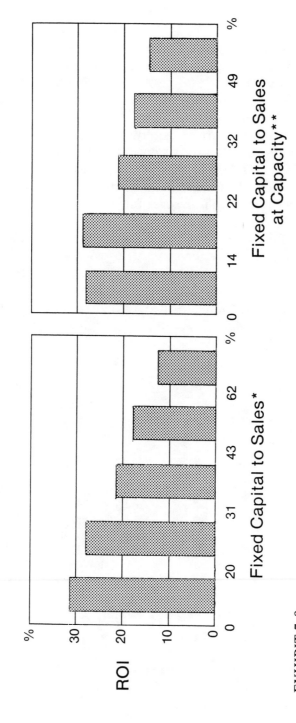

EXHIBIT 7-8
Fixed Capital Intensity Hurts Profitability

*Gross book value of plant and equipment per dollar of sales.
**Gross book value of plant and equipment per dollar of sales at 100%.

75%) earn ROEs that are less than half of the ROEs earned by companies with investment to sales less than 30%.

Fixed-Capital and Working-Capital Intensity

Let's return to the PIMS data base and analyze separately the effects of fixed and working capital on ROI. When we compare ROI to the plant and equipment component of capital intensity, we again find a strong negative relationship (Exhibit 7-8). This relationship remains strong and negative even after we use four-year averages and also control for more extended differences in capacity utilization. These findings mean that the negative relationship between fixed-capital intensity and ROI is not just due to fluctuating good and bad years in the business cycle or to differences between start-up and ongoing operations.

When we examine the effects of fixed-capital intensity and working-capital intensity together, we find that they each have an independent negative relationship with profitability. Exhibit 7-9 shows the negative relationship between pretax ROI and both fixed-capital and working-capital intensity for PIMS business units. Exhibit 7-10 shows the negative relationship between aftertax ROE and both fixed-capital and working-capital intensity for companies in the Compustat data base. The negative relationship between capital intensity and profitability also shows up when we use other measures of financial performance (free cash flow to investment) and capital intensity (investment to value added).

All in all, the evidence shows there is a powerful, robust, basic, negative relationship between capital intensity and profitability.

WHY DOES CAPITAL INTENSITY DEPRESS PROFITABILITY?

To understand why capital intensity hurts profitability we need to understand why capital intensity differs from one business unit to the next. Capital intensity differs not only across industries, but also among competitors within an industry. Differences in capital intensity across industries reflect different product and process technologies and different distribution systems. Differences in capital intensity among competitors within an industry reflect differing degrees

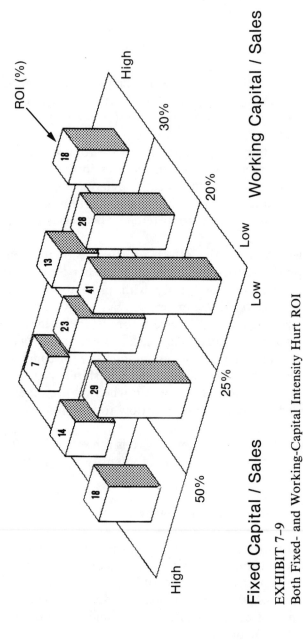

Fixed Capital / Sales

Working Capital / Sales

ROI (%)

EXHIBIT 7-9
Both Fixed- and Working-Capital Intensity Hurt ROI

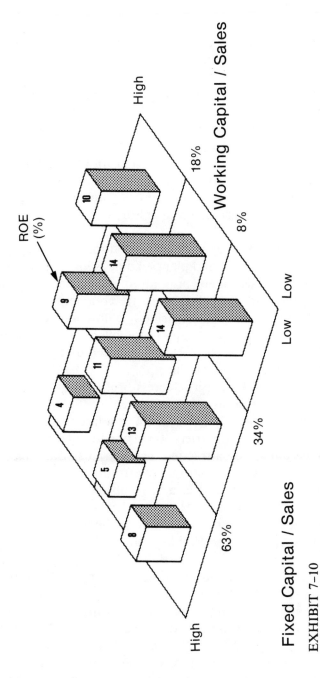

Fixed Capital / Sales

EXHIBIT 7-10

Both Fixed- and Working-Capital Intensity Hurt Corporate Return on Equity

SOURCE: Compustat data base, 1982–1985. Return on equity is aftertax.

of operating effectiveness as well as differences in technology or distribution.

The negative relationship between capital intensity and profitability stems from four main causes:

- Capital intensity leads to aggressive and often destructive competition.
- Heavy capital investment often acts as a barrier to exit from an unprofitable business.
- Management sometimes sets a normal profit to sales target for businesses that have heavier than normal investment to sales.
- Capital-intensive businesses may be less efficient in using fixed or working capital than are competitors.

Capital intensity leads to aggressive competition, especially when economic conditions are poor and plant loading is low because managers may be willing to accept any price above variable costs. In such environments, price and marketing wars are common. Classic examples of such industries include airlines, aluminum, corrugated boxes, commodity chemicals and paper. Moreover, we've found that ROI is negatively related to capital intensity even after we control for the effects of capacity utilization.

Why else does capital intensity depress profitability?

To some people the phrase "capital intensity" conjures up an image of huge investment requirements (in absolute size). To them, capital intensity means high barriers to entry and good rates of return without the danger of attracting new entrants. But, since we measure capital intensity as a ratio to sales, a high level of capital intensity doesn't necessarily reflect a large absolute investment requirement or a barrier to entry. However, heavy fixed investment relative to sales does act as a barrier to exit, and barriers to exit tend to prolong the depressed profitability of capital-intensive businesses.[4]

The behavior of some managers when they set targets for profit margins is a third reason for the negative relationship. They may establish the wrong profit margin goals by focusing on a normal return on sales for all businesses. In doing so, they fail to recognize that a heavier-than-normal investment per dollar of sales requires a better-than-normal margin to achieve a decent return on investment. This failure to reflect structural differences among businesses in target profit margins may explain why the pattern of return of sales versus investment to sales that we saw earlier is relatively flat instead of sharply rising.

There is a fourth key reason why capital intensity and profitability are negatively related. Businesses that are more efficient than their competitors tend to have lower investment per dollar of sales. Japanese automobile companies, for example, tend to have far lower levels of work-in-process inventories than their U.S. or European competitors, because the Japanese use a "just-in-time" inventory system. This means that for Japanese companies, the *relative* investment intensity is lower than it is for their U.S. competitors. Given a comparable return on sales, the competitor with lower capital intensity will earn a higher return on investment.

The FTC data base illustrates the importance of this relative investment intensity phenomenon. In the FTC's *industry* data base, where none of the difference in capital intensity is due to differences among competitors within an industry, return on sales and capital intensity are positively related.[5] (Remember, however, that—despite slightly higher profit margins—capital-intensive industries still fall short of the returns on sales required to earn a pretax ROI of 20%). By contrast, in the Lines of Business data base, like the PIMS data base, where part of the difference in capital intensity represents differences among competitors *within* an industry, return on sales and capital intensity are negatively related or uncorrelated depending on the time span studied.

Being capital intensive because you're in a capital-intensive industry makes it tough to beat the cost of capital. But being capital intensive because you have more plant and equipment and/or more working capital per dollar of sales than your competitors makes beating the cost of capital even tougher.

Strategic versus Business-Cycle Focus

Why focus on investment to sales being low rather than on sales to investment (investment turnover) being high? Aren't they both the same? Arithmetically, yes. But culturally they are different. People tend to focus on the numerator rather than both parts of the ratio. And most managers habitually look at sales to investment *one year at a time.* By tracking profit performance and turnover over time they gain an understanding about how the business cycle affects their short-term profit performance.

In contrast, by using a four-year average of investment to sales we tend to remove differences in profit performance due to cyclical effects and focus on how much investment is used to run the business over a longer time frame that includes good and bad years. And, by comparing profit rates across businesses in the PIMS data base, we shift the focus away from short-term swings in sales to a focus on long-term structural differences among businesses, in their investment employed to support a given volume of sales. Remember that in investment intensive situations, on average, only the market leaders came close to earning a 20% pre-tax ROI, and even they fall a little short (Chapter 5, Exhibit 5–10).

WHY DO BUSINESSES BECOME CAPITAL INTENSIVE?

If the evidence shows a powerful, negative relationship between capital intensity and profitability, why do businesses become capital intensive? Typically, strategies that wind up increasing capital intensity were intended to achieve some other objective. Let's list some examples:

- A business trying to offer better credit terms increases its receivables relative to sales.
- A business aiming at better product availability increased its finished goods inventory relative to sales.
- Businesses protecting against a shortage of supplies may carry high levels of work-in-process inventory relative to sales.
- When businesses vertically integrate backward to assure a source of supply or to coordinate better the different stages of the value adding process, they assume the value-adding activities of suppliers, and thereby increase the amount of investment tied up in their business without increasing their sales (see Chapter 8).
- Changes in technology may make equipment more expensive. Successive generations of plants making semiconductors have cost much more than earlier setups.
- Businesses also tend to become capital intensive over time as their products and markets mature and the value-added activity shifts away from innovation and marketing to operations (see Chapter 10).
- Some businesses invest ahead of the market to establish preemptive capacity.

- Some businesses become capital intensive when hit with a secular shortfall in demand or caught with obsolete equipment.
- Some businesses invest to increase output per employee or, in other words, to attempt to cut variable costs and thereby boost profits.

Let's take a closer look at each of the last three examples.

Establishing Preemptive Capacity

As Michael Porter notes,

> "The essence of the (capital investment) dilemma, then, is to add capacity to further the company's objectives, improving its competitive position or market share while avoiding obsolescence and industry overcapacity."[6]

In industries that produce commodity products (basic chemicals and metals, building products and paper) many companies have been led to focus solely on cost and to neglect relative service quality and relative investment intensity, which are key dimensions of competitive success. Furthermore, as noted in Chapter 5, the relationship between cumulative volume and relative profit margins has often been miscalculated and overemphasized. Many companies were tempted to pursue a preemptive capacity expansion and price-cutting strategy to obtain cumulative volume leadership.

As Porter has observed, these preemptive strategies are risky because specific conditions must be satisfied for them to be successful. First, your preemptive capacity expansion must be very large in relation to expected market size; otherwise it will not be preemptive. Second, you must benefit from economies of scale or a significant learning curve to offset your low capacity utilization. Third, you must have the credibility that leads competitors to believe that you are committed and able to carry out a preemptive strategy. Fourth, there must be entry barriers to prevent competitors from jumping in later. Fifth, you must have competitors who will back down. Even when most of these conditions seem to be present, the market environment can change to unravel a growth-oriented share-gain strategy that would have preempted the market.

In the early 1970s DuPont led the titanium dioxide market with over one-third of the U.S. production capacity.[7] (Titanium dioxide is a commodity chemical used in paints, papers, and plastics.) Three methods of producing titanium dioxide were then in use: (1) chloride ilmenite, (2) chloride rutile, and (3) sulfate. But 1970 and 1971 saw a jump in rutile ore prices and the introduction of new pollution control legislation that sharply increased waste disposal costs. These developments undercut the positions, respectively, of the rutile chloride and sulfate producers. As the only producer using ilmenite chloride technology (which accounted for 70% of its total capacity in 1972), DuPont profited from these events and developed an aggressive growth strategy to double its market share by 1985.

By early 1975, however, a number of factors dictated a revision of the capacity plans that DuPont had made in 1972. First, new forecasts of market demand through 1980 came in well below the 1972 projections. Second, new uncertainty about demand made attempts at preemption seem risky. Third, unexpected leniency in the enforcement of pollution controls had let competitors' sulfate units continue to operate. Fourth, low capacity utilization and sharp increases in chlorine prices and construction costs meant that cash flow from the titanium dioxide business would be below 1974 predictions at a time when there was a corporate shortage of capital. Consequently, a number of major decisions were made in February 1975 to postpone indefinitely the construction of some planned new capacity and to delay expansion of existing plants. Thus, even a business that at first seemed to meet all the conditions for a successful strategy to capture all of the market growth ran into problems that forced it to abort that strategy.

Capacity Overkill

In a recent book about the chemical industry, Joseph Bower notes that every competitor keeps hoping the other guy will be the one to cut back. "The willingness of companies to bleed each other is awesome," wrote Bower.[8]

There is a strong tendency to overbuild capacity, particularly in commodity businesses, that goes far beyond mistakes in attempts to preempt the market. The pressures that lead many industries to repeatedly overbuild have been thoroughly catalogued by Michael Porter. A few of these pressures are summarized here.

Economies of scale often mean that capacity must be added in large lumps. When these lumps are large relative to industry output, and especially when some economic event triggers several competitors to bunch their capacity decisions, serious overcapacity can result. This happened, for example, in color TV picture tubes in the United States in the late 1960s.

Plant additions frequently involve long lead times that require companies to project demand and competitive behavior far into the future. To avoid the risk of being left behind without sufficient capacity, some companies are tempted to plunge ahead and take the risk of uncertain future conditions. Investments in capacity are largely irreversible; hence, if capacity overshoots demand, barriers to exit cause the overcapacity to persist for a long time.

The probability of overcapacity is also related to an industry's structure and to competitive conditions. The tendency to overbuild is severe when there are many companies vying for market position and no clear leader with the clout needed to enforce an orderly expansion process. If competitors in the industry are integrated downstream, pressures for overbuilding rise even higher because each company wants to ensure a source of supply for its downstream operations. If barriers to entry are low, new entrants often create or aggravate the problem of capacity overbuilding.

Capital Intensity and Output per Employee

Businesses often substitute capital for labor in an attempt to increase output per employee, reduce unit costs and improve profitability. When these projects are actually undertaken, output per employee typically does go up. But, for most businesses, capital intensity doesn't improve labor productivity enough to keep ROI above the cost of capital.

Businesses in the PIMS data base show a wide range of value added per employee, from less than \$10,000 to more than \$90,000.[9] The most powerful determinants of output per employee are the level and mix of capital per employee. Plant and equipment (measured at gross book value) per employee is the most powerful single factor; working capital per employee is second. Using these two factors alone, a rough productivity benchmark can be established (Exhibit 7-11). This benchmark shows dramatic differences in the amount of value added per employee that is normal for different combinations of fixed and working capital per employee.

The net effect of investment per employee and value added per employee on ROI is shown in Exhibit 7-12. The few businesses that achieve high productivity despite low investment per employee are

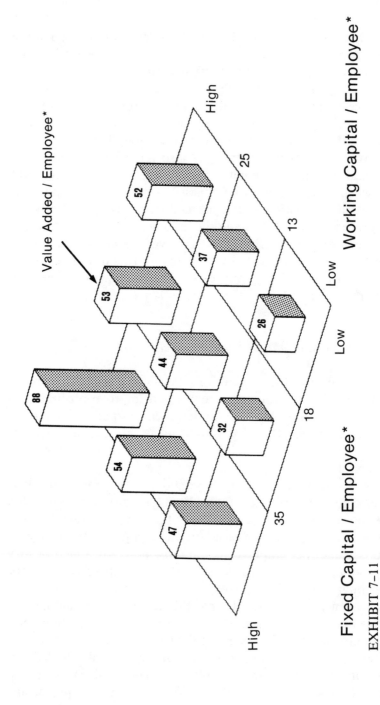

Value Added / Employee*

Working Capital / Employee*

Fixed Capital / Employee*

EXHIBIT 7-11
Investment per Employee Boosts Labor Productivity
*1980 U.S. ($000).

154

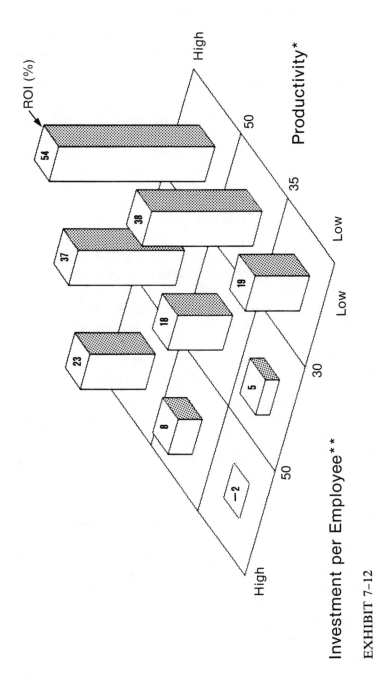

ROI (%)

Productivity*

Investment per Employee**

EXHIBIT 7-12
Heavy Investment per Employee Hurts ROI but High Productivity Can
Offset the Damage

*Value added per employee, 1980 U.S. ($000).
**1980 U.S. ($000).

155

extremely profitable, while the few that have heavy investment per employee and poor productivity earn very low returns. These low returns occur because output doesn't keep pace with investment as these businesses mechanize, computerize or automate.

Since investment per employee and value added per employee usually go together, some 60% of the businesses lie on the diagonal from low investment and value added to high investment and value added. Of these businesses, the ones that are high in both investment and value added earn higher returns on investment. From this we conclude that businesses that become more mechanized or automated, in the sense that investment increases relative to *employees,* can maintain or even slightly increase their profitability if value added per employee increases dramatically.

By contrast, businesses that become more capital intensive in the sense that investment increases relative to *sales* suffer a decline in ROI even if they achieve a normal increase in labor productivity (Exhibit 7–13). Usually, these businesses were not following a conscious strategy of increasing investment relative to sales. Rather, they were substituting capital for labor to improve productivity. Typically output per employee does increase, but not enough for sales and profits to keep pace with the increased level of investment.

As Peter Drucker has observed, the paper industry

". . . has been unable, in most years (since WWII) to produce any but marginal profits . . . The break-even point of most up-to-date paper mills is just barely below 100 percent of capacity operations . . . The paper industry . . . has substituted capital for labor on a massive scale. But the trade-off was a thoroughly uneconomical one. In fact, the paper industry represents a massive triumph of engineering over economics and common sense."[10]

Sometimes profits don't keep pace with investment because of unanticipated price declines. Capital-intensive businesses become more desperate to load their plant and equipment. In other cases, the investment balloons because the strategy requires increased working capital to an extent not fully realized in the analysis supporting the request for a capital expenditures. Many companies scrutinize lumpy fixed-capital investments more carefully then gradual build-ups in working capital.

Some businesses suffer a decline in ROI because they wind up adding capital to labor rather than substituting it for labor. The headcount doesn't fall as much as anticipated because white-collar workers replace blue-collar workers. And even if anticipated unit cost

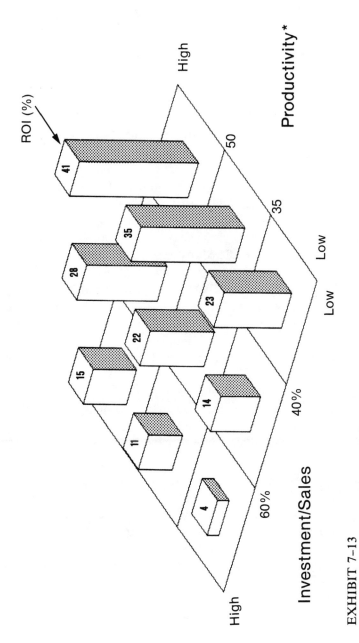

EXHIBIT 7-13
Heavy Investment to Sales Drags Profitability Down and High Productivity
Only Offsets Some of the Damage

*Value added per employee, 1980 U.S. ($000).

157

declines are realized, returns on the larger investment base may fall because the benefits of lower costs are competed away in the form of lower prices to customers or bargained away by unions in the form of higher wages.

WHEN DO CAPITAL INVESTMENTS PAY OFF?

Small, single product companies usually turn to the capital markets for investment funds, but diversified companies' own executives (rather than outside market forces) allocate capital to their business units. Thus their decisions play a key role in determining which capital allocation requests are funded. Most executives intuitively grasp the key principle of capital budgeting and value-based planning: Invest (when and if you can) to beat the cost of capital. Note that this can mean *lowering* average ROI! Many executives, however, are unhappy with the results of their current capital allocation process and would like to improve dramatically the odds of winning.

In theory, companies should make investments if the discounted cash flow plus the discounted future market value of a strategy exceeds the current market value of the investment. Such investments will enhance the company's return on equity and ultimately its stock price.

Many companies have used value-based planning on historical data to better understand how past investments in different business units have either created or destroyed value for the corporation. Making value-based planning calculations for investments in the *future,* however, is a bit more problematic because future cash flows and future market values must be estimated. For ways to validate future cash flows and sustainable ROI, see Chapter 11. Without reasonable reality-checks on financial pro formas, value-based planning can easily become a garbage-in–garbage-out process.

Capital Allocation in Practice

How then does the capital appropriation process typically work in a large diversified corporation? Initially, the corporate office sets a corporate-wide hurdle rate based on its cost of capital. This hurdle may be modified slightly to reflect differing business-unit risks. To get projects approved, business-unit managers frequently juggle the numbers (usually boosting their sales estimates or ignoring the possibility of price reductions) in order to exceed the hurdle.

Business-unit managers reason that if corporate management wants numbers designed to clear the hurdle rate, that's what they will get. But they feel uneasy in submitting rosy financial plans.

The corporate capital-appropriation committee reviews all funding requests. Most projected profit rates are a little above the hurdle rate by design. (It is useless to come in under the hurdle rate, and it is dangerous to come in much above the hurdle rate.) Yet funding all projects with projected returns above their designated hurdle rates would be unwise even if sufficient funds were available. Many of the projects are known to be overly optimistic.

Therefore each capital appropriation committee must decide which projections to believe and which to question. They often cross-check business-unit sales forecasts. The tendency is to back managers with good financial track records.

Betting on Past Profitability versus Strategic Position

To identify a better way of investing capital, we examined businesses that increased their investment base and used our findings to determine what measures might predict the incremental return on their incremental investment. The chance of achieving an incremental ROI greater than 20 percent is measured as the percentage of businesses achieving an increase in pretax profit that is at least 20 percent of the increase in their investment base. While the odds of beating a 20 percent incremental return on future investment are only somewhat related to current profitability, we found that they are tremendously influenced by the current strategic position of a business. As Exhibit 7-14 shows, when the investment dice are rolled, capital investments in businesses with good strategic positions (and, hopefully, sound strategies) pay off. This finding is further supported by evidence that long-run value enhancement (measured as the discounted cash flow plus discounted future market value expressed as a percentage of current market value) is strongly related to a business's strategic starting position (see Chapter 11).

The overall measure of a business's strategic position used in Exhibit 7-14 is its par ROI. Par ROI is a benchmark of what profitability level is normal given a business unit's profile of strategic characteristics. Rather than funding separate projects solely according to

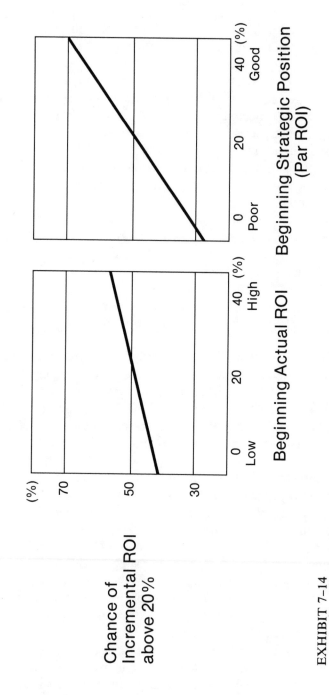

EXHIBIT 7–14
Capital Investments in Businesses with Good Strategic Positions and Sound Strategies Pay Off

160

financial calculations, companies should fund coherent strategies for business units that currently enjoy a good strategic position, or strategies that will reposition a business from a poor to a good strategic position for profitable growth.

SUMMARY

Capital intensity has a critical effect on profitability, just like relative perceived quality and market share. Yet while investment and sales data are often easier to obtain than data on market share or relative quality, managers in most companies don't systematically track the long-term capital intensity of their own businesses. The few managers that do track the capital intensity of competitors' businesses and sister businesses within their own companies as well as their own business typically gain insights that allow them to operate at lower capital intensity than their competitors.

The evidence shows a powerful, negative relationship between capital intensity and profitability. This does *not* mean that companies should not make capital investments. It means that most companies should try to allocate capital more effectively so that they have a better chance of beating the cost of capital. There are several points that a company should remember to ensure that its investments pay off:

- Avoid capacity overkill by reviewing the characteristics that tend to lead to an overbuilding of capacity. Remember that investments in flexible, general purpose plant and equipment can be less risky than investments in equipment that is highly specialized.
- Don't think of your business as a commodity producer or it will surely be one. Creating differentiation and superior product/service quality provide protection against price and marketing wars by building uniqueness, customer loyalty, and repeat purchases (Chapter 6).
- Make sure that when capital is substituted for labor that the improvement in labor productivity realized (not just planned) is sufficient to keep pace with the increased investment per employee so that capital intensity, relative to sales, is not increased.

- Above all else, it is important to fund sound business strategies in businesses that have or are attaining strong competitive positions.

In times like the present, when markets are in flux and change is the rule, managers should strongly consider reality-testing their strategies to see that (1) the projected financial performance is consistent with the business's evolving strategic position and (2) the targeted strategic position is attainable. Investments in individual projects by businesses with poor strategic positions may appear to beat incremental financial hurdles, but they tend to build up "assets" in businesses that may never be able to reposition themselves and may ultimately have to be written off.

Chapter 8 _____

When Does Vertical Integration Pay Off?*

For many types of businesses, decisions about the "vertical scope" of the operation are of key strategic impotance.[1] In some situations, it is claimed, an adequate degree of vertical integration is a necessity for survival. For example, in the mid-1970s Bowmar Instrument Company, the early market leader in hand-held calculators, depended on Texas Instruments—a competitor—for its supplies of integrated circuits. Bowmar's higher costs for this key component, and its inability to get adequate quantities to meet a seasonal surge in demand, were important factors in the company's eventual demise. Conversely, some commentators have attributed a part of the American automobile industry's woes to excessive vertical integration. As Robert Hayes and William Abernathy put it: "In deciding to integrate backwards [into the production of various components] because of apparent short-term rewards, managers often restrict their ability to strike out in innovative directions in the future."[2] Thus, for example, until recently General Motors justified its extensive vertical integration by claiming that it "saved the supplier's profit by making its own components."[3] But in December 1986 GM announced a component plant closing, saying that it hoped to keep the

*This chapter is based on Robert D. Buzzell, "Is Vertical Integration Profitable?," *Harvard Business Review,* January–February 1983, pp. 92–102.

plant operating as an independent supplier, thereby achieving lower costs!

While most would agree that decisions regarding vertical integration often have important effects, there are few guidelines for managers in this area. Consultants and academic authorities on strategic planning and strategic management have offered numerous prescriptions for success in designing corporate portfolios, market segmentation, pricing, and product development. But they have little to say about vertical integration, beyond suggesting lists of possible advantages and risks. Nor does economic theory offer much in the way of guidance. Economists have made numerous studies of vertical integration, both from a general theoretical viewpoint and in specific industries. In spite of this extensive research literature, according to Dennis Carlton, "Vertical integration has never been a well-understood phenomenon."[4]

In this chapter, we summarize the evidence provided by the PIMS data base on the subject of vertical integration. Specifically, we compare the performance of businesses with different degrees of vertical integration in order to shed some light on the following questions:

- Are highly-integrated businesses in general more or less profitable than those that are less integrated?
- Under what conditions is a high degree of vertical integration most likely to improve profitability?
- Apart from its impact on profits, what other benefits and risks are associated with vertical integration strategies?

DEFINING AND MEASURING VERTICAL INTEGRATION

A traditional way of defining vertical integration is that it is the combination, under a single ownership, of two or more distinct stages of production and/or distribution that are usually separate. This concept is well-understood in such industries as oil, chemicals, and textiles, where a sequence of activities beginning with raw material extraction and ending with the distribution of finished products has traditionally been divided into physically distinct steps with independent businesses responsible for each one. In the oil industry, for example, the sequence running from the well to the service station is divided into four stages: crude oil production, transportation, refining, and marketing. Some companies specialize in just one of these, such as Buckeye Pipeline Company in the transportation stage.

Other firms combine two or three stages, and the fully integrated major oil companies are involved in all four.

Not all industries, of course, have distinct stages comparable to those of the oil industry. But almost every type of business does have to make choices about the extent to which it makes rather than buys various components of its products and various services. Examples include:

- Whether to operate a company-owned trucking fleet or utilize independent owner-operators;
- For a retail chain, whether to operate its own warehouse or to rely on wholesalers;
- Whether to make or buy containers (Coors, for instance, makes all of its own beer cans and bottles, while Anheuser-Busch buys about half of its requirements from outside suppliers);
- Whether to utilize an in-house sales force or independent, commissioned sales representatives.

All of these and many other similar choices make up the broad area of vertical integration strategy.

While the basic idea of vertical integration is straightforward, measuring the extent of integration is not—at least, not in a way that permits comparison across different industries. In our analysis of the experiences of the PIMS businesses, we use two types of vertical integration measures: an absolute measure and a relative one. The absolute measure is *value added as a percentage of sales* for each business unit. "Value added" is defined as sales and lease revenue minus *all* purchases (materials, components, supplies, and energy) by a business from other businesses. (Purchases from another business within the same parent corporation are treated as "outside" purchases.) Thus, value added as a percentage of sales is simply:

$$\frac{\text{Sales} - \text{Purchases}}{\text{Sales}} \times 100$$

In order to explore how differences in the value added/sales ratio are related to profitability, an adjustment is necessary. Because each business unit's value added measure *includes* net profit, any increases in profitability arising from sources other than actual vertical integration will also increase value added, thus creating an automatic positive relationship between the two factors.

To eliminate the tautological relationship between the value added/sales ratio and profitability, we use an adjusted ratio in which each business unit's *actual* net profit is replaced by an *average* rate of return on its invested capital. (The method of calculation is explained in Appendix A.)

In the analysis that follows, adjusted value-added as a percentage of adjusted sales (VA/S) is used as the primary measure of each business unit's degree of vertical integration. The businesses in the data base vary greatly in terms of the VA/S ratio, from a low of around 20% to a high of 90%.

Differences in business units' VA/S ratios are, without doubt, attributable primarily to the fact that they operate in different industries or product-markets, with corresponding variations in industry norms and in the range of possibilities for vertical integration. To supplement the VA/S measure of vertical integration, therefore, we use an additional measure of *relative* vertical integration. This relative measure is based on PIMS participants' responses to the following question: *Compare the degree of (1) backward and (2) forward vertical integration of this business to that of its three leading competitors: is it less, about the same, or greater?*

Responses to this question indicate that the majority of the PIMS businesses (over 60%, in fact) are integrated to about the same extent as their competitors. The performance of these businesses can be compared with those that are less integrated and those that are more integrated than competitors.

POTENTIAL BENEFITS OF VERTICAL INTEGRATION

The experiences of companies that have pursued vertical integration strategies suggest that vertical integration can lead to several different kinds of competitive advantages. These include lower costs of buying and selling, assurance of supply or distribution, better production and inventory control, enhanced technological capabilities, and increased barriers to the entry of new competitors.

Lower Buying and Selling Costs

In many cases, a major objective of vertical integration is to eliminate, or at least substantially reduce, the costs of buying and selling that go with separate ownership of two stages of production. Integration may lead to lower physical handling costs as well. Thus, an integrated circuit producer that also manufactures finished products could operate with little or no sales force, advertising, sales promotion, or market research as compared with another producer selling to independent customers.

Assurance of Supply or Distribution

A frequent rationale for integration into the production of raw materials or components is that it may be necessary to ensure adequate supplies. Certainly this aspect of vertical integration has been a major attraction in the oil industry since its beginnings.[5] More recently, the successive crises of 1973–74 and 1979 made oil producers tempting candidates for acquisition by large users. Thus, when DuPont bought Conoco for $7.3 billion in 1981, Chairman Edward Jefferson stated that the merger would give his company "a captive hydrocarbon feedstock source (and) reduce the exposure of the combined companies to fluctuations in the price of energy and hydrocarbons."[6]

On the selling side, companies may adopt strategies of forward vertical integration because of a lack of qualified independent distributors or a belief that full control over sales and service functions will provide them with a competitive advantage. The Singer Sewing Machine Company, for example, developed its own network of retail stores in order to provide the customer-training and installment credit services that were needed to build primary demand for home sewing.

Better Production and Inventory Control

Even when supplies of materials are not subject to great uncertainty, vertical integration may permit cost reductions through better coordination of production and inventory scheduling between stages. An in-house supplier can, it is argued, schedule production more effectively when dealing with a captive downstream customer than with independent and less predictable buyers. Similarly, buying from a sister business can give a business greater assurance of supply, permitting lower reserve inventories.

Technological Capabilities

Integration, especially backward integration, may give a business better access to information about technological change, thus reducing risks of obsolescence. More generally, it is claimed that vertically integrated businesses or companies are better equipped to innovate because they participate in more of the production/distribution activities in which change can occur. This argument rests, in part, on the notion that a critical requirement for successful innovation is adequate coordination of marketing and technical functions, and that coordination is improved by integration.[7]

Increased Entry Barriers

A final motive for vertical integration may be to increase entry barriers. The more vertically integrated a business is, the greater the financial and managerial resources required to enter and compete in it. Established firms in an industry may integrate their operations as a way of raising the stakes and discouraging potential new entrants. Of course, this gambit is effective only if vertical integration becomes necessary for competing.

DISADVANTAGES OF VERTICAL INTEGRATION

If a strategy of vertical integration offers so many potential gains, why is it not more widely employed? Obviously there must be offsetting costs and risks associated with operating on an integrated basis. Among the more important ones are increased capital requirements, problems of balancing throughput, reduced flexibility, and loss of specialization.

Capital Requirements

When a business integrates either backward or forward, it must provide the capital required for the newly integrated operations. Especially in the case of backward integration, the result usually is that a high degree of vertical integration carries with it a higher level of capital intensity, i.e., more investment per dollar of sales or value added. As we have shown in Chapter 7, high capital intensity tends to *depress* profitability.

Balancing Throughput

An inherent problem in combining different stages of production or distribution is that the stages may differ in terms of what scale of operation is required for efficient operation. For example, a very high volume of production of integrated circuits may be required to achieve costs competitive with those of independent suppliers. The minimum efficient scale of operation for ICs may therefore be much greater than the volume needed for efficient production of, say, minicomputers.

The fact that scale requirements differ among vertically linked activities suggests that integrated businesses must either (1) operate on a large enough scale to satisfy the requirements of the most volume-dependent components, or (2) suffer the penalties of inefficient scale at one or more stages. An implication of this line of reasoning is that vertical integration is more likely to be feasible for businesses with large market shares. A big share of a given market or industry represents large scale, relative to competitors in that market. It seems reasonable to expect that, in general, opportunities for vertical integration will be greater for businesses with large market shares than for their smaller competitors. This is consistent with the experience of the automobile industry: according to one estimate, General Motors buys 10% to 15% of its standard components from outside suppliers, compared with 40% to 50% for Ford.[8]

Reduced Flexibility

Vertical integration can be extremely risky because it implies commitment to a particular technology or way of operating. If the products or methods of one stage in a vertically integrated system are rendered obsolete by technological or market changes, the integrated firm may find it very difficult to change. A classic example is that of Jonathan Logan, a women's apparel producer. In the 1960s, the company committed itself to double-knit fabrics by investing in its own textile mill. Later, when double-knits had gone out of fashion, Jonathan Logan "continued to turn them out, mainly to use up the mill's production." When the mill was finally closed in 1981, the company reported a $40 million write-off.[9]

Loss of Specialization

A somewhat intangible, but often important, danger in vertical integration is that different stages of production or distribution may have very distinct managerial requirements. Retail or wholesale distribution, in particular, seem to need quite different forms of organization, control systems, and management style than do manufacturing or processing. Up to the mid-1930s, the major U.S. oil companies were moving in the direction of increased ownership of retail service stations. Then the company-owned stations began to be phased out in favor of independently owned, franchised dealers. A major reason for this shift was "the pricing and operating inflexibility displayed by the company-owned and -operated service stations."[10]

Other industries have had problems similar to those of the oil refiners when they have attempted to integrate forward into retailing. The company-owned stores operated by the major tire producers, for instance, had severe problems in the 1960s when mass merchants began competing with them and consumers moved to the suburbs. Similarly, integrated men's clothing producers like Robert Hall and Bond, and Sherwin-Williams, an integrated paint producer, all had difficulties during the 1970s. While there may have been other reasons for these companies' troubles, it appears that their efforts to manage geographically dispersed retail chains were handicapped by a "manufacturing mentality."

VERTICAL INTEGRATION AND PROFITABILITY

Since vertical integration entails both potential benefits and potential risks, it is reasonable to expect that the payoff from a strategy of increased integration will vary according to the market and competitive conditions in which a business operates. To determine when vertical integration strategies are most likely to improve profitability, we can compare the results achieved by PIMS businesses with low versus high degrees of integration, using both the absolute and relative measures we have described.

Exhibit 8–1 shows average pretax profit margins, investment-to-sales ratios, and rates of return on investment for businesses with differing levels of vertical integration as measured by VA/S percentages. As expected, profit margins expressed as percentages of sales rise as VA/S increases. There is no difference in profit margins up to a VA/S ratio of 60%, but from that point onward profits rise consistently with increasing integration. Investment intensity, however, rises along with VA/S over the whole range of the data. As a result, the pretax rate of return on investment (ROI) declines up to the point where VA/S is between 50% and 60%. Beyond an integration level of 60%, investment intensity increases more slowly than profit margins, and ROI consequently rises with increasing vertical integration.

The V-shaped relationship between VA/S and ROI suggests that profitability is highest at the two opposite ends of the spectrum. Either a very low or a very high level of integration yields an above-average rate of return, while profits are lowest in the middle. This pattern is identical to one reported by Edward Bowman in a study of minicomputer and computer peripherals manufacturers. Bowman's interpretation of the pattern was that a company:

> . . . can do most of its work itself, such as research and development, production, and service, and be relatively successful. On the other hand, it can be low on value added, be essentially a purchased-component assembler, and also be successful. Middle ground is apparently a questionable strategy.[11]

Additional evidence of the V-shaped relationship between vertical integration and ROI is provided by a special analysis of 163 chemical industry business in the PIMS data base.[12] This group included 50 or more SBUs in each of three categories—basic chemicals, such as chlorine and plasticizers; intermediate products (e.g., fertilizers); and end products including paints, soaps and detergents, and explosives. Among these chemical producers, ROI was highest (averaging 34%) when VA/S was below 40%, and lowest (average 14%) for those with an intermediate VA/S ratio (between 50% and 60%).

The figures in Exhibit 8–1 demonstrate clearly how rising investment requirements act to offset the higher profit margins associated with increased vertical integration. If integration can somehow be achieved without the penalty of a proportionally higher investment base, then increasing vertical integration should be extremely beneficial. Exhibit 8–2 shows that this is indeed the case. Here the PIMS businesses are sorted into nine subgroups on the basis

172

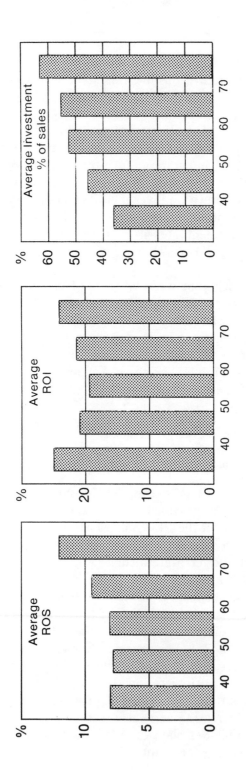

Adjusted Value Added—% of Sales

EXHIBIT 8–1
Vertical Integration, Profitability, and Investment Intensity

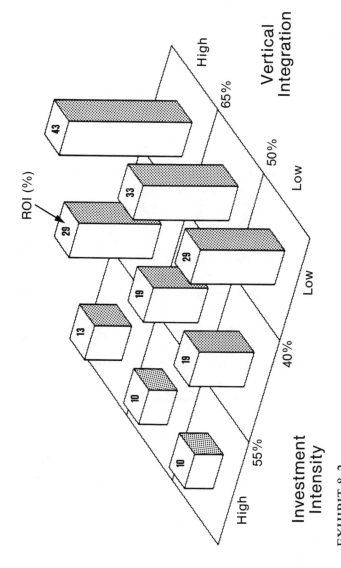

EXHIBIT 8-2
Vertical Integration, Investment Intensity, and ROI

173

of both VA/S and investment intensity. The data indicate that, for any given level of investment intensity, higher levels of VA/S are accompanied by steady increases in ROI.

The moral seems clear: if a strategy of increased integration can be carried out without increasing investment intensity, it usually leads to higher profitability. But the data also show that the winning combination of a high VA/S ratio and low investment intensity is uncommon. Of the 616 businesses in the highest VA/S group (over 65%), only about one-fifth had low levels of investment intensity.

RELATIVE VERTICAL INTEGRATION AND PROFITABILITY

As noted earlier, cross-sectional differences in the VA/S ratio among businesses are primarily due to differences in the nature of the markets or industries in which they operate. To the extent that this is true, we might conclude that the main implication of the pattern shown in Exhibit 8-1 is that it pays to be in those kinds of businesses where VA/S is (inherently) very low or very high. Beyond this, however, in many cases there are strategic choices to be made about a business unit's relative degree of vertical integration. Is it profitable to be more highly integrated than the industry norm? Exhibit 8-3 shows average ROI performance for PIMS businesses that reported varying degrees of relative vertical integration. These data are given separately for Consumer and Industrial Products businesses; as men-

EXHIBIT 8-3
Relative Vertical Integration and Profitability

Degree of Integration, Relative to Competitors	Average ROI	
	Consumer Products	Industrial Products
Backward Integration:		
Less	18	20
Same	22	23
More	25	26
Forward Integration:		
Less	22	23
Same	22	22
More	19	23

tioned earlier, the feasibility of forward and/or backward integration depends on where a business is located in a production-distribution system.

The data in Exhibit 8-3 suggest that, for both consumer and industrial product manufacturing businesses, ROI is usually enhanced by a high degree of *backward* integration, but there is no connection at all between ROI and differing degrees of *forward* integration.

VERTICAL INTEGRATION, SCALE, AND PROFITABILITY

As mentioned earlier, larger businesses should more often be able to use vertical integration strategies than their smaller competitors because they are more likely to be able to operate at efficient scales in each stage of activity. Of course, sometimes a company can integrate backward or forward on the basis of the shared requirements of two or more businesses that operate in separate product-markets. For example, Black & Decker produces a wide variety of motor-driven tools and appliances, and can make its own motors in sufficient quantities to be competitive with independent producers. Thus, there are ways of achieving efficient scale other than simply having a large share in a single market. Nevertheless, other things being equal, large-share businesses should derive greater benefits from increased vertical integration.

Exhibit 8-4 shows that the effects of vertical integration do, indeed, depend on size. Here the PIMS businesses are grouped according to their relative market shares. For businesses with small relative shares—less than 25% that of the 3 largest competitors combined—ROI is slightly lower when a business is highly integrated vertically. This relationship applies both to the absolute level of integration, as measured by VA/S, and to relative backward integration at the business unit level. For businesses with relative market shares over 25%, ROI is highest for the high and low extremes of integration based on the VA/S measure. When relative share is greater than 60%, however, ROI rises consistently with increasing *relative* backward integration.

The impact of relative *forward* integration on profitability is not clear: surprisingly, ROI declines as this form of integration goes up except for small-share businesses. This may not reflect any real difference, however, because of the small number of SBUs in this particular category.

EXHIBIT 8-4
Vertical Integration, Relative Market Share, and Profitability

	Relative Market Share		
Adjusted VA/S	*Under 25%*	*25%–60%*	*Over 60%*
	Average ROI		
Under 50%	15 (280)*	24 (251)	31 (223)
50%–65%	12 (266)	18 (281)	31 (257)
Over 65%	12 (154)	21 (200)	34 (262)
Relative Vertical Integration:			
Backward			
Less	13 (227)	22 (182)	29 (112)
Same	14 (402)	20 (457)	32 (474)
More	11 (71)	22 (93)	35 (156)
Forward			
Less	13 (135)	24 (95)	37 (87)
Same	13 (516)	21 (576)	31 (582)
More	17 (49)	17 (61)	31 (73)

*Number of businesses in each group shown in parentheses.

The figures in Exhibit 8-4, then, provide some support for the idea that the net effects of vertical integration vary according to the size of a business unit. The data also show that large-share competitors are more likely to pursue vertical integration strategies. For instance, more than 35% of the businesses with relative shares greater than 60% reported VA/S ratios over 65%, compared with around 20% of the small-share business units.

VERTICAL INTEGRATION AND INFLATION

As mentioned earlier, a rationale advanced for some vertical integration moves (such as DuPont-Conoco) is to the effect that integrated organizations are less vulnerable to increases in raw materials costs. If this is a valid theory, then a high ratio of VA/S should have a bigger impact on profitability in markets with high inflation rates. To test this, the PIMS businesses were separated into high-inflation and low-inflation groups, with the dividing line at a 10% annual rate of increase in selling prices.[13] Within each of these two groups, we compared the *relative direct costs* of businesses with differing degrees of integration—see Exhibit 8-5. (The index of "relative direct

EXHIBIT 8–5
Vertical Integration, Inflation, and Relative Direct Costs

	Rate of Inflation	
Adjusted VA/S	*Under 10%*	*Over 10%*
	Index of Relative Costs	
Under 50%	102	102
50%–65%	102	102
Over 65%	101	104

cost'' is an estimate of how an SBU's per-unit costs of materials and production compare with those of its major competitors. An index of 100 means that direct costs are equal to the average of leading competitors.)

If it is true that integration shields a business from inflationary cost increases, then highly integrated SBUs should have a real cost advantage in high-inflation markets. This, however, does not appear to be the case. While vertical integration has little or no impact on relative costs when prices are rising at less than 10% per annum, it seemingly increases relative costs under high-inflation conditions. At minimum, this casts doubt on the notion that integration offers any insurance against the effects of inflation.

VERTICAL INTEGRATION AND INNOVATION

Are highly integrated businesses more innovative? Exhibit 8–6 shows, for businesses with low, medium, and high rates of VA/S, the percentages of sales accounted for by new products. (New products are defined here as those introduced during the preceding 3 years.) Separate figures are shown for consumer and industrial businesses; for those competing in mature versus growth markets; and for situations in which major technological change had occurred recently as opposed to those where it had not.

The results indicate that highly integrated businesses *do* generate more new products. (In Exhibit 8–6, a cut-off of 50% is used to separate high from low VA/S ratios because levels of new-product activity were essentially the same for all businesses beyond the 50% level.) In mature as well as growing markets, high levels of integration went along with higher rates of new product introduction. The same pattern holds regardless of whether or not technology is chang-

EXHIBIT 8-6
Vertical Integration and Product Innovation

	Adjusted VA/S	
Types of Business	*Under 50%*	*Over 50%*
	Average % of New Products	
Consumer Products	5%	10%
Industrial Products	7	10
Recent Technological Change:		
Yes	10	15
No	5	7
Product Life-Cycle Stage:		
Introduction/Growth	14	17
Maturity/Decline	5	7

ing, and for consumer as well as industrial product marketers. Thus, the experience of the PIMS businesses lends support to the notion that vertical integration facilitates product innovation. In some instances, this might justify a vertical integration strategy even if it involves some decrease in short-term profitability.

EVALUATING VERTICAL INTEGRATION STRATEGIES

To return to the question posed at the beginning of this chapter: is vertical integration profitable? Not surprisingly, the answer seems to be sometimes yes, sometimes no. The evidence summarized here does not, of course, provide any formula for determining just how a specific integration strategy will affect performance. But the experience of the PIMS businesses, together with other evidence drawn from various industries, does suggest some general guidelines for evaluating possible benefits and risks of integration.

1. *Beware of Heightened Investment Needs*

As noted earlier, when a high level of vertical integration hurts ROI, it is usually because of rising investment intensity. An ideal strategy is one in which value added is increased without a corresponding expansion in the investment base. No doubt the best way to accomplish this is to develop proprietary products or processes whose value derives from superior performance rather than from extensive in-house manufacturing or processing activities. Successful producers of cosmetics and other personal care products, for example, often enjoy value-added-to-sales ratios of 70% or more without heavy investments in plant and equipment. In much the same way, some firms in the computer industry have modest in-house manufacturing operations but very high VA/S ratios. These companies add value through technical skills in design and/or customer service, not by in-house production of numerous product components.

Unfortunately, it appears to be far more common for rising capital requirements to accompany increasing vertical integration. Many businesses, it would seem, follow the path from "Southeast" to "Northwest" in Exhibit 8–2. When this happens, the rate of return on investment tends to fall. Does this imply that most decisions to increase vertical integration are mistakes? No doubt many of them are. Managers probably underestimate the investment needed to support moves into their suppliers' or customers' businesses. They may also view vertical integration moves as a means of defending a profitable core business. This reasoning is no doubt sometimes valid, and it is perfectly reasonable to accept modest profits in one part of a business if this, in fact, provides greater security for a high rate of return elsewhere. The question is, how much is this kind of insurance worth? The data in Exhibit 8–2 indicate that the cost is often excessive.

2. Consider Alternatives to Ownership

Vertical integration, in the traditional sense of the term, is an arrangement based on *ownership* of vertically-linked activities. In some cases, at least some of the benefits of integration can be achieved without combined ownership. A manufacturer might, for example, be able to reduce transaction costs via long-term contracts with independent suppliers. This approach apparently is more common in Japan than in American industry. Hayes and Abernathy were quoted earlier on the dangers of excessive vertical integration by major U.S. corporations, especially in the automobile industry. The same authors go on to suggest that:

> Long-term contracts and long-term relationships with suppliers can achieve many of the same cost benefits as vertical integration without calling into question a company's ability to innovate or respond to innovation.[14]

3. Avoid "Part-Way" Integration

The V-shaped relationship between vertical integration and profitability (Exhibit 8–1) suggests that some businesses may suffer from integration strategies that are not carried far enough. Recall that the most profitable businesses were those at one extreme or the other on the spectrum of vertical integration. The least profitable position, in general, was an intermediate one. The implication is that, on this dimension of strategy, a clearly defined position—one way or the other—is most likely to succeed. Managers should be wary of gradual, piecemeal increments in the vertical scope of a business which may lead to the unprofitable middle ground.

4. Carefully Analyze Scale Requirements

A significant risk in many vertical integration strategies is that one or more of the stages of production/distribution is too small to be cost-competitive with independent suppliers or customers. Presumably for this reason, the PIMS data show that integration is much more likely to pay off for businesses with reasonably large market shares.

Just what scale of operation is required to make a given integration strategy viable will, of course, depend on the specific technologies available in a particular situation. The moral to be drawn from the statistical data, however, is that mistakes are fairly common. Quite a few small-share businesses *are* highly integrated, and on average they are not successful. Some of them, at least, suffer from what Peter Drucker calls "being the wrong size." Excessive vertical integration is not the only route to becoming wrong-sized, but it may well be one of the most common ones.

5. Be Skeptical of Claims that Integration
Will Reduce Raw Material Costs

Economist have long questioned the idea that vertically integrated businesses or companies are somehow insulated from fluctuations in the costs of key raw materials. Unless materials supply is monopolized, they ask, why should a vertically integrated enterprise be able to supply itself at anything less than open market prices? The data in Exhibit 8–5 indicate that skepticism about cost advantages is often well-founded.

All of these guidelines may seem unduly negative. Each points to possible dangers or illusions associated with increased vertical integration; and, given the fact that integration strategies often involve major investments, caution does seem advisable. On the other side, though, vertical integration often *is* a highly successful strategy. Especially for businesses and companies that enjoy strong market positions, increased integration can pay off both in current profitability and in increased product innovation.

Strategies for Market Leaders and Followers

The strategic options available to management, and the results that can be expected from a given strategy, both depend on a business unit's competitive position. In this chapter, we explore variations in the linkages between strategy and performance for SBUs that occupy differing positions in their served markets. As our primary measure of competitive position, we use a business unit's market share *rank,* just as we did in the discussion of scale economies and other sources of competitive advantage in Chapter 5. Here, we focus specifically on how various strategic choices affect profitability and growth for market *leaders*—businesses with the largest shares of their served markets—and market *followers.*

MARKET LEADERS

In every marketplace there is just one leader. These top-ranked competitors are well-represented in the PIMS data base, accounting for just over a third of the total.

How do leaders attain their positions? When we compare leaders and followers, three factors stand out as important differences:

- Leaders are more likely to have entered their markets early. Nearly 70% of them reported that they had entered as "one of the pioneers," compared with about 40% for followers.[1]
- A much higher proportion of leaders (47%) than followers (36%) benefit from patents or trade secrets related to products, processes, or both.
- Leaders' products and services are generally of considerably higher quality, relative to competition, than those of followers.

These three factors are not, of course, unrelated: often, early entry into a market is based on proprietary technology or designs, which are protected by patents and/or secrets. The products or services developed by a pioneering entrant frequently set the standard for later entrants and thereby achieve a leading quality position among customers—at least, until a new and better concept is developed.

Early market entry provides a business with some other advantages in addition to the opportunity for quality leadership.[2] Especially for the first successful entrant, being there before competitors arrive can mean better access to distribution channels, a strong and lasting "image" among users, and the possibility of achieving low costs through greater scale and experience. Some leaders have advantages over competitors along all of these dimensions. A striking example, described by Michael Porter, was that of Procter & Gamble in the disposable diaper business in the 1970s.[3] P&G's Pampers, introduced in 1966, was the first successful large-volume product in its category, and by 1980 it had a 70% share of a market that had grown to over $1 billion. According to figures cited by Porter, as of 1975 a prospective "me-too" entrant into the market would have faced the prospect of huge losses for up to 4 years, in addition to a massive capital investment, to attain a viable market position. Even after 5 years, Porter estimated that a challenger would suffer from a serious cost disadvantage and still have a profit margin only about half as large as P&G's! This example illustrates the powerful leverage that can be achieved by an early entrant that is energetically exploited. (It turned out that Pampers was not invulnerable, however, as explained later in this chapter.)

While early market entry is usually a potential source of advantage, it is by no means a guarantee of success. Of the PIMS businesses ranked fourth or lower in their markets, over 30% were "pioneer" entrants! How do such businesses lose the potential advantages of a head start? In some cases, they lacked the financial or technical resources to exploit their positions. Royal Crown, for example, introduced a diet cola before Coca-Cola or Pepsico but soon fell behind the diet colas introduced by these much larger companies. Similarly (as mentioned in Chapter 8), Bowmar Instrument Company pioneered in the hand-held calculator business in the early 1970s, but lacked the resources to compete with Texas Instruments.

Pioneer market entrants often falter because they make poor or unlucky choices of technologies in the unstable early stages of a market's development. The first commercial version of a product, after all, seldom survives for long without substantial modifications. A case in point was the Docutel Corporation in the mid-1970s. Docutel introduced the first workable automatic bank teller machine in 1971 and, five years later, had a market share of over 90%. In 1976, however, the company introduced a second-generation product line which had serious flaws. Moreover, owners of first-generation Docutel machines could not upgrade their equipment without substantial expenditures. As a result, Docutel's market share fell to 8% by 1978.[4]

How High Is Up?

By definition, the market leader enjoys the largest share of all competitors in a market. But the relative strength of the leader's position, or "degree of dominance," varies enormously among markets. Among the PIMS businesses, the leader's market share ranges from a low of less than 10% to a high of 75%, averaging 40%.

What accounts for differences in the leader's degree of market dominance? Exhibit 9-1 compares the characteristics of leaders with relatively low and high market shares. This comparison suggests that the leader is likely to have a high degree of dominance when:

- Products or services are mostly standardized;
- Customers are concentrated, i.e., a few large customers account for a big percentage of total sales;
- The leader was a pioneer entrant and/or has patents on products or processes.

EXHIBIT 9-1

Contrasting Low and High Market Leader Dominance

	Degree of Dominance	
	Low	*High*
Averages:		
• Leader's Market Share	21%	60%
• Ratio to Number 2's Share	1.6×	4.2×
Market Characteristics:		
• Percent of Custom Products	25%	20%
• No. of Large Customers Accounting for 50% of Sales	330	240
• Scale Economies: Minimum EfficientCapacity Addition as % of Market	4%	14%
Leader's Competitive Position:		
• Percent with Patents		
On Products	18%	28%
On Processes	20	31
• Percent Who Entered Market		
As Pioneers	66%	76%
As Early Followers	24	19
As Late Followers	10	5
Average Performance:		
ROI	23.8	39.5
ROS	9.6	15.9
Number of Businesses	(306)	(319)

NOTE: Based on 877 market leader business units in the PIMS data base.

The most dramatic difference between the situations of high and low market leader dominance shown in Exhibit 9-1 is in the importance of scale economies. Our measure of scale economies is an indirect one: we asked managers of each business to estimate the size of the minimum efficient addition to capacity in their served market. In Exhibit 9-1, this is expressed as a percentage of the total market. In situations of low leader dominance, the minimum capacity addition (either new plant or addition to an existing plant) averaged 4%. In contrast, where the leader's dominance was high, the minimum capacity addition represented, on average, 14% of the entire market volume. Obviously, this kind of situation acts as a significant barrier to entry for prospective new market entrants and for would-be challengers among a leader's existing competitors.

WHEN CAN A LEADER BUILD SHARE?

As Exhibit 9-1 shows, the degree of dominance that a leader can achieve depends on the situation. When market conditions change, the leader may be able to gain additional market share. For example, as an industry's products become more standardized or customer concentration increases over time, the industry tends to consolidate and an aggressive leader can gain at the expense of smaller rivals.

The strong relationship between the leader's market share and scale economies suggests an avenue for the leader to gain share: by raising the stakes. If the leader can somehow increase the importance of scale economies, smaller competitors will typically be unable to follow suit and will suffer from increasing cost disadvantages. A classic example of this process was the motorcycle industry in the 1960s and 1970s:

> Prior to 1960, the leading producers of motorcycles were Harley-Davidson in the U.S. and two British companies, Norton and Triumph. Each of these companies employed small-scale, labor-intensive, job-shop manufacturing systems. Beginning around 1960, Honda (and later, other Japanese producers) developed a mass market for small motorcycles in Japan. In the early 1960s the Japanese producers entered the U.S. and European markets. By 1970, Honda had achieved market leadership in all of the Western countries.
>
> As their production levels grew, the Japanese manufacturers adopted highly automated production systems. By 1974, Honda's investment amounted to over $8,000 per worker, compared with about $4,000 for Harley-Davidson and $3,200 for NVT, the British company that had been created by a merger of Norton and Triumph. Moreover, a cost-efficient plant would have required output of at least 100,000 units annually, more than twice the yearly production of either Harley or NVT. As a result, either of the two companies would have been forced to make a huge investment, relative to its existing asset base, to regain market share. Neither of them was willing, or perhaps able, to make such investments.[5]

A strategy of raising the stakes by automating or otherwise increasing the investment requirements of a business can be self-defeating. As explained in Chapter 7, increased investment-intensity usually leads to a lower average ROI, even for market leaders. But up to a point, it still makes good sense to invest more in a business even at the expense of a lower overall ROI, as long as the return on additional investments is greater than the applicable cost of capital. When the leader can also protect its future market position by making competitive challenges more costly, raising the stakes can be a powerful strategy.

Leaders can also sometimes continue to gain market share by the same means that challengers use against them: by broadening their product lines, introducing new products, and increasing outlays for sales force, advertising, and promotion. For example, Heinz ketchup has been the leading brand in its category for many years. Throughout the 1960s the brand's market share seemed to be on a permanent plateau at about 35%. By 1982, however, Heinz's share had reached 46%, primarily through addition of new forms of packaging, larger sizes, and increased advertising support.[6]

When the leader can raise the stakes via increased spending on R&D and new product introductions rather than increased investment in fixed assets, the result can be continued growth *and* higher profitability. Needless to say, this is the ideal combination!

LIMITS ON MARKET LEADERSHIP

While managers of almost all market-leading businesses would no doubt like to increase their shares, there are usually limits to such growth. One kind of limit, in the U.S. and some other countries, is the possibility of legal action. American antitrust laws are intended to prevent excessive market dominance and have served to inhibit many companies from pursuing some approaches to building market share.[7] In the mid-1980s, antitrust concerns appear to be less of a constraint on market leaders than in the past. Thus, especially in mature industries or in lines of business threatened by import competition, growth via acquisition may be an increasingly feasible and attractive option for leaders.

A second and far more pervasive kind of limit on most leaders' market shares is what might be called "the erosion syndrome." It is reflected in the fact that, among the PIMS businesses, those with leading market positions are considerably more likely to lose share than smaller competitors are. Leaders are especially likely to suffer from erosion when their market shares are very large:[8]

Leader's Market Share	Percent Losing Share
Under 20%	16%
20–29	24
30–39	34
40–49	41
Over 50	46
All Leaders	31%

WHY LEADERS TEND TO LOSE SHARE

Leaders usually have significant advantages over their competitors in terms of product quality, costs, and reputation, as already noted. In view of these advantages, why do leaders so often see their positions erode? To some extent, it is probably inevitable and in many ways desirable that leaders' market shares decline over time. The leader is, after all, the natural target for competitors to imitate or attempt to surpass. Moreover, as a market grows and evolves, customer needs and preferences almost always become more varied: some want full service, others little or none, some want convenience features, others don't. Seldom can a single supplier effectively provide all of the desired combinations of product types, services, and prices.

Above and beyond what might be termed "natural erosion," leaders also sometimes experience share losses that could (with hindsight) have been avoided. One common reason is an excessive concern about cannibalization of existing product sales as a result of introducing new products. An apparent example of this, in the late 1970s, was the Sterling Drug Company, which produces Bayer aspirin:

> For many years, Bayer aspirin was the leading brand in the U.S. market for pain relievers. In 1975, Johnson & Johnson began large-scale advertising of Tylenol, a non-aspirin pain reliever. Sterling marketed a similar product overseas but was apparently reluctant to do so in the U.S. because it might damage Bayer's sales. Not until 1983, when non-aspirin products accounted for over 40% of pain reliever consumption, did Sterling combat Tylenol directly by introducing the Panadol brand. By that time Bayer aspirin's share of the overall pain reliever market had fallen to 8%.[9]

In its most extreme form, a market leader's reluctance to respond to change reflects what Thomas Bonoma has called "marketing inertia." Bonoma suggests that:

> A company much enamored of its own marketing success . . . does not find changing easy. A marketing strategy introduced long ago by people still in positions of power can acquire the status of dogma.[10]

Examples of marketing inertia are not hard to find. Consider just two of them:

- Wrigley, long the dominant leader in the chewing gum business, stood pat from the mid-1960s until 1975 while competitors introduced a series of new sugarless and "soft bubble gum" products. Among Wrigley's brands, the newest had been introduced in 1914! By the late 1970s Wrigley's share had declined to about 33%, while American Chicle had grown to virtual co-leadership.
- American LaFrance, a producer of fire trucks, " . . . once dominated its marketplace as well as any American company ever dominated a business."[11] But the company went out of business in 1985, victim of competition from better designed, more durable trucks aggressively marketed by 11-year-old Emergency One. American LaFrance failed to change its product designs, its materials (aluminum vs. steel) or its manufacturing methods, and eventually found itself too far behind to catch up.

It is tempting to dismiss incidents of marketing inertia like these as simply examples of gross mismanagement, perhaps due to overly conservative family control of a company or to the obsession of a conglomerate parent corporation with current profits. We believe, however, that the problem is deeper and more pervasive than this. Even Procter & Gamble, generally regarded as one of the most effective marketers in the world, is not immune. Earlier in this chapter we cited Michael Porter's glowing appraisal of P&G's disposable diaper business, whose 70% share of the market in 1980 seemed to be "well protected by significant mobility barriers."[12] Notwithstanding these barriers, Kimberly-Clark introduced a new type of diaper, featuring reclosable tapes, in 1978–79. By mid-1985 P&G's market share (for two brands, Pampers and Luvs) had fallen to just over 50%, and Kimberly-Clark's had reached 32%. *Advertising Age* quoted some industry analysts who termed P&G's experience "a prime example of marketing miscalculation."[13] The moral of the story, in our view, is that there is no such thing as an impregnable position of market leadership. Even the best managed and most successful businesses must be prepared to change technologies, redesign products, and alter their marketing approaches in response to changing competition and customer preferences.

GROWTH STRATEGIES FOR SMALL-SHARE COMPETITORS

The vulnerability of market leaders to market-share erosion suggests how smaller competitors can often grow: by innovating in precisely those ways that the leader would be most reluctant to do or would find most costly or disruptive to match.

More generally, followers that improve their market positions usually do so through a combination of improvement in product/ service quality, introduction of new products, and increasing marketing expenditures. Exhibit 9-2 shows the types of changes made by market followers that gained share, as compared with those that stayed even or lost share.[14] Followers who gained share typically improved quality, maintained or increased their new product introductions, and increased all categories of marketing expenses at rates faster than the growth rate of the served market. (The percentage changes shown in Exhibit 9-2 are differences between changes in spending and market growth rates. For example, a business that in-

---

EXHIBIT 9-2

Strategic Changes by Market Followers that Lost, Held, or Gained Market Share

Strategic Changes	Market Share Change		
	Losers	Holders	Gainers
Relative Product Quality	−0.6	+0.6	+1.8
New Products, % of Sales	−0.5	+0.1	+0.1
Price, Relative to Major Competitors	+0.2%	+0.2%	+0.3%
Marketing Expenditures (Adjusted for Market Growth)			
Sales Force	−8%	±0	+9%
Advertising			
—Consumer Products	−9%	+1%	+13%
—Industrial Products	−14	−6	−1
Promotion			
—Consumer Products	−5	+5	+13
—Industrial Products	−10	−1	+7

creased its sales force outlays by 10% in a market that grew by 6% would be shown as having a 4% relative rate of change in spending.)

Exhibit 9-2 also shows that market share gainers generally did not reduce their prices relative to competition. In fact, among *all* of the PIMS businesses, changes in relative prices among major competitors are rare. Obviously price *is* used as a competitive weapon, as illustrated by the recent history of the semiconductor industry and others. But in most markets, price changes by one competitor are apparently matched by rivals so that relative prices tend to remain unchanged.

Whether a market follower should attempt to grow by gaining market share will depend, of course, on how much it would cost to achieve the gains.[15] According to the conventional wisdom, a manager who sets out to build a business's share should be prepared to pay a price, at least in the short term. To make matters worse, a costly effort to wrest business away from competitors may be in vain, and even backfire, as we have seen happened when Yamaha challenged Honda.

While the costs of gaining share are often high, it is also true that most businesses that gain share improve their profitability at the same time. Among the PIMS businesses that made the biggest year-to-year gains in share, ROI improved by an average of 4 points. In contrast, the SBUs that suffered the largest share losses had an average ROI decline of around 4 points.

Why do market share and ROI usually rise or fall together? In many cases, because a business's competitive position improves through competitors' mistakes or inertia. Thus, for example, A's relative quality can rise because B's quality has deteriorated. Another explanation is that a rising or falling trend in market share usually persists for several years: there is such a thing as momentum, both positive and negative, in market position. For this reason, many year-to-year gains or losses reflect moves made in the past—which may involve little or no current costs.

FOLLOWER STRATEGIES FOR PROFITABILITY

As we have already mentioned (see Chapter 5), some commentators have been critical of earlier publications based on PIMS for having exaggerated the importance of having an adequate market share. Richard Hamermesh and Carolyn Woo, among others, have pointed out that some small-share competitors are highly profitable.[16] There is no doubt that cases of this kind do exist. But, as we have tried to demonstrate, the fact that a minority of small-share competitors earn high rates of return does not imply that, given a choice about it, managers would rationally prefer a small market share to a larger one.

How can market followers maximize their profitability, or at least earn adequate rates of return? One answer, as just suggested, is to try harder on all of the other dimensions of strategy that influence performance. Exhibit 9–3 illustrates the point: it shows how ROI is affected by product/service quality, fixed capital intensity, and employee productivity, for followers as compared with leaders. (A more complete comparison of profit determinants for leaders versus followers is given in Exhibit B–7, Appendix B.) Each of the factors shown in Exhibit 9–3 has a strong impact on ROI for both leaders and followers. The difference between the two groups is that market leaders can earn adequate or even good rates of return even when they have only average quality, high capital intensity, or low em-

EXHIBIT 9–3

How Quality, Capital Intensity, and Productivity Affect ROI for Market Leaders versus Followers

| | | Average ROI | |
| | | Market Followers | |
Profit Influences	Market Leaders *(No. 1)*	*No. 2 or 3*	*No. 4 or Lower*
Product/Service Quality:			
Low	23	17	10
Average	28	20	14
High	38	25	18
Fixed Capital Intensity:			
Low	39	23	14
Average	31	20	16
High	23	16	8
Employee Productivity:			
Low	25	17	10
Average	30	20	13
High	38	21	16

NOTE: For fixed capital intensity, "low" is under $.10 of net book value per $1 of capacity, "average" is $.10–$.20, and "high" is over $.20. For productivity, "low" is under $25,000, "average" is between $25,000 and $35,000, and "high" is over $35,000.

ployee productivity. In contrast, market followers—especially those ranked fourth or lower—can achieve satisfactory returns only by doing well on one or more of these key dimensions. Otherwise, their profitability is likely to be below their costs of capital.

While many of the major profit-influencing factors affect market followers and leaders in the same ways, others operate quite differently depending on a business unit's competitive position. As we have already mentioned in Chapter 8, a high degree of backward vertical integration typically increases profitability for high-share businesses but decreases it for low-ranking competitors. Some other market characteristics and dimensions of strategy that have differing impacts for leaders versus followers are shown in Exhibit 9-4. The data in the exhibit suggest that:

- For followers, current profitability is adversely affected by a high level of product innovation, measured either by the ratio

---

EXHIBIT 9-4

How Some Profit-Influencing Factors Affect ROI for Market Leaders versus Followers

	Average ROI		
	Market Leaders *(No. 1)*	Market Followers	
Profit Influences		*No. 2 or 3*	*No. 4 or Lower*
New Products, % of Sales:			
Under 1%	31	20	13
1%–5%	31	21	17
Over 5%	32	17	9
R&D Expense, % of Sales:			
Under 1%	29	21	13
1%–5%	34	19	14
Over 5%	28	14	1
Marketing Costs, % of Sales:			
Under 5%	29	20	15
5%–12%	33	20	14
Over 12%	32	17	7
Rate of Inflation:			
Under 5%	33	20	11
5%–10%	31	19	11
Over 10%	30	20	16

NOTE: For a more complete statistical comparison, see Exhibits in Appendix B.

of new product sales to total sales or by R&D spending. (The effects of these two aspects of innovation cannot be clearly separated because they are highly correlated—see Exhibit B–0, Appendix B.) The penalty paid for innovation is especially heavy for businesses ranked No. 4 or lower in their served markets. Market leaders' profitability, on the other hand, is not hurt by new product activity or R&D spending, one way or the other.

- High rates of marketing expenditure depress ROI for followers, but not for leaders.
- Low-ranking market followers benefit from high inflation in selling prices. For businesses ranked first, second, and third, inflation has no relation to ROI.

Some additional, relatively minor differences between leaders and followers may be noted:

- Followers tend to do better in markets, or in market segments, where services are important to users. This no doubt reflects the fact that followers suffer from smaller cost disadvantages in the provision of services than they do in basic product costs.
- Charging premium prices is an especially dangerous strategy for small-share competitors. Average ROI for businesses with market shares less than half that of the leader and with different combinations of price and quality reflect this:

Product/Service Quality	Price, Relative to Competition		
	2% or More Below	*About the Same*	*5% or More Above*
Low	11	12	8
Average	13	16	13
High .	15	20	16

In contrast, market leaders' profitability was usually higher with premium prices than with parity pricing. Perhaps a leader's reputation, or the greater security that goes with buying from a leading supplier, is enough to justify a price premium.

It should be pointed out that some of the actions that hurt current profitability the most for market followers—high levels of new product activity and market expenditure—are precisely the ones that are usually necessary to build market share (see Exhibit 9-2). What this means is that for market followers there is often a clear-cut trade-off between earning reasonable current profits and growing through an increase in market share. For leaders, it is more often possible to grow without paying a similar penalty.

FOCUS STRATEGIES

A common strategic prescription for small-share businesses is to focus on one or a few segments within the served market, defined in terms of particular product and/or customer types; the businesses must then develop the specialized skills or resources needed to serve that sector. If a segment has requirements that are distinctive and enduring, the business can develop "barriers to entry" into it in much the same way that a leader can for a broader marketplace.[17] (Indeed, if the differences between a segment and the rest of a market are very great, it probably should be regarded as a separate "market." In such a case, the small-share business may, in fact, be a market leader—the classic "big fish in a small pond.")

There are many examples of successful focus strategies. Savin Business Machines, working with the Japanese company Ricoh, built a $200 million business in just two years by offering customers a simple, low-priced copying machine with reasonably good quality.[18] At the time Savin was penetrating the market, Xerox was emphasizing large, high-priced machines designed for centralized copying facilities. The Savin-Ricoh model opened up the possibility of distributed copying (several machines dispersed through an office) with greater user convenience. This approach was so successful that by 1978 Savin was the largest-selling small machine in the market. The company's profits that year amounted to 64% on equity!

Sometimes opportunities for new focus strategies emerge because a market, overall, is becoming more concentrated and its products more standardized. In the 1980s this appears to be happening in the U.S. brewing industry. While an ever-growing proportion of beer sales is being made by a few national brewers, operating ever-larger plants, "microbrewers" are also flourishing at the same time. These companies produce premium beers with local identities, such as the "Samuel Adams" brand in New England and the "Sierra Nevada" brand in California.

REDEFINITION STRATEGIES

Market followers can sometimes go one step beyond a focus strategy and redefine their businesses. One example is the Pasquale Food Company of Birmingham, Alabama:

> Pasquale, originally based in Ohio, was a franchise chain of pizza restaurants. When larger companies such as Pizza Hut and Godfather's Pizza began expanding rapidly in the 1970s, Pasquale's profits fell and franchisees defected in droves. The management of Pasquale developed a new way of doing business: selling fresh, unbaked pizzas through delicatessen departments in supermarkets. The company installs equipment and trains the supermarket workers in proper preparation methods. In late 1985, Pasquale had an estimated 5,000 supermarket outlets and had multiplied its sales six-fold in a 5-year period.[19]

Another example of apparently successful redefinition of a business is that of Honeywell in the large computer business.[20] Honeywell, having tried to become a major competitor by acquiring the computer divisions of General Electric (in 1970) and Xerox (1976), had only a 3% market share in the early 1980s. The company then began a shift away from computer production by entering into agreements with Groupe Bull and NEC Corporation to market their machines in the U.S. By 1985, Honeywell's computer division, largely transformed into a marketer of imported products, earned a healthy 10% operating profit on sales of $2 billion.

Chapter 10 _____

Market Evolution
and Competitive Strategy

In Chapter 4 we discussed market growth rates at some length, and showed how performance is affected by the characteristics of the market in which a business participates. In this chapter we build on that discussion, exploring how market evolution affects the nature of competition, business strategies, and performance.

As a market evolves over time, many of its characteristics change. What was a very attractive market at one stage of its development can become an unattractive arena later on—and vice versa. As a result, managers must modify their profit expectations for a business as it passes through key transitions from one evolutionary market stage to another. Moreover, the strategic options open to a business, and the results that can be expected from them, also shift because of evolutionary forces. Changes take place in virtually all aspects of the competitive environment: customer buying behavior, the number and relative strength of competitors, production methods, and marketing methods. Some managers take an active part in creating these changes; others adapt to them successfully; and still others fail to cope with the new demands that accompany market evolution.

MODELS OF MARKET EVOLUTION

If we examine the histories of different markets or industries, some common denominators in their patterns of evolution quickly become apparent. In the beginning, most pass through a period of infancy, characterized by erratic demand and considerable trial and error in technology, product design, and marketing. Those that survive this volatile period then enjoy a phase of rapid growth, which is eventually succeeded by a period of maturity and relative stability. Finally, in many instances, comes a stage of decline which may be abrupt or prolonged depending on the forces that cause it.

The stages of evolution just outlined correspond to those of the familiar "product life cycle" (PLC) model. While the life cycle is conventionally described as a process of change for *products,* it is also widely accepted as a useful model for entire markets and industries.[1] As Michael Porter puts it, the life cycle is "the grandfather of concepts for predicting the probable course of industry evolution."[2]

The life cycle model has been used not only to predict the future evolution of markets and industries but also as the basis for "strategic prescriptions." As a market evolves, according to many management consultants and textbook authors, so too must the strategy employed for a business unit or product line. In the heyday of "strategic management" during the 1970s, some companies developed elaborate formal guidelines for competitive strategies based, in part, on the PLC model. For example, in the early 1970s the General Foods Corporation's guidelines called for one set of objectives and performance measures to be employed for managing those market-leading products with prospective real growth rates of 5% or better, and a different set for those with lower anticipated growth. For the first group, pricing was to be used to stimulate volume growth; for the second, pricing was aimed at maintaining margins. Similarly, "aggressive" new product development was prescribed for high-growth categories, while "line extensions for market share maintenance" were expected for low-growth categories.[3]

While the PLC model is widely accepted, it has also been widely criticized.[4] Among the more frequent criticisms are:

- The duration of life cycle stages varies greatly among industries. Some products may even "skip" stages, moving (for instance) directly from growth to decline.
- Changes in market structure and competition do not follow the same kinds of patterns in all markets. Some industries, for example, go through dramatic "shake-outs" during early maturity, while others do not.
- Most important, if managers uncritically accept the strategic

prescriptions that are made for different life cycle stages, these prescriptions can become "self-fulfilling prophecies." For example, cutting back on new product development efforts because a market is regarded as mature may guarantee that little or no innovation will take place.

We believe that there is some merit in these criticisms. Patterns of market or industry evolution *do* vary, and the risk of the self-fulfilling prophecy is a real one. Nevertheless, we think that there *are* some common basic patterns of change in competition and performance as markets evolve. Understanding how these patterns typically operate can, in turn, help managers to develop and modify their strategies to meet the changing situation. In the remainder of this chapter we utilize the PIMS data base to show some of the ways in which markets evolve, and we explore the implications of these changes for management. We do not, however, want to suggest that anyone should blindly follow a series of standard strategic prescriptions based on the perceived stage of their market's evolution. Instead, managers should use the typical patterns of evolution, along with the other general relationships between strategy and performance discussed elsewhere in this book, as a starting point for analyzing their specific situations.

ACTUAL PATTERNS OF EVOLUTION

The PIMS data base includes three different indicators of the stage of evolution for each business unit's served market: its age (when the products or services involved were first marketed), its growth rate, and management's assignment of the market to one of the four conventional PLC stages. (For the definitions of the four stages used in the data collection process, see Appendix A, p. 260. Only a few businesses reported that they competed in Introductory stage markets, so we cannot analyze this group separately.) If all markets evolved in exactly the way described by the PLC model, these three measures would be in virtually complete agreement: newer markets would always have high growth rates and be designated as falling into the "Introduction" or "Growth" stage, and so on. The only exception to this might be that, in a given time period, a growth-stage market might exhibit low actual growth, or a mature market might show high growth, because of the impact of macroeconomic business cycles, shortages, or other external factors.

In fact, as we have already mentioned in Chapter 4, PLC stages are strongly related to market growth rates, but with numerous exceptions. Particularly among markets classified as "mature," real growth rates for 4-year reporting periods vary widely: almost a fifth (19%) of these markets were *declining* in real terms by at least 5% annually, while a third (32%) were growing at the rate of 5% or more.

A market's *age* is generally related to both its PLC stage and its growth rate, but again there are many departures from the usual pattern. Exhibit 10–1 shows how life cycle stage and growth rate vary in relation to market age. Note that while most old (pre-1930) markets are classified as mature or declining, some are still seen as growing. Conversely, although most "adolescent" markets were expanding rapidly, some were actually declining in real volume—at least, during the 4 years covered by these figures.

Given the diverse patterns of evolution, no system of classifying markets by "stages of evolution" is completely satisfactory.[5] The approach we use here is to accept the PLC stage designations made by the business units' managers, with one modification. The businesses operating in "mature" markets represent over 70% of the data base; we have subdivided them into three groups:

- *"Growth Maturity"* businesses—those classed as mature, but with real market growth rates of 5% or higher (534 businesses);

EXHIBIT 10–1
Market Age, Product Life Cycle Stages, and Real Growth Rates

Life Cycle Stage/ Real Growth Rate	When Products/Services Were First Marketed			
	Prior to 1930	*1930– 1949*	*1950– 1959*	*1960 or Later*
Percent of Markets in:				
Growth Stage	6%	12%	29%	45%
Mature Stage	87	80	68	53
Decline Stage	7	8	3	2
	100%	100%	100%	100%
Number of Cases	567	796	478	456
Real Growth Rate:				
Average	1.2%	2.4%	4.1%	8.1%
⅓ of Cases Were Below:	−4.9	−4.9	−4.1	−1.9
⅓ of Cases Were Above:	+7.5	+9.5	+11.7	+18.5

- *"Stable Maturity"* businesses—designated as mature, with real market growth rates between −5% and +5% (830 businesses); and
- *"Declining Maturity"* businesses—designated as mature, rather than in the Decline stage, but operating in markets that were contracting by at least 5% annually (327 businesses).[6]

These three sub-stages of maturity will now be compared with each other and with the Growth and Decline stages of evolution.

MARKET EVOLUTION, MARKET STRUCTURE, AND INNOVATION

Exhibit 10-2 compares some key structural characteristics of markets in different evolutionary stages. As shown there, growth markets are much more likely to attract new entrants than markets in later stages. This reflects the well-known phenomenon of "jumping on the bandwagon" that almost invariably accompanies a market's first sustained period of expansion. A good example is the counter-top microwave oven (MWO) business: in the late 1960s, only Amana (a division of Raytheon), Litton, and General Electric marketed MWOs. The market grew rapidly in 1972–77, attracting a host of new entrants, and by the late 1970s there were more than two dozen competitors in the field. The same kind of inrush has occurred dur-

EXHIBIT 10-2
Market Evaluation and Market Structure

		Stage of Evolution			
Market Structure	Growth	Growth Maturity	Stable Maturity	Declining Maturity	Decline
Percent of Markets:					
With New Entrants	43	25	21	18	25
With Competitors Exiting	21	14	17	19	23
Combined Share of					
4 Largest Competitors	74	73	70	70	73
Market Leader's Share	36	35	32	33	34
Market Share					
Instability (Index)	5.7	4.4	3.7	3.7	3.8
Average Real Market					
Growth Rate	10.5	12.3	0.3	−10.5	−1.7
Number of Businesses	(474)	(534)	(830)	(327)	(124)

ing the last two decades in color television, recreational vehicles, minicomputers, personal computers, hard disk drives, and many other markets.

The rate of new entry falls sharply with the transition from Growth to Growth Maturity, as does the rate at which competitors exit from markets. In the Declining Maturity and Decline stages, entry and exit are approximately equal, reflecting stability in the number of competitors. The tendency for markets to become more stable as they evolve is also shown by a drop in the index of market-share instability in Exhibit 10-2. (This index is simply the sum of all year-to-year market-share changes during a 4-year period, plus and minus, for the 4 largest competitors.)

Surprisingly, market concentration—measured by the combined share of the 4 largest competitors—does not display any clear pattern of change with successive stages of evolution. As discussed in Chapter 9, the market share of the market *leader* tends to decline over time but at a very slow rate.

As Exhibit 10-2 shows, Growth Maturity markets actually grew at a higher annual rate, on average, than Growth markets did. Also, Declining Maturity markets had a greater average rate of decline than those in the Decline stage. Since, however, these growth or decline rates are for particular 4-year periods, some of them including the recessions of 1974–75, 1979, and 1981, they may consequently not be reliable indicators of growth rates over a longer term.

Exhibit 10-3 illustrates a second major aspect of market evolution: the tendency for innovation to diminish. This shows up most clearly in the figures for new product sales as a percentage of total market volume. From a high of more than 10% for Growth Markets, this measure of innovation falls to 5.4% during Growth Maturity, to 3.5–3.7% during later stages of Maturity, and to less than 3% in the Decline phase.

The reduced pace of innovation is also reflected in typical rates of R&D spending, which fall from over 3% during Growth to 1.7–2.0% in Maturity and 1.2% in the Decline phase. Moreover, as markets evolve, the proportion of R&D devoted to *product* innovation falls while *process* R&D increases in relative importance. This shift in the allocation of R&D resources is consistent with the findings of previous research on "process life cycles" by Utterback and Abernathy. They suggested that increased relative emphasis on process R&D is due, at least in part, to increasing pressure to improve productivity and reduce costs during maturity.[7]

EXHIBIT 10-3
Market Evolution and Product/Service Innovation

Measures of Innovation (Averages)	Stage of Evolution				
	Growth	Growth Maturity	Stable Maturity	Declining Maturity	Decline
New Product Sales, % of Market	10.2	5.4	3.5	3.7	2.8
R&D Spending, % of Sales	3.1	2.0	1.7	1.7	1.2
Product R&D, % of Total R&D	72%	67%	67%	70%	60%
Percent of Markets: With Major Changes in Technology	49	27	18	21	23
Where New Product Development Takes 2 Years or More					
—Industrial	51	43	43	42	28
—Consumer	30	28	31	28	27

NOTE: New Products (those introduced during the preceding 3 years) are, for the 4 largest competitors only, expressed as a percentage of those businesses' total sales. (On average, the 4 largest competitors accounted for 72% of total market volume.) R&D expenditures are for the reporting business only.

The chances of major technological changes occurring in a market are less than half as great during the later stages of Maturity and Decline as they are during the Growth stage (see Exhibit 10-3). It is important to note, however, that major technological changes did take place in almost one in four of the Decline stage markets—clearly implying that the stability of existing technology must not be taken for granted in *any* market!

One final indicator of innovation, shown in Exhibit 10-3, is the proportion of markets in which the process of new product development takes 2 years or more. For consumer products manufacturers, this figure is virtually the same (around 30%) in all stages of evolution. But for industrial product manufacturers it falls sharply in early Maturity and again in the Decline phase. We interpret this as an indication of the reduced frequency of major product innovation as a market evolves. In mature markets, and even more so in declining ones, product innovation consists more and more of improvements in existing products, and in product line extensions, which typically have relatively short development cycles.

All of the evolutionary trends summarized in Exhibit 10-3 suggest that less innovation—especially less major innovation—takes place as a market matures. This does not, however, mean that successful innovation is impossible or that it is less profitable in mature or declining markets. Indeed, the very scarcity of opportunities for significant innovation makes the innovations that do happen all the more powerful as competitive weapons. We return to this point later in this chapter.

MARKET EVOLUTION, COMPETITION, AND PERFORMANCE

As a market evolves, the extent of differentiation among competitors tends to decline. Some measures of differentiation are given in Exhibit 10-4. The first is an index of product/service differentiation, which reflects the degree to which PIMS business unit's products or services are either superior or inferior to those of major competitors. (Our measure of relative product service quality and differentiation are discussed at some length in Chapters 3 and 6.) As measured by this index, differentiation is greatest in Growth Markets and falls off steadily through maturity to reach a low point in the Decline stage. As might be expected, declining differentiation in the products and services of competing sellers is typically accompanied by greater sim-

EXHIBIT 10-4
Competitors Become More Alike as Markets Evolve

Measures of Competitive Differentiation	Stage of Evolution				
	Growth	Growth Maturity	Stable Maturity	Declining Maturity	Decline
Product/Service Differentiation (Index)	51	43	42	40	32
Price Differentiation (Index)	7.0	6.3	6.2	6.0	5.4
Percent of Markets Where Major Competitors: Have Similar Product Line Breadth	32	36	39	39	42
Serve Same Types of Customers	58	60	63	58	69
Have Similar Number of Customers	30	34	36	38	50

ilarity in pricing. This is reflected in lower values of the index of price differentiation during later life cycle stages, as shown in Exhibit 10-4.

Three additional indicators of competitive differentiation in Exhibit 10-4 all present the same picture of progressively smaller variations among market rivals. These indicators show the percentages of PIMS businesses in each stage of evolution that were about the same as their major competitors in terms of (1) product line breadth, (2) types of customers served, and (3) number of customers served. Each of the three measures of similarity is lowest in the Growth stage, rises during the Maturity stages, and reaches a maximum during Decline.

The tendency for competitive differences to be homogenized as a market evolves results from a series of competitive moves and counter-moves made over time, and perhaps also from progressive redefinitions of served markets. Some examples illustrate this tendency:

- During the 1960s and most of the 1970s, the major fast-food chains were highly differentiated from each other. Some specialized in hamburgers; others in chicken, seafood, or pizza. As overall market growth slowed, the leading competitors invaded each others' "turfs" by broadening their product lines. In the mid-eighties, differences in emphasis still exist, but the extent of direct, product-versus-product competition is much greater.
- At one time, most of the major U.S. marketers of distilled liquors were known as "Bourbon houses" or "Scotch houses," and they competed with each other only indirectly via efforts to build consumption of their primary liquor types. In the 1970s and 1980s, static or declining demand for hard liquor led many of the larger companies to broaden their product lines, as well as to acquire wines. Brown-Forman, for example, added Canadian Mist, Bolla and Cella imported wines, and Korbel brandy to its long-established bourbon whiskey brands.[8]

Not only does competition become more direct as a market evolves, but patterns of spending and profitability shift, too. Exhibit 10-5 compares gross margins, marketing expenditures, profitability, and cash flow for businesses at different stages of evolution. The

EXHIBIT 10-5
Changing Patterns of Spending and Performance by Stage
of Market Evolution

		Stage of Evolution			
Averages	Growth	Growth Maturity	Stable Maturity	Declining Maturity	Decline
Gross Margin	30.5%	26.2%	26.0%	23.8%	21.8%
Marketing Expenses:					
Consumer Products	14.1	11.5	13.2	11.2	10.9
Industrial Products	9.9	7.5	7.5	7.2	5.9
ROS	10.1	9.4	9.1	8.7	7.2
ROI	23.8	23.4	22.5	20.8	17.9
Cash Flow, % of Investment	−1.9	3.8	4.5	5.9	6.2

pattern is clear: over the course of the life cycle, gross margin falls, and so do marketing expenditures, profit margins (ROS), and ROI. The sole exception to this is a rise in marketing outlays in the stable maturity phase for consumer product manufacturers. This presumably occurs because of the promotional wars that often break out when major competitors in a market first recognize that primary market demand is no longer growing much. During the 1970s and 1980s, for example, there were sharp increases in advertising and promotion expenditures in such mature product categories as soft drinks and distilled liquors.

As many writers on marketing and business strategy have pointed out, declining profit margins over successive stages of the life cycle reflect a shift in the focus of competition toward price rivalry. In the computer industry, where product life cycles are short, this kind of shift has taken place again and again, usually within just a few years. William Sahlman and Howard Stevenson, in a study of the dramatic expansion of the Winchester Disk Drive industry between 1977 and 1984, observed: "The computer industry had exhibited the same pattern repeatedly: technological-based competition evolved into service-based competition evolved into price competition."[9] While few other industries display this kind of evolution in such a short time span, most do tend to move in the same direction.

Although profit margins typically fall as a market evolves, net cash flow tends to rise (see Exhibit 10-5). This, of course, happens because the need to increase assets diminishes as market growth ebbs. There is consequently an improved possibility of cashing in on a business in the later stages of market evolution—assuming, of course, that its market and other strategic characteristics are sufficiently favorable.

MARKET EVOLUTION, STRATEGY, AND PROFITABILITY

A recurring theme in discussions of strategy is the need for major changes in strategy as a market evolves, especially during the transitions from Growth to Maturity and from Maturity to Decline. A *Fortune* article on "How to Make Money in Mature Markets," for example, warned that

> "Running a business in a declining industry . . . takes an entirely new game plan from the one that saw the company through the era of market growth."[10]

How should strategic game plans be modified as a market moves from one stage of evolution to the next? The discussion of changes in market structure, declining rates of innovation, increasing competitive similarity, and diminishing profitability suggest some of the changes that are appropriate. Specifically, in later stages of the PLC, managers should anticipate greater stability in market shares, fewer new products, increased head-on competition with their rivals, and a greater price sensitivity among customers. These are general tendencies, of course, and trends in particular markets can and do diverge from them.

By analyzing the experiences of businesses in the PIMS data base, we can compare the relationships between profitability and key strategic factors at different stages of market evolution. Does market share, for instance, become more or less important as a market evolves? For most of the major profit influences discussed in Chapter 2, the answer is no—their impacts on profitability are more or less the same in all stages of evolution. This is true for all of the factors listed in Exhibit 10-6. (For a detailed statistical analysis, see Exhibit B-9, Appendix B. The profit impacts of some of these factors do vary somewhat from stage to stage, but not in any systematic fashion.)

Some strategic factors *do* appear to change in importance with market evolution, and some of these are shown in Exhibit 10-7. For one thing, vertical integration appears to boost profits most in de-

---

EXHIBIT 10-6

Profit Influences with Similar Effects in Most or All Stages
of Market Evolution

- Market Share (+)
- Fixed Capital Intensity (−)
- Capacity Utilization rate (+)
- Percent of Employees Unionized (−)
- Inventory, % of Sales (−)
- Typical Purchase Amount by Customers (Low +, High −)
- Rate of Inflation in Selling Prices (+)
  (Exception: impact not significant in Stable Maturity)

---

clining markets. This is probably because of the relative competitive
and technological stability of markets in later stages of evolution.
As mentioned in Chapter 8, vertical integration is often unsuccessful
because of unanticipated changes in technology or demand.

Exhibit 10-7 also reflects the increasing importance of labor pro-

---

EXHIBIT 10-7

Profit Influences with Varying Effects at Different Stages
of Market Evolution

Profit Influences	Average ROI		
	Growth	Maturity	Decline
Vertical Integration			
Low	27	23	15
Average	20	20	16
High	24	24	28
Employee Productivity			
Low	18	18	14
Average	25	21	11
High	28	26	26
Newness of Plant Requirement			
Low	30	22	16
Average	23	23	19
High	21	20	21
New Products, % of Sales			
Low (under 1%)	27	22	14
Moderate (1–10%)	26	24	26
High (over 10%)	20	21	17

NOTE: Markets in the Growth Maturity, Stable Maturity, and Declining Maturity phases are
combined into a single group because the patterns were similar for these three groups.

ductivity, and of operational efficiency more generally, as markets mature. The most profitable businesses in declining markets are those with high value added per employee *and* those with relatively new and presumably more efficient facilities.

The profit impact of a high level of new product activity is clearly negative in growth markets but insignificant in mature and declining ones. As we have already suggested, it may be that scarcity of new products in later stages of evolution makes the ones that do emerge all the more valuable, so that businesses with no new products to offer are at a significant disadvantage.

HARVESTING STRATEGIES

A frequent prescription for businesses in mature or declining markets, especially for those that are not leaders, is that they be "harvested" or "milked" to generate cash. To accomplish this, it is recommended that management should:

- Minimize additions to the asset base, or better yet, *reduce* assets;
- Reduce all discretionary expenses, such as R&D and marketing; and
- To the extent possible, raise prices.[11]

Exhibit 10-8 illustrates some of the differences between "cash users" and "cash generators" among PIMS businesses that operated in mature or declining markets. Cash generators typically have higher gross margins, lower R&D and marketing expenses, fewer new products, lower levels of receivables and inventories, and older facilities than cash users. Not all of the cash generators were necessarily pursuing harvesting strategies, of course. But the overall pattern does give some indications about how such a strategy can be carried out.

PLANNING FOR STRATEGIC CHANGE

In some companies, managers use past experience to anticipate evolutionary changes in patterns of competition and performance. Planners at E.I. du Pont de Nemours and Company, for example, recognize that their chemical products typically pass through a

EXHIBIT 10-8
Profiles of Cash Users versus Cash Generators
(Mature and Declining Markets)

Percentage of Sales	Cash Users	Cash Generators
Gross Margin	20.3	29.8
R&D Expenses	2.0	1.6
Marketing Expenses	12.9	12.3
Receivables	15.1	13.6
Inventories	22.2	17.3
New Products	8.9	4.9
Newness of Plant & Equipment	56.6	50.4
(Net Book Value, % of Gross Book Value)		
Number of Businesses	(418)	(824)

NOTE: "Cash Users" had negative cash flows of at least 5% of investment, while "Cash Generators" had positive cash flows of 5% or more.

"competitive life cycle."[12] The cycle, as they conceive it, has five stages:

1. *Sole Supplier:* the first producer to introduce a product which has no direct competition, although there are usually substitute products available.

2. *Competitive Penetration:* one or more competitors enter the market, almost always by offering lower prices. The pioneer lowers his price but maintains a premium over the later entrants that declines as cumulative output increases.

3. *Share Stability:* overall market growth slows in this stage. Competing producers' market share stabilize, and capacity additions "tend to be orderly and in proportion to market shares."

4. *Commodity Competition:* at some point all suppliers in the market offer virtually identical products and services, and "price premiums cannot be sustained."

5. *Withdrawal:* finally, when industry growth stops, weaker competitors begin to drop out. Stronger producers have a choice between withdrawing and remaining in the hope of improved margins for the "survivors." To evaluate profit potential, especially in the withdrawal phase, Du Pont planners analyze a product line's long-term profitability using a statistical model derived from the PIMS data base.

Chapter 11 _____

Managing for Tomorrow*

Since 1980, American managers have been widely criticized for over-emphasizing short-term profits at the expense of their companies' future competitive strengths. In a widely quoted article, Robert Hayes and the late William Abernathy indicted what they called a "new management orthodoxy," based largely on financial analysis, for stifling investment in new plant and equipment and in R&D and quality improvement programs. As a result, according to Hayes and Abernathy, there has been a "broad managerial failure . . . that over time has eroded both the inclination and the capacity of U.S. companies to innovate."[1]

According to the critics, American managers evaluate proposed strategies primarily in terms of their expected effects on near-term profits, without paying much attention to long-term consequences. In such industries as steel, automobiles, and electronics, according to this view, U.S. and perhaps also European companies have not invested heavily enough in automation, quality improvement, or product innovation to maintain their competitiveness with Asian producers. There are many possible explanations for this, including government trade policies, labor-management relations, and antitrust regulations.[2] While some of these are beyond management's control, one weakness *can* be corrected without assistance from the

*The approach to performance measurement suggested in this chapter is adapted from one originally developed by Mark Chussil of the Strategic Planning Institute. (See Robert D. Buzzell and Mark J. Chussil, "Managing for Tomorrow," *Sloan Management Review*, Summer 1985, pp. 3–14.)

government: the way business performance is measured. According to some observers, if managers and investors would only use performance measures that reflect both short-term *and* long-term profitability, companies and industries would do a better job of improving their economic vitality.[3]

In preceding chapters we have discussed linkages between strategy and performance largely in terms of conventional measures of *current* profitability. While we have used 4-year averages of ROI and ROS in order to avoid too much of a short-term focus, we might still be criticized for reinforcing managers' existing bias toward current "bottom line" results. In this chapter we introduce a different kind of performance measure that is expressly designed to incorporate both short-term and long-term effects. Using this measure, which we call "value enhancement," we can explore a key issue: how do strategies that enhance value in the long run differ from those that maximize current profitability?

DEFINING "THE LONG TERM"

To measure and explain the long-term performance of a company or one of its component business units, we obviously must observe its actions, the situation in which it operates, and its results over a sufficiently long period of time. Just how long a period constitutes the long run is debatable, and it no doubt varies among industries. In the forest products industry or in wine growing, the full results of a major investment may not be apparent for a decade or more because of the long lead times required to develop (i.e., grow) new production capacity. At the other extreme, according to an old industry adage, for makers of fashion apparel "the short run is next week and the long run is next season."

For our analysis of how strategic factors affect long-term performance, we utilize a portion of the PIMS data base for which we have at least 7 years of financial, market, and strategic information. This enables us to use the first 2 years as a "base period" in which to assess each business unit's starting position. Given that starting position, we then measure changes in strategic factors and in performance over a 5-year "planning horizon," and again assess the unit's position at the end of Year 7.

The data base available to us, based on a minimum of 7 years worth of information, includes 620 business units—about one fourth of the main PIMS data base. The time spans covered by this "long term" data base range from 1970–76 up to 1979–85, and thus include periods of both recession and economic expansion as well as high and low rates of inflation.

It should be noted that the data base used for the analyses summarized in this chapter was first available in April 1986. For this reason, the results presented here represent only a "first pass" effort to explain long-term business performance.

MEASURING LONG-TERM PERFORMANCE

How should the performance of a business unit be measured over a five-year period? Our economic-value approach involves two components: discounted cash flow (DCF) and discounted future market value (DFMV).

DCF, the first of these, is straightforward. We simply calculated the net cash generated or absorbed by each business during each of the five years and then discounted these amounts to equivalent values at the beginning of the five-year period. (The procedure for calculating net cash flow in each year is described in Appendix A.)

Analyzing projected cash flows is a business planning tool of well-established value. The notion that future cash flows should be discounted to equivalent "present values" is also generally accepted and widely practiced.[4] What discount rate should be used is a more debatable matter. Ideally, the discount rate should be based on the "cost of capital" that is applicable to a particular company, SBU, or individual investment project. Since we don't have adequate information to calculate specific capital costs for each business, we use the same discount rate for all—20%—in the analyses reported here.[5]

The second component of our long-term performance measure, DFMV, is less familiar than DCF. The rationale for estimating a market value for a business unit is borrowed from corporate financial analysis.

For a publicly owned company, market value is perfectly clear: it is the value placed by investors on the equity portion of a firm's assets. The market value of a stock often differs considerably from the book value shown on a company's balance sheet. Most top managers of major corporations recognize the importance of the market values of their companies' stock and actively seek to increase their market-to-book ratios. Since management is responsible for maximizing shareholder value, increasing the market value of common stock should be a primary goal of corporate strategy.

The importance of enhancing market value at the company level is well accepted in the financial community. For example, *Fortune's* annual survey of the 500 leading industrial corporations includes information on the "total return to investors" achieved by each company. "Total return" in a given time period is defined as the sum of dividends paid and the net change in a stock's market value, expressed as a percentage of the stock's beginning value. Of the two components, the change in market value is usually considerably larger (plus *or* minus!) than the return obtained via dividends. For example, one of the best-performing companies in the decade 1975–85 was VF Corporation, with an average *annual* total return of 28.6%. Most of this total return was accounted for by appreciation in the market value of the company's stock, which rose from around $6 in 1975 to over $50 in 1985.

We suggest that the same logic used in measuring or forecasting corporate performance should be applied in planning for business units, and that explicit estimates should be made of how a strategy will affect future market value. After all, corporate results are derived from the performance of the corporation's business units.

But how can market values be determined for business units within a corporation, given that they do not issue and sell their own common stocks? In our analyses we determined market values by applying a technique developed by SPI researchers. Their approach is conceptually similar to ones advocated by several strategy consulting firms and used in quite a few major corporations.[6] Using actual stock market price data for 600 corporations, the researchers built a statistical model to explain company market-to-book-value (M/B) ratios. They found that the most important determinants of the M/B ratio are a company's recent return on equity, its growth rate, its rate of spending on R&D, and its "interest coverage ratio."[7]

Exhibits 11–1 and 11–2 illustrate the connections between M/B ratios and three of these factors—return on equity (ROE), growth rate, and R&D spending. Not surprisingly, both ROE and growth are positively related to M/B ratios. On average, a combination of high growth (over 12% annually) and high ROE (over 15%) produces an M/B ratio nearly three times as large as that for the opposite extreme of low ROE and low growth (Exhibit 11–1). Perhaps less expected is the fact that a high rate of R&D spending tends to go with a high M/B ratio (Exhibit 11–2). Apparently, investors

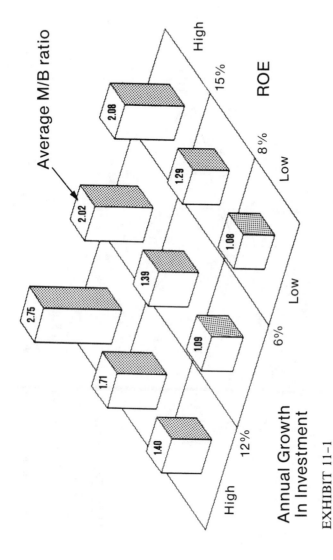

Average M/B ratio

Annual Growth
In Investment

ROE

High   15%
Low   8%
Low   6%
High   12%

2.08
2.02
1.29
1.39
1.08
2.75
1.71
1.09
1.40

EXHIBIT 11-1
High Profitability and Growth Boost a Company's M/B Ratio*

*Market value of equity divided by book value of equity.
SOURCE: Compustat data base, 1982–1985.

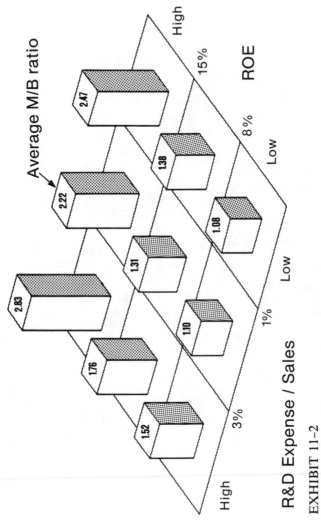

R&D Expense / Sales

EXHIBIT 11-2
R&D Spending Increases the M/B Ratio*

*Market value of equity divided by book value of equity.
SOURCE: Compustat data base, 1982–1985.

interpret heavy R&D spending as an indicator of future growth prospects, and reward it via an M/B premium above and beyond that awarded for recent actual growth.

We used an M/B model with business unit ROI, growth rate, and R&D spending rates, along with parent corporation interest coverage ratios, to assign an M/B ratio to each business unit as though it were a stand-alone company.[8] We simulated each business's market value by multiplying its M/B ratio by the book value of its investment at the end of the five-year planning period. Finally, we discounted the market values to equivalent values at the beginning of the period, just as we discounted the cash flows.

Our measure of long-term performance, then, is based on *total economic value:* the sum of the cash flows earned by a business over a five-year period plus its estimated market value at the end of the period, all discounted to their present values at the outset of the planning period.

Assessing Performance

Obviously, some businesses are much better positioned than others to realize high rates of profitability, cash flow, and future market value. Those with large market shares, weak competitors, low investment intensity, and well-differentiated products, for example, can be expected to perform much better than those with the opposite characteristics.

Performance standards should take a business's position into account. For this purpose, we calculated each business unit's market value at the *beginning* of the 5-year planning period in the same way that we computed its ending market value—by estimating its M/B ratio and multiplying it by the beginning investment's book value. This beginning market value is an appropriate measure of a business unit's "going-in" position, relative to which we can assess the total value it produces in the form of discounted cash flows (DCF) and discounted future market value (DFMV).

Our measure of "Value Enhancement" for a business unit, then, is calculated as follows:

$$\text{Value Enhancement} = \frac{\text{DCF} + \text{DFMV}}{\text{Present Market Value}}$$

Exhibit 11–3 shows illustrative calculations of Value Enhancement for two hypothetical business units, "A" and "B." In these examples, Unit A is investing heavily during the 5-year planning period (Years 3–7), perhaps in new plant and equipment and R&D programs. As a result, its cash flow for the period is negative. But these programs have paid off by the end of the period in terms both of growth—the investment base has doubled—and of a sharply increased M/B ratio. As a result, the *combined* value produced by this SBU (the ratio of DCF + DFMV to initial market value, expressed as a percentage) is 122%. Unit B, in contrast, has produced positive cash flows during Years 3–7, but its investment base has grown by only 50% over the 5-year span. Moreover, its M/B ratio has fallen from 0.8 to 0.6, so that DFMV is less than 40% (29/80) of the unit's initial market value. Unit B's Value Enhancement Index, accordingly, is a dismal 61%.

These hypothetical examples are designed to illustrate, in an exaggerated way, the trade-off that must sometimes be made between investing in a business for maximum future value and generating cash in the short term. Among the 620 businesses in our long-term data

EXHIBIT 11–3
The "Value Enhancement" Measure of Business Performance:
Two Illustrations

	Business A	Business B
Year 2:		
Book Value of Investment	100	100
Market/Book Value Multiplier	1.2	0.8
"Market Value"	120	80
Discounted Cash Flows, Years 3–7	−15	20
DCF, % of Market Value	−12.5%	25%
Year 7:		
Book Value of Investment	200	120
Market/Book Value Multiplier	2.0	0.6
"Market Value"	400	72
Discounted Market Value (as of Year 2)	161	29
Discounted Cash Flow + Discounted Market Value in Year 7	146	49
DCF + DMV, % of Initial Market Value	122%	61%

EXHIBIT 11-4
Patterns of Long-Term Performance: Discounted Cash Flow
and Market Value
(Number of Businesses)

Discounted Cash Flow, Years 3-7	Discounted Market Value, Year 7 % of Market Value in Year 2	
% of Market Value in Year 2	*Under 100%*	*Over 100%*
Positive	326	100
Negative	118	76

base, some performed well in terms of generating cash, some built long-term value, some did both, and some did neither. Exhibit 11-4 shows the breakdown on both dimensions. More than half of the SBUs (326 out of 620) had positive cash flows but suffered declines in market value (after discounting). Fewer than one fourth as many (76) followed the opposite path of building future market value while being net users of cash. The disparity in the size of these two groups appears to support the criticism of American managers we cited earlier: near-term cash flow does seem to be preferred over long-term value enhancement.

Exhibit 11-4 also shows that some businesses—about one in six—generated positive cash flows *and* increased their long-term values. A slightly larger number, however, performed poorly on both measures. Just as there are big differences in current performance, measured by ROI or ROS, there is also considerable variation in long-term performance as measured by Value Enhancement.

VALUE ENHANCEMENT AND COMPETITIVE POSITION

What kinds of businesses are most likely to perform well in terms of long-term Value Enhancement? Our analysis of the 620 PIMS businesses shows that SBUs with strong *initial* competitive positions are more likely to enhance their value than those with weak positions. Exhibit 11-5 shows average value enhancement scores, DCF, and DFMV, for businesses with weak, average, and strong initial competitive positions. As a measure of initial competitive position for each business we use its Par ROI rating. (The Par ROI measure

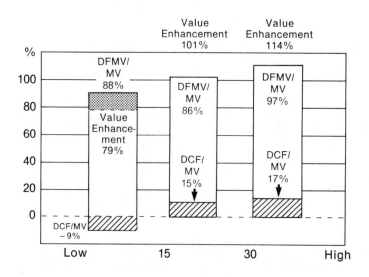

Beginning Par ROI (%)

EXHIBIT 11-5
Competitive Position and Value Enhancement

is estimated on the basis of a comprehensive statistical model developed by SPI. This model includes all of the strategic factors listed in Chapter 3, and some additional ones besides.)

As the exhibit shows, strongly positioned businesses improved their overall values by an average of 14%. Those with average profit potential at the beginning of the 5-year planning period stayed about even, while the weakest third of the group lost overall value by an average of more than 20%. These weak businesses typically had negative cash flows.

Finding that weaker businesses typically perform the worst may, on the surface, seem obvious; after all, it is generally recognized that market position, growth, and the other factors reflected in the Par ROI scores strongly affect performance. But our calculations of initial market value take these factors into account: small-share, slow-growth businesses have lower initial market values than do large-share, robust-growth businesses. Our results suggest not only that weaker businesses suffer from lower profitability, and hence from less favorable starting points, but also that they are less likely to improve upon their initial values.

The fact that short-run profitability and long-term value enhancement usually go together suggests that most of the strategic factors that improve performance work in similar ways regardless of the time period involved. Businesses with strong competitive positions, above-average employee productivity, and efficient use of assets tend to maintain and improve on their high performance levels. Conversely, strategically weak businesses typically remain weak, at least over time spans of 7 years. Exceptions to these general tendencies will be discussed in the next section of this chapter.

The fact that strong businesses get stronger and weak ones get weaker may also reflect overly simplistic use of portfolio planning approaches by managers. The portfolio approach has been criticized on the ground that it leads managers to neglect all but the "star" divisions and products in their companies. Allocating attention and resources to "stars" and "cash cows" that dominate their markets may unduly penalize businesses with viable positions as number two, three, or even four. Moreover, as some critics allege, prescribing that managers channel investments into fast-growing markets may lead them to undernourish businesses whose markets, while mature, still offer substantial opportunities for growth in sales and profits.

VALUE ENHANCEMENT AND STRATEGIC CHANGE

While long-term performance depends to a considerable degree on a business unit's initial competitive position, there are many exceptions to the general pattern. Some relatively weak SBUs achieve very good performance, and some strong competitors fall from grace and dissipate their initial values. To see how strategies affect long-term performance, it is especially useful to compare these exceptions to the rule with their more normal counterparts.

Exhibit 11-6 compares the initial positions and long-run performances of four groups of businesses:

> *"True Stars"*—These are SBUs with strong initial competitive positions (Par ROI over 30%) that achieve *excellent* long-term performance (DCF + DFMV at least 110% of beginning market value.)
>
> *"Fading Stars"*—Businesses with strong initial positions, similar to those of True Stars but poor long-term performance (DCF + DFMV/MV under 50%).

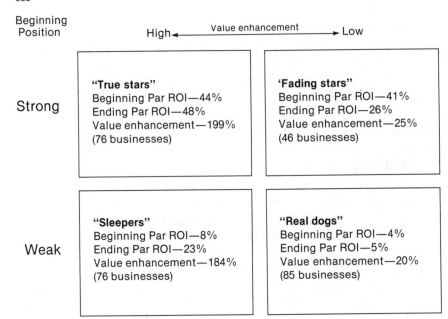

EXHIBIT 11-6
Performance Profiles: "True Stars," "Fading Stars," "Sleepers," and "Real Dogs"

> *"Sleepers"*—These businesses overcame adversity: despite weak initial competitive positions (Par ROI under 15%), they had outstanding records of value enhancement (110% or better).
> *"Real Dogs"*—SBUs with weak initial positions (similar to Sleepers) and poor long-run performance (under 50%).

To highlight the strategic factors that most strongly influence long-run performance, we compare True Stars with Fading Stars, and Sleepers with Real Dogs.

TRUE STARS VERSUS FADING STARS

True Stars and Fading Stars had roughly equal competitive positions at the beginning of their planning periods, with Par ROI scores of 44 and 41, respectively. But while True Stars' value enhancement averaged 199%, Fading Stars on average achieved values of only 25%. Put another way, the best performers *doubled* their initial market values, while the worst ones on average lost three-fourths of their market values. What accounted for this huge disparity in results? Exhibit 11-7 contrasts some of the key market and strategic differences for the two groups.

True Stars typically increased their market shares, while Fading Stars suffered losses in share. Since True Stars' served markets also grew at a faster pace—5.4% vs. 2.1%—their sales and investment bases expanded much more rapidly than was true for Fading Stars. (Since both types of businesses had large initial market shares, the disparity in real market growth rates was probably influenced to some extent by the True Stars' strategies.)

How did True Stars achieve their growth? In comparison with Fading Stars, they:

- spent more on R&D in the base period;
- spent more on marketing in the base period;

EXHIBIT 11-7
Strategic and Market Differences: "True Stars" versus "Fading Stars"

	Beginning Position	Ending Position	Change
True Stars (77 Businesses)			
Market Share	40.6	43.1	+2.5
Relative Quality	73	72	−1
Relative Price	105	106	+1
Relative Cost	98	99	+1
% New Products	5.1	5.7	+0.6
R&D, % of Sales	2.1	1.9	−0.2
Marketing, % of Sales	8.4	7.7	−0.7
Annual Rate of Capacity Expansion	—	—	+7.5%
Real Growth Rate of Market	—	—	+5.4%
Fading Stars (46 Businesses)			
Market Share	34.4	31.2	−3.2
Relative Quality	68	64	−4
Relative Price	103	105	+2
Relative Cost	100	102	+2
% New Products	5.1	7.8	+2.7
R&D, % of Sales	1.6	2.1	+0.5
Marketing, % of Sales	7.7	9.2	+1.5
Annual Rate of Capacity Expansion	—	—	+3.4%
Real Growth Rate of Market	—	—	+2.1%

- had higher relative product quality levels and maintained them, while Fading Stars' quality declined;
- maintained product costs below those of competitors, while Fading Stars' relative costs increased.

The differences between the two groups on each of these dimensions are not great, but their collective effect on long-term performance (as seen in Exhibit 11-6) is substantial. As Exhibit 11-7 shows, True Stars also expanded their real output capacities at a much faster rate than Fading Stars—by 7.5% per annum versus 3.4%. In many cases, no doubt, True Stars' capacity additions simply *reflect* their growth. But, to the extent that capacity expansion decisions were made in *anticipation* of increased future sales, they represent a dimension of strategic aggressiveness that paid off in terms of long-term value enhancement.

SLEEPERS VERSUS REAL DOGS

The performance gap between Sleepers and Real Dogs is even more dramatic than that between True Stars and Fading Stars. As Exhibit 11-6 shows, a typical Sleeper started from a very weak position, with a Par ROI score (pretax, remember) of around 8%—lower than anyone's cost of capital. These businesses nevertheless achieved value enhancement scores averaging 184% (including a positive 5-year cash flow of 35%) and *tripled* their Par ROI ratings by the end of year 7! At the other extreme, Real Dogs averaged just 20% on the value enhancement score, had *negative* cash flows, and ended Year 7 with Par ROI scores scarcely changed from those of Year 2.

Exhibit 11-8 compares Sleepers and Real Dogs in terms of market and strategic factors. Just as True Stars benefitted from (and perhaps stimulated) faster market growth than Fading Stars, so did Sleepers. They also made substantial gains in market share, while Real Dogs achieved only slight increases. Several strategic factors stand out as probable explanations of the excellent long-run performance by Sleepers:

- They typically started with a higher level of product/service quality *and* increased it substantially. (While Real Dogs also improved their relative quality, it was still lower at the end of the planning period than Sleepers' quality was at the outset.)

EXHIBIT 11–8
Strategic and Market Differences: "Sleepers" versus "Real Dogs"

	Beginning Position	Ending Position	Change
Sleepers (46 Businesses)			
Market Share	17.1	21.2	+4.1
Relative Quality	44	54	+10
Relative Price	102.4	102.2	−0.2
Relative Cost	103.0	101.1	−1.9
% New Products	12.0	9.5	−2.5
R&D, % of Sales	1.7	1.1	−0.6
Marketing, % of Sales	8.4	7.9	−0.5
Annual Rate of Capacity Expansion	—	—	+6.2%
Real Growth Rate of Market	—	—	+3.7%
Real Dogs (85 Businesses)			
Market Share	13.3	13.9	+0.6
Relative Quality	34	43	+9
Relative Price	102.8	102.9	+0.1
Relative Cost	104.9	105.2	+0.3
% New Products	5.0	8.0	+0.3
R&D, % of Sales	1.7	1.5	−0.2
Marketing, % of Sales	7.5	7.9	+0.4
Annual Rate of Capacity Expansion	—	—	+4.3%
Real Growth Rate of Market	—	—	+0.3%

- Sleepers' prices (relative to competition) were slightly *lower* than those charged by Real Dogs, and decreased slightly during the 5-year planning period while those of Real Dogs rose. Coupled with the difference in quality between the two groups, this means that Sleepers provided their customers with significantly better *value*.
- Sleepers' product lines included a substantially higher proportion of *new products* (12%) in the beginning period than those of Real Dogs (5%). Presumably in order to promote these new products, Sleepers also spent more on marketing—8.4% of sales versus 7.5%.
- As did Real Stars, Sleepers added to capacity at a faster rate than their poorly-performing counterparts.

Based on the comparisons in Exhibits 11–7 and 11–8, what can we conclude about the differences between short-term and long-term performance? As already noted, most of the things that help or hurt short-term ROI affect Value Enhancement in the same direction. The main exceptions to this are new product introduction and heavy spending on marketing and R&D. High rates of new product introduction and heavy spending on marketing and R&D tend to depress ROI, as shown in Chapter 3. But each of these factors is positively related to long-run performance, because all three contribute to growth. Similarly, although in some cases maintaining or improving relative quality has a short-run cost, it also has a beneficial long-run impact on a business unit's value.

The profiles of True Stars and Sleepers also suggest the importance of expanding a business's production capacity rapidly enough to support its growth. This point seems obvious, but when additions to capacity must be made before sales increases have materialized the investment decisions are risky and require courage. Nothing is more certain to depress profitability than the addition of capital-intensive new capacity that ends up not being utilized!

The Challenge for Management

There is general agreement that management's primary responsibility is to maintain and enhance shareholder value. While this may sometimes best be accomplished through acquisitions or divestitures, most of the time the value of a company is increased only by making its component parts—its business units—more valuable. We have proposed one way to measure business unit value: our index of value enhancement. There are other approaches to calculating value, but all of them, like the one outlined here, are based on the same idea. "Value" is not just short-term profitability or cash flow; it must also reflect the strength or weakness of a business at the end of the period during which products or cash flows are measured.

The ideal approach to maximizing shareholder value is to construct a portfolio that includes only strong SBUs that have high inherent profitability. Even then, there is a risk that some "star" businesses will become "fading stars." To avoid this, management must closely monitor even the best-performing businesses. Some of the warning signals that might point to a potential fading star are a deterioration in relative product quality, eroding market share, rising relative costs, and insufficient marketing effort (see Exhibit 11-7).

DEXTER CORPORATION'S VALUE-BASED PLANNING SYSTEM[10]

Dexter Corporation, with 1985 sales of $633 million, is a producer of coatings and encapsulants, life science products, nonwoven papers and fabrics, and water treatment products. For planning purposes the company groups its products into 26 "strategies business segments." One business segment, for example, is responsible for semiconductor molding powders, while another handles teabags.

Dexter's "Strategic Business Segment Valuation System," developed in 1984–1985, is designed to show whether or not each of the company's business segments (units) is creating value for the company's shareholders. Estimates of the "market value" of a unit are derived by:

1. Projecting the unit's financial performance over a 5-year planning horizon. Typically, the financial projections are based on an assumption of constant market share. Plant and equipment requirements are estimated in light of anticipated rates of inflation and productivity improvement. Key operating expense ratios are projected on the basis of historical experience. Each business unit's profitability forecasts are also "reality-tested" by comparing them with estimates derived from the PIMS "PAR" profitability model.
2. Assigning a cost of capital to each business segment. To do this, the analysts assign an appropriate mix of debt and equity to each unit and calculate a unit-specific "risk index." Based on a unit's debt/equity ratio and its risk index, an overall cost of capital is computed.
3. Each unit's projected 5-year cash flows and projected future value are discounted by its cost of capital to arrive at a *net present value* (NPV). If a unit's NPV is greater than the book value of its investment, it is making a positive contribution to shareholder value. If NPV is *less* than book value, the business segment is assigned to one of five strategic missions—FIX, HOLD, HARVEST, SELL, or LIQUIDATE. ("FIX" means that unit managers must change some of its characteristics to improve its cash flows.)

In late 1985 Worth Loomis, Chairman of Dexter, cited four examples of strategic decisions in which the value-based planning system had played a role. Each of the decisions, in Loomis's view, improved the company's long-term value. In addition, he pointed out, at least some of these decisions were contrary to the ones that would have been prescribed by "typical portfolio-planning approaches."

Since some of these key barometers are measures of an SBU's position relative to leading competitors, it follows that accurate, up-to-date competitive intelligence is essential for informed evaluation.

Almost every company has some weak and some strong businesses in its portfolio. In dealing with the weaker components, the challenge for management is to distinguish between the potential sleepers and the "terminally ill" cases that may appear much the same. To do this, managers need to focus on strategic fundamentals rather than current financial results. Our analysis suggests that a typical sleeper has a reasonable competitive position in terms of market share, relative quality, and relative costs. It may also have a substantial number of new products, or developmental projects that promise future new product potential. Given these characteristics, the key requirement for awakening a sleeper is adequate support in the form of marketing effort and capital investment. Providing this kind of support may depress profitability and cash flow in the short run, but the long-term payoff can be enormous.

Some corporations are using "value-based planning" approaches that are designed to show how business strategies affect long-run value. One example, the Dexter Corporation's "Strategic Business Segment Valuation System," is described in the set-off material on page 227. Two other companies that have used similar approaches are TRW, Inc. and Sonoco Products Company. TRW uses PIMS profitability models, along with other inputs, to estimate business units' future cash flows and residual values at the end of a planning period. These estimates are then discounted to arrive at a unit's net present value. Sonoco, a major supplier of paper and packaging materials, also uses PIMS models to evaluate business unit potential. According to Donald R. Russell, Senior Vice President of Corporate Development, the company has been able "to discover additional opportunities to enhance economic value (which) may have gone unnoticed, especially in mature businesses."[9]

Chapter 12 _____

Integrating Strategies for Clusters of Businesses

For individual business units, strategy involves creating a sustainable competitive advantage (better technology, superior perceived quality, larger market share, lower capital intensity) in the product/market segments that the business has chosen to serve. In Chapters 3–11 we have shown how these and other strategic and market factors affect the performance of individual SBUs. In addition to formulating strategies at the business-unit level, a primary goal of corporate strategic management is to create sustainable competitive advantages by carefully building *clusters* of interrelated business units that reinforce each other. (We use the term "cluster" to designate either an overall company portfolio or, in a larger corporation, a group or "sector" of related SBUs.) The goal is not to invest in isolated projects that produce incremental benefits, but to develop well-positioned business clusters whose synergy creates advantages that beat the cost of capital and build lasting shareholder value. To achieve this goal, management must develop strategies for related business clusters, not just for one business at a time. Companies that have benefited from the powerful impact of synergies based on the interrelatedness of their businesses include General Electric, General Motors, Phillips, and RCA.[1]

Early portfolio matrix displays were designed to focus corporate management's attention on the need to invest in individual businesses whose competitive positions and strategies have a good chance of beating the cost of capital, rather than investing in individual projects based solely on financial analysis. These matrix approaches were useful for appraising questions of cash flow balance, but they didn't really deal with the issues of relatedness, sharing, synergy, and the need to integrate strategies for clusters of interdependent businesses. While they bore the name portfolio matrices, they were really only systems for classifying individual business-unit data on such dimensions as market growth and relative market share.

Heightened global competition and merger, disposition, and leveraged buyout activity in the 1980s all point to the need for focusing more attention on the broader portfolio issues of interrelatedness, sharing, synergy, and dedicated roles for specific businesses. What is synergy? How does synergy create value? How can the effects of synergy on performance be measured? How can a cluster of businesses be analyzed systematically to uncover pervasive problems or opportunities? How can a cluster of businesses be assessed relative to competitors? What specialized roles should be assigned to specific units so as to strengthen the overall cluster effectively?

SYNERGY

What is synergy? We define synergy as the performance of a cluster relative to what its performance would be as the sum of its components. How would its effects show up in operating results? Ongoing synergistic benefits are those sources of value that allow the business units in a portfolio to achieve higher profitability levels than they would normally achieve as stand-alone operations. For instance, when business units share the costs of a particular activity, economies of scale will probably allow each to enjoy lower unit costs than if it had been operating independently. This reduced cost would be reflected in a higher level of profitability than indicated by the strategic position of each business unit.

There are four basic mechanisms through which ongoing synergies create value:

- *Shared resources/activities:* common activities (R&D/engineering, procurement, production/operations, pooled sales forces, marketing programs, distribution channels) that are shared to achieve scale economies.

- *Spill-over benefits of marketing and R&D:* even when marketing and R&D activities aren't shared, businesses in a cluster often capture some of the indirect benefits of marketing and R&D expenditures that are made by sister businesses. For example, GE's research in turbine engines helped its aircraft engine business.
- *"Similar" businesses:* knowledge and skills (both technical and managerial) can be shared across businesses in similar domains of knowledge (high technology industries or situations where marketing skills are the key).
- *Shared image:* individual business units in a company gain in value by being strongly identified as members of the highly-regarded corporate whole.

The research insights summarized below are based on an analysis of a data base of sixty companies that have performed a PIMS portfolio analysis across all or most of their businesses.[2]

Shared Activities and Spill-overs

Shared functional costs represent a key type of potential synergy across units. How much synergy can be attained depends on the following:

- which functional components of the value chain are most subject to scale economies across units (A value chain is the collection of activities that a business performs to design, produce, market, deliver, and support its product/service offering.)
- how important each function is in the cost structure of the value chain
- the degree to which functional costs can be shared across units.

Production and purchasing costs are variable in the sense that they are closely tied to a business's level of output. By contrast, R&D and marketing costs are relatively fixed and decline more rapidly on a per unit basis as a business's rate of output gets larger. This *a priori* knowledge of which costs are relatively fixed, and strong evidence from the SPI data base of portfolios of businesses, together indicate

EXHIBIT 12-1

Assessing Potential Synergy Across the Value Chains of Related Business Units

Cost Element	Activities Included	Relative importance in cost structure	Opportunities	
			Scale Economies	Sharing Costs
R&D	Product and process development	Very low	High	High
Marketing	Advertising, promotion, sales	Medium	High	Medium
Production	Manufacturing distribution	High	Low	Low
Purchases	Purchased goods and services	High	Very low	High

NOTE: Double line separates value-added costs from purchases.

that R&D and marketing (advertising and sales) costs are more subject to scale economies across units; on the other hand, production and purchasing costs are usually more important components of the cost structure (Exhibit 12-1). Portfolios whose value chain is relatively intensive in marketing and R&D achieve above-average synergy and therefore outperform the profitability they might achieve if they were stand-alone businesses. These results reflect not only the effects of economies in shared functional costs, but also the spillover benefits that businesses in a cluster receive from the marketing and R&D expenditures of sister businesses. By contrast, portfolios whose value chain contains relatively little marketing and R&D activity realize below-average synergy.

Similar Businesses: Shared Knowledge, Skills

Some companies seem to develop a distinctive competence that enables their units to perform effectively in certain business contexts or knowledge domains. For example, a company might be particularly good at operating in high-technology industries (Hewlett-Packard), or in industries where marketing skills are key (Procter & Gamble), or in labor-intensive industries where people skills are especially important.

If a company consciously focuses on the business context that it has mastered, it should be able to outperform corporate portfolios that include several dissimilar kinds of businesses. Companies that stray outside their domain of knowledge usually have difficulty developing a recognized corporate competence or a "culture" that accommodates all the businesses in their portfolio. As one might expect, they have trouble trying to run high-tech businesses in tandem with low-tech businesses, or labor-intensive businesses alongside capital-intensive businesses.

Research on related versus conglomerate diversification strategies has produced mixed results.[3] Rumelt found that firms that diversified horizontally into areas closely related to their core skills were more profitable than conglomerates or companies whose units were vertically related. But two groups of academics have disputed Rumelt's findings. One group took a subsample of Rumelt's data and corrected for market structure effects. Once these corrections had been made, they found no significant differences in performance. They found that companies following a closely-related diversification strategy happened to have strong positions in each of the markets in which they operated, and it was this that explained why they performed so well. Another pair of academics found no statistically significant difference in profitability between related and unrelated companies once they had taken into account what they thought to be the undue influence of the pharmaceutical industry on their own results and Rumelt's.

Looking at the PIMS data base of start-up businesses, Ralph Biggadike found that financial and market-share performance depended on the type of relatedness between the venture unit and its parent.[4] He classified start-up businesses into three categories:

- Forward integration
- Technology link
- Marketing link

Using the median performance of businesses in each category, Biggadike found that start-up businesses with marketing links to sister businesses outperformed, on all performance measures (cash flow,

EXHIBIT 12–2

Start-up Success Depends on Type of Relatedness Between Venture Unit and Parent

| Performance Measures (%)* | Type of Relatedness | | |
	Forward Integration (n = 31)	Technology (n = 28)	Marketing (n = 54)
Cash flow/Investment	−83	−73	−69
Return on investment	−33	−47	−22
Return on sales	−38	−70	−16
Relative market share	7	3	14

*The results were achieved during the first two years of entry by start-up businesses.

ROI, ROS, and relative market share), start-ups that had technology or upstream vertical links.

Biggadike's findings were based on a sample of 29 of the 40 units in the PIMS start-up business data base in 1976. Using a sample of 113 of the more than 200 businesses in the 1986 start-up data base, we replicated Biggadike's research and found that this larger sample confirmed his original results (Exhibit 12–2).

For several dimensions of portfolio relatedness, research on the PIMS portfolio data base indicates that clusters of businesses competing in similar environments outperform those clusters competing

EXHIBIT 12–3

Portfolio Profitability and the Degree of Similarity Among Business Units*

Characteristic	Measure	Profit Performance of Consistent versus Dissimilar Clusters of Business Units
Marketing intensity	Marketing/Sales	+3.5
Technology	R&D/Sales	+2.9
Capital intensity	Fixed Capital/Sales	+3.5
Industry concentration	Share of Top 4 Companies	+1.8
Innovation	% Sales from New Products	−2.4
Growth	Real Market Growth	−0.2

*The degree of similarity was captured by using the standard deviation of the measure in question within each portfolio. For each characteristic, the portfolios were divided into similar and dissimilar groups on the basis of the average degree of similarity for the 60 portfolios.
SOURCE: John Wells, "In Search of Synergy," doctoral thesis, Harvard Business School, 1984.

in dissimilar environments. Portfolios of businesses that have roughly comparable marketing intensity, or R&D spending levels, or capital intensity almost inevitably outperform portfolios that try to accommodate both high tech and low tech, or both marketing-intensive and non-marketing-intensive, or both capital-intensive and non-capital-intensive businesses. They generally do so by about 3 points of ROI (Exhibit 12–3).

Innovation, however, is one key characteristic that thrives on dissimilarity. The evidence indicates that in introducing new products, portfolios in which each business introduces some new products earn lower returns than portfolios composed of a balance between businesses that actively introduce new products and those that do not (Exhibit 12–3).

Shared Image

A business unit's reputation for superior (or inferior) quality may spill over onto its sister businesses in the cluster. If a portfolio is made up of businesses that are consistently superior in quality relative to their competition, we would expect that portfolio to achieve performance levels that exceed par projections based on individual business-unit characteristics. Conversely, if relative quality is consistently inferior across a portfolio, the portfolio will tend to underperform the par of its individual units.

The SPI portfolio data base confirms these expectations (Exhibit 12–4). Portfolios with consistently superior quality outperform par by 2.5 points of ROI. Portfolios with consistently inferior quality underperform par by 2.9 points of ROI.

Notice what we have just observed. "Synergy" can be negative as well as positive! Most executives (and researchers) focus on positive synergies—not negative synergies. When stand-alone businesses are clustered together they hope for (1) economies of scale in shared activities, (2) spill-over benefits from marketing and R&D expenditures of sister businesses and (3) economies of shared knowledge and skills in running similar businesses. Many people even define synergy as $2 + 2 = 5$. But, our definition of synergy focuses on the performance of a cluster as such, relative to what its expected performance would be as the sum of its components. Clearly, a portfolio made up of businesses that were suffering from the spill-over effects of their inferior quality reputations would be better off broken up.

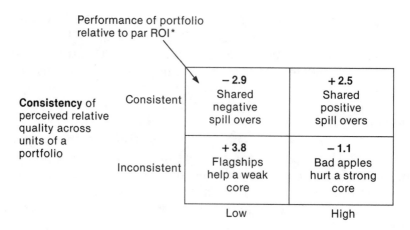

EXHIBIT 12-4

How the Level and Consistency of Relative Perceived Quality
Affects Portfolio Performance

*Actual ROI earned minus Par ROI.
SOURCE: John Wells, "In Search of Synergy," doctoral thesis, Harvard Business
School, 1984.

This two-edged sword of shared-image synergy may be one reason
why researchers have not been very successful in finding significant
performance differences between the related and conglomerate categories of diversified companies.

The more intriguing effects of shared image are seen in portfolios
that contain a mix of inferior and superior quality businesses. There
are two very interesting manifestations.

At one end of the spectrum, we find portfolios where nearly all
the business units are superior in quality but a few are markedly
inferior. These "bad apples" benefit from the excellent image of the
core of the portfolio and therefore outperform their individual pars.
But they also drag the performance of the core below par. The net
effect is negative. "Bad apples" generally reduce the overall portfolio ROI by about one point (Exhibit 12-4).

At the other end of the spectrum, we find portfolios of business
units typically inferior in quality, whose few superior-quality, flagship businesses spark overall portfolio performance. Although the
low quality environment may undermine the profitability of the flag-

ships themselves, the strong image that the latter SBUs project is sufficient to pull up the performance of the rest of the portfolio and more than compensate. Strong flagships can generally pull up overall portfolio performance by almost 4 points of ROI (Exhibit 12-4).

These findings offer dramatic proof of the need to track the competitive positions of business units in a portfolio rather than just focusing on their financial performance. Companies that don't track the relative perceived quality and performance of their business units versus their par ROI may allow "bad apples" to make a deceptively good showing and, what's worse, pull down the performance of the entire business cluster. Alternatively, companies may under-reward the spark-plug performance of flagship units.

VERTICAL INTEGRATION

So far in this chapter we have discussed the horizontal dimensions of relatedness among businesses. Businesses in a cluster can also be linked by selling to and buying from each other. In Chapter 8 we analyzed the effects of the absolute and relative levels of vertical integration on financial performance within a *single* business. Here we outline a way to keep track of vertical relationships among businesses within a cluster.

In some industries the vertical relationships among businesses can become quite complex. An input/output table showing the internal sales by SBU seller and SBU buyer can help to reveal these vertical linkages (Exhibit 12-5). The rows represent businesses in their role as (upstream) suppliers. The columns represent these same businesses in their role as (downstream) buyers. The flow from upstream to downstream units can be clarified by listing the businesses by the percentage of sales they make internally to sister businesses.

It is often difficult to assess the financial performance of vertically-linked businesses because in many cases there are no readily available normal market prices. In tight vertical clusters, the historical profit performance of each business should be assessed relative to its Par ROI. If the supplier businesses are mostly below par and the downstream businesses are mostly above par, it is likely that the internal transfer price has been set below the price that would exist if all the businesses were stand-alone operations.

The potential benefits and disadvantages of SBU vertical integration were discussed in Chapter 8. The same factors affect per-

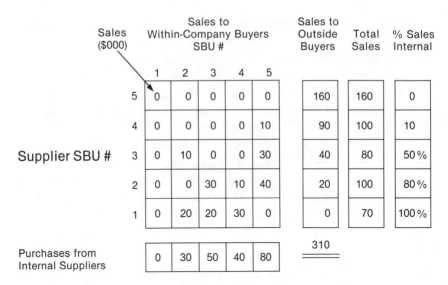

EXHIBIT 12-5
Keeping Track of Vertical Relationships Among Businesses Within a
Cluster

formance for vertically-linked clusters of SBUs. A cluster of vertically related businesses that has succeeded in capturing the benefits
without the disadvantages will tend to perform above the Par ROIs
of the individual businesses. A cluster of vertically related businesses
that is performing below par may want to rely more on market forces
to dictate the sources of its supplies, and less on common ownership
and buy-internal rules.

ANALYZING CLUSTERS FOR COMMON PATTERNS

To develop a successful integrated strategy for a cluster of businesses, you must learn as much as you can about both the individual
business units and the structure of your cluster relative to competitors. To accomplish this, you must first put the units into a common
strategic framework and then examine existing and potential clusters
to identify problems and opportunities.

The entire process comprises the following steps:

- Collect financial and strategic data to compare business units
  and to assess each one's competitive position in its markets.

(The major dimensions of strategy were described in Chapter 2.)

- Validate the internal consistency of business-unit data by comparing actual financial performance against benchmarks based on its competitive position.
- Assess interrelatedness and synergy among potential clusters.
- Determine how to strengthen individual businesses and what special roles should be assigned to specific units so as to reposition the cluster effectively.

Assessing the Business Units

The first major task is to assess the strategic positions of individual business units in the corporate portfolio. This is where the basic strength of a cluster begins. Is each unit serving attractive markets? Does each have strong technology, perceived quality, and market share relative to its competitors? In each case, how does capital intensity, employee productivity, and overall operating effectiveness compare to competitors?

To answer these questions, management needs to assemble and maintain *both* financial data and equally reliable strategic data. We retrace here some of the points covered in Chapter 2, "Linking Strategies to Performance," to emphasize the importance of maintaining comparable, reliable strategic data for a corporate portfolio of businesses. While all companies routinely maintain comparable financial data for their businesses, they frequently ignore strategic data or gather it only on an ad hoc, non-quantitative, non-comparable basis. Financial data alone do not provide enough information to develop clusters of businesses that reinforce each other. Companies that are put together largely on the basis of a financial analysis are frequently taken apart later. The history of IT&T in the 1970s and 1980s is a case in point.

The procedures for assembling financial data are well known. The Financial Accounting Standards Board (FASB) has developed a set of generally accepted accounting principles that apply to collecting and reporting financial data. Using these principles, controllers prepare financial statements that enable operating management to compare individual business units, making any subjective judgments that are needed to reflect market or industry-specific circumstances. But no official Board exists to monitor "Strategic Accounting Standards." On the other hand, since the 1950s there has been an on-going effort to develop increasingly reliable measures of competitive position and market attractiveness. During the 1950s the General Electric Company's Measurements Task Force developed a set of standard non-financial measures (such as productivity, perceived quality, market share) for use at the business unit level within the company. These measures were implemented at G.E. during the 1960s. During the 1970s these non-financial measures were refined, expanded and implemented on a multicompany basis by the PIMS Program in cooperation with the Harvard Business School and companies participating in PIMS.

A PIMS strategy profile provides essential data that rest on generally accepted principles for defining business units and their served markets. Even though companies contributing data compete in many different industries, generic measurements can be fine-tuned by management to increase their accuracy relative to specific markets or industries. These strategic measurements provide a good starting point for comparing the strategic positions of the various business units in the portfolio.

Once comparable financial and strategic data are developed for the clusters of businesses, they can and should be validated. Perhaps the most reliable method is to examine the business-unit data in reference to benchmarks based on the experience of "look-alike" businesses in the PIMS data base. Look-alikes may be in different industries but they are businesses in similar strategic positions to your own. These benchmarks enable management to (1) check the internal consistency of the financial and strategic data, (2) confirm the business and served market definition and (3) subject the unit's plans to the test of reality.

Viewing the Clusters from Different Perspectives

Once strategic and financial data have been assembled and validated, management can identify pervasive problems and opportunities by viewing the clusters through a number of displays, each based on a methodology that assesses the portfolio from a different angle to produce useful insights. In the remainder of this chapter we illustrate several ways in which clusters of businesses have been evaluated using analysis derived from PIMS data.

Actual Versus Par ROI

Par ROI is the normal rate of return on investment for a business given its profile of strategic characteristics.

A plot of each unit's actual ROI versus Par ROI is first used to validate the internal consistency of your financial and strategic data and to confirm the business and served market definition. Businesses that are well above or well below par should be able to cite industry-specific or operating reasons that explain why actual performance differs so much from the norm. If unit management is unable to identify such reasons, it may be that the served-market boundaries, market share, or relative perceived quality position have not been determined properly.

Once each unit's data have been validated, the actual and the par displays can be used to diagnose the cluster's current strategic position and operating performance. Businesses may achieve poor financial results for very different reasons and therefore may require different corrective steps. For example, suppose two businesses, "A" and "B," are both earning low returns. Business A (par and actual ROI both equal 5%) has a low Par ROI and needs to be strategically repositioned to improve its financial performance. Business B (Par ROI is 25% but actual ROI is only 5%) has a good strategic position but is performing well below par. It needs to take action to improve operating effectiveness or to offset a negative market-specific factor. Non-financial incentives in Business A should be tied to improving strategic position; in Business B, they should be tied to improving operating effectiveness.

A cluster in which most businesses are performing above par may be vulnerable to a drop-off in profitability. For example, many financial service companies saw their profits fall markedly when the government deregulated their markets.

A cluster in which businesses are performing below par may face a pervasive operating or human relations problem. The division may have an inappropriate compensation system, poor recruitment practices, ineffective employee training, or some other problem may cut across all the units.

PIMS research indicates that over a period of time businesses that are above par tend to move down toward par, while those that are below par tend to move up toward par. Businesses that are at par may be temporarily pushed either above or below par by industry-specific events.

A well-positioned cluster will have most of its units in the high-par portion of the actual versus par plot. A portfolio with most of the units below a Par ROI of 20 needs radical surgery to reposition the fixable units and to eliminate the lost causes, or at least to diminish their number.

The Dexter Corporation, which makes and markets specialty chemicals and specialty materials, has been a leader in applying strategic and financial planning concepts and tools to its operating clusters of businesses.[5] As shown in Exhibit 12–6 most of its units were well positioned with Par ROIs greater than 20 as Dexter entered the 1980s. During the 1980s, Dexter's corporate ROE has persistently been in the top quartile among chemical companies and its sales growth has been well above the industry median.

Whereas the Dexter illustration includes all of the major, established units in the corporate portfolio, and is based on historical data,

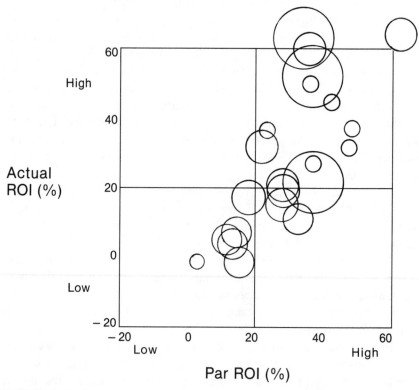

EXHIBIT 12–6
A Well-Positioned Cluster, Mostly High-Par Businesses

Exhibit 12-7 shows plan data for a cluster of start-up businesses. This exhibit is taken from the Test Systems, Inc. case, a disguised version of the experiences of a medical devices company with its start-up ventures group. Four of these businesses (B, C, D and H) were anticipating profit rates far in excess of their profit norms. Business D's financial pro formas were projecting an ROI of about 50 percent supported by an evolving strategic position that suggests it would be normal to earn only 10 percent.

The case was first presented at the 1984 SPI Member Conference. At that time, newly-introduced government policies regarding medical-care reimbursement were removing those forces that had traditionally sheltered medical equipment competitors from price competition. The resulting dramatic upheaval and new profit pressures forced the company to step back and take a fresh look at the

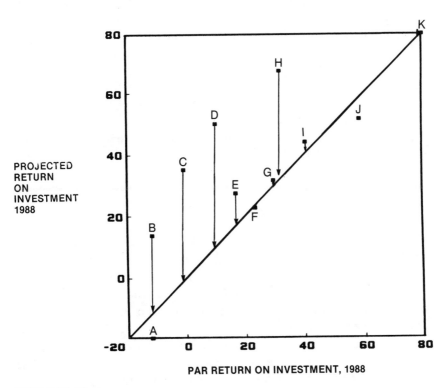

EXHIBIT 12-7
Reality Check on Profit Projections
SOURCE: Test Systems Inc.-SVG.

prospects for new businesses being generated in its New Ventures Group.

The New Ventures Group used a series of empirical benchmarks for individual businesses and analytical tools for the entire cluster to reassess its changing business situation and set priorities for business development. The analysis helped the group decide which new businesses the company should back and to what level it should invest in these businesses.

Along the way the company developed:

- A framework for comparing investment opportunities under differing business conditions;
- Objective and realistic benchmarks for evaluating proposed strategies;
- A common language for discussing strategic options;
- A company-accepted system for allocating resources among competing start-up ventures;
- Guidelines for proven successful start-up strategies.

The telling point of the analysis was that the company was able to quantify the difference in profitability between having its start-up businesses perform at (1) the optimistic but not always realistic levels predicted by their managers, and (2) the conservative and reality-tested levels predicted by the real-life experiences of look-alike businesses in the PIMS data base.

Actual Versus Par Value Added per Employee

Value added per employee is a partial productivity measure. It is partial in the sense that it keeps track of the labor input but not the inputs of capital, energy, or materials. Par value added per employee does keep track of capital inputs. Businesses that have high investment per employee do need, and typically achieve, high value added per employee.

The actual versus par value added per employee display can be used to complement the actual versus Par ROI plot. It focuses on the amount of value added that is normal per employee. As we have seen, the Par ROI display focuses on the part of value added that normally drops down to the bottom line, relative to dollars tied up in investment.

Exhibit 12–8 shows actual versus par value added per employee

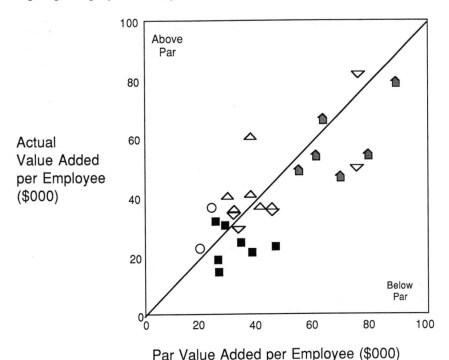

Actual
Value Added
per Employee
($000)

EXHIBIT 12-8
Division Clusters Pinpoint Two Divisions with Low Operating
Effectiveness

for a disguised corporate portfolio. Although quite a few businesses were somewhat above par, a larger number of businesses were considerably below par, indicating a possible productivity problem. When the display was refined to reveal the business clusters by division, the productivity problem was pinpointed as existing in two major divisions. Once the problem was identified, these divisions used an analysis that contrasted strategic look-alikes who were above par with those that were below par for each of their businesses. The insights from this analysis allowed each division to formulate plans to improve operating effectiveness, plans tailored to the specific situation of their individual businesses.

Value Map

A value map is frequently used to compare a business to its competitors; however, since its dimensions are relative price and relative quality, it can also display the units of a business cluster. Businesses in the better-value zone (superior quality, lower price) tend to gain share, while those in the worse-value zone are vulnerable to share loss.

You can use the value map to analyze where your cluster's growth will come from and which units will gain or lose competitive position.

You can estimate how much share will probably be gained or lost for various zones of the value map and, with customized analysis, calibrations can pinpoint share change more precisely for individual units.

Exhibit 12-9 shows a value map for a disguised corporate portfolio. It reveals a sizable cluster of businesses receiving premium prices that are not fully supported by superior quality positions of each business taken as a stand-alone unit. Perhaps they are able to

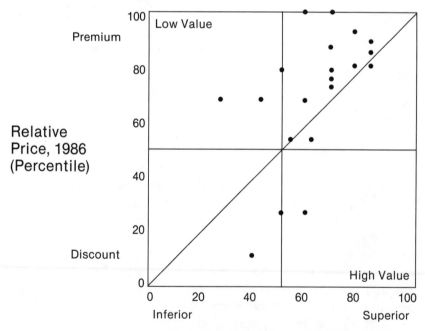

EXHIBIT 12-9
Premium Prices Not Fully Supported by Superior Quality May Mean
Vulnerability to Margin Declines or Share Loss

charge premium prices because they are part of a business cluster in which the superior perceived quality of each business spills over onto sister businesses. If the spill-over effect does not fully account for the premium prices, or if it begins to erode, these businesses are vulnerable to slipping profit margins. Alternatively, they may be vulnerable to share loss if the price premiums are maintained without quality improvements. This highly profitable company launched a relative perceived-quality improvement program to ensure its continued success.

Differentiation Map

The 1980s have been a turning point for Dow Chemical and many other chemical giants.[6] They were beset first by high-priced U.S. dollars and then by low-priced chemicals from Saudi Arabia and other new competitors. Over the past several years Paul F. Orreffice, Dow's chairman, has relentlessly attacked Dow's reliance on basic chemicals, such as chlorine and ethylene. These, sold by the ton and delivered by the tankerful, have always been Dow's core, and until recently they brought in all but a fraction of Dow's earnings. Orreffice wants to see half of Dow's earnings flowing from the specialty side by 1987, and close to two-thirds by mid-1990.

Acquisition money of $1 billion has gone into pharmaceuticals, industrial specialties such as superstrong ceramics and plastics, and branded products for households. In the consumer-products division, newly acquired Spray'n Wash spot remover and Yes detergent have joined Dow's well-known products such as Saran Wrap and Ziploc storage bags giving Dow more clout in bargaining for shelf space with retailers.

In addition, the adjective "basic" rather than "commodity" is chosen for chemicals like chlorine and ethylene to remind Dow managers that they should also try to differentiate and improve their service quality relative to competitors to prevent these bulk chemicals from being pure commodity product/service offerings.

Displaying both market differentiation and relative perceived quality on a differentiation map (first described in Chapter 6) can help teach executives who have been reared in businesses like commodity chemicals to track the performance of their old-core and new-specialty clusters as their company with its shifting mix moves away from the commodity zone to offerings that are differentiated and

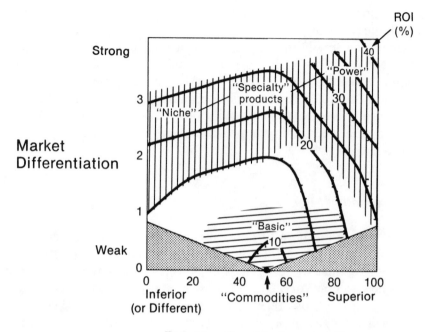

Relative Quality (percentile)

EXHIBIT 12–10
Differentiation Map: Shift the Mix from Commodity to Speciality
Offerings
SOURCE: SPI's Quality/Differentiation Data Base.

superior in perceived quality (Exhibit 12–10). Even a quick glance at
the map helps to sort out power brands, niche businesses, and commodity businesses. ROI contour lines indicate expected profitability
for the various positions on the map. Businesses in the commodity
zone (bottom middle) have the lowest profitability; power brands
(upper right) have the greatest potential for profitability. For any
unit spotlighted, a customized par ROI analysis can produce a more
precise profitability benchmark.

Competitive Position Map

Displaying both market-share rank and relative perceived quality on
a competitive position map can help a multi-business general man-

ager size-up the image that that particular business cluster is projecting in the marketplace.

Market-share rank is the simplest measure of relative market share. Although customers and non-customers may not know your market share relative to competition for each business in your cluster, they probably know your market-share rank for several businesses. Similarly, they may not know your relative product/service quality for each business, but they probably have a perception of your quality position in some businesses, based on usage or reputation. This perception of relative quality position may carry over to other businesses where customers and non-customers have little experience, no experience, or experience that is obsolete.

Perceived relative quality is an indicator of the cluster's ability to obtain premium prices and gain market share. Market-share rank is a good proxy for the relative costs of marketing the product/service offering to the served market. Together, relative perceived quality and market-share rank indicate a cluster's prospects for market competitiveness, profitability, and growth.

By analyzing the pattern of market-share rank and relative perceived quality in a competitive position map, a cluster manager can pinpoint which businesses may be able to move up in market-share rank and which businesses may be vulnerable to being knocked down a notch or two. Businesses whose quality position is high relative to their share rank are candidates for moving up toward number one. Businesses whose quality position is low relative to share rank may be vulnerable to a loss in market share. Additional knowledge of the interrelatedness among businesses may enable the cluster manager to assign special roles to sister businesses that will help a unit to move up in rank or to hold its current position against competitors. Head-to-head quality profiles (attribute by attribute) versus key competitors, together with data on the market shares of your businesses and your competitors', provide the knowledge base for formulating action plans to strengthen the market position and image of your cluster.

The cluster's cost competitiveness can be analyzed using a competitive advantage map that displays relative direct cost versus relative perceived quality. This display complements the competitive position map and is especially useful when evaluating clusters where global competitors are present and direct costs are large relative to marketing costs.

We have described several of the many interesting two-dimensional displays that allow us to evaluate a cluster of businesses from different angles. Once the basic strategic and financial data for a cluster of businesses has been assembled on a common, systematic basis, the cluster can be analyzed using these portfolio displays. The PIMS data base provides benchmarks of performance measures and operating ratios for various zones in these two-dimensional portfolio displays. More importantly, the PIMS data base also allows us to provide more exact, customized benchmarks for individual businesses in the cluster.

Assessing the Structure of Your Cluster Relative to Competitors

Once you've sized up your cluster of units from different angles, you need to examine how the structure of your cluster differs from that of competitors. This requires several steps.

First, list your products and market segments and construct your product/market matrix (Exhibit 12–11). The basic strategic data already assembled should enable you to assess your market share, quality, cost, and technology position, relative to each of your leading competitors, for each cell of the product/market arena in which you are active.

To understand how competitors' business clusters differ from yours, you need to expand the product/market matrix to include those product lines you do not offer, and customer groups you do not serve (Exhibit 12–12). Be especially careful to include additional products or markets that may allow competitors to realize economies of scale or to share costs across product lines or market segments. For example, United Technologies (UT) might include turbine generators because UT's jet engine business competes with GE's aircraft engine business which has a technology-linked sister business that makes turbine generators. As a further step, you should also include related products or markets where neither you nor your competitors are yet active. This augmented product/market matrix sets the stage for analyzing how economies of scale across products or markets can strengthen your basic competitive position in individual products or markets.

Next you can summarize the data by grouping product/market

EXHIBIT 12-11
Assess Your Relative Share, Quality, Cost, and Technology Position in Each Cell of the Product/Market Matrix

Market segments

Products	Your Relative Position*	1. _____	2. _____	3. _____	4. _____
A. ____	Share	_____	_____	_____	_____
	Quality	_____	_____	_____	_____
	Cost	_____	_____	_____	_____
	Technology	_____	_____	_____	_____
B. ____	Share	_____	_____	_____	_____
	Quality	_____	_____	_____	_____
	Cost	_____	_____	_____	_____
	Technology	_____	_____	_____	_____
C. ____	Share	_____	_____	_____	_____
	Quality	_____	_____	_____	_____
	Cost	_____	_____	_____	_____
	Technology	_____	_____	_____	_____
D. ____	Share	_____	_____	_____	_____
	Quality	_____	_____	_____	_____
	Cost	_____	_____	_____	_____
	Technology	_____	_____	_____	_____

*Key: Relative Share: small, average, large
   Absolute share: percent
   Quality: inferior, same, superior
   Cost: lower, same, higher
   Technology: behind, same, ahead
     (Product)
     (Process)

EXHIBIT 12-12
Extend Your Product/Market Matrix to Include Portions of the Total
Arena Where You Are Not Active but Your Competitors Are

Products	Market segments						
	1.	2.	3.	4.	5**	6.	7.
A. _____							
B. _____							
C. _____							
D. _____							
E.* _____							
F. _____							
G. _____							
H. _____							

*Include related products offered by your competitors.
**Include related markets served by your competitors.
A served market typically consists of several closely related market segments that purchase
goods and services from a product-line offering.
3b. Circle or shade product/market segments that belong in the same served market.

segments into key product-line businesses serving markets that are
made up of closely related segments. You can then construct a grid
showing your own market share and that of each of your major competitors in relationship to the key served markets in the competitive
arena (Exhibit 12-13). This display of served market and each competitor's share reveals the structure of your business cluster relative
to that of your competitors.

EXHIBIT 12-13

How Does Your Company (Division) Compare to Leading Competitors in Each of the Served Markets Within Your Competitive Arena?

Relative Position*	Served Market (Cluster of Product/Market Segments)				
Competing Suppliers	*SM 1*	*SM 2*	*SM 3*	*SM 4*	*SM 5*
Your Company					
Competitor 1					
Competitor 2					
Competitor 3					
Competitor 4					

*Key: Relative market share: small, average, large
Absolute market share: percent
Relative quality: inferior, same, superior
Relative cost: lower, same, higher
Relative technology: behind, same, ahead

CHECKLIST: DEVELOPING AN INTEGRATED STRATEGY FOR THE CLUSTER

To develop an integrated strategy for your cluster of businesses you need to take the following steps:

1. Adopt a common language for discussing strategy and competitive advantage.

2. Use a common framework for structural analyses of markets and competitors.
3. Assemble comparable financial data for each business.
4. Maintain comparable strategic data for each business.
5. Review unit management's knowledge of the market or industry-specific factors affecting each business.
6. Validate your strategic data, competitor data, and financial plans against benchmarks based on the experience of look-alike businesses in similar strategic positions.
   —check the internal consistency of your financial and strategic data
   —confirm the business and market definition
   —test unit plans for reality
   (A plan has not been validated unless it is based on evidence that can be supported.)
7. Assess the structure of your cluster relative to competitors.
8. Decide how the businesses in the cluster are interrelated.
9. Calibrate how cluster interrelatedness affects shared costs, shared knowledge, and shared quality image.
10. Restructure your portfolio toward an interrelated cluster that builds and reinforces your position at the individual unit level.
11. Assign special roles to individual units.

Special Roles for Individual Units: A Final Step

In other chapters we have focused on competitive position and market attractiveness at the individal unit level. Here we have focused on sizing up the portfolio with common strategic data, measuring interrelatedness, and creating synergy. The final step involves explicit recognition of cases where an individual unit's objective is not to produce profits itself, but to help the core portfolio of sister businesses perform better.

In some portfolios a unit is assigned the key defensive role of blocking entry into the served market or preventing cannibalization by a competitor who is lower down on the quality-for-price curve. Japanese companies have penetrated many motor-driven markets in North America (motorcycles, automobiles and tractors) by beginning at the lower, and often neglected, end of the quality-for-price curve and then moving up.

Since a key part of the Japanese advantage is derived from the motors themselves, one might have expected them quickly to penetrate the marine outboard market with their small efficient engines. But the North American brands (Evinrude, Johnson, and Mercury) had been supplying a full spectrum of engine sizes for years. While the Japanese are now active in the marine outboard market in North America, their initial entry was not aided by an unguarded end of the product spectrum, as happened with motorcycles and cars.

A second specialized role played by some units in a portfolio is to serve as a window to gain information about style or technology in leading markets. For example, an Italian apparel manufacturer maintains a high fashion clothing unit in the U.S. to keep an eye on where demand is headed. Similarly, many companies locate a unit in the country that leads in a particular technology to see where that technology is headed.

In some portfolios, a unit is assigned the role of attaining a beachhead market-share position in the home market of a global competitor. Rather than attempting to earn a profit itself, the unit aggressively tries to track the competitor's unit and to disrupt profitability in the competitor's core home market.

The PIMS Data Bases

This Appendix provides a more detailed description of the PIMS data base, and more detailed definitions of the measures used in the research than those contained in Chapter 3. It is organized in five sections: Basic Concepts, Composition of the Data Base, Descriptive Information, Financial Statement Measures, Market and Competitive Information, and Satellite Data Bases. The contents are drawn from various publications of the Strategic Planning Institute.

I. BASIC CONCEPTS: BUSINESS UNIT AND SERVED MARKET

The concepts of the "Business Unit" and "Served Market" are explained in Chapter 3, pp. 31–34. In the instructions provided to the companies that supply the information, some additional considerations are mentioned:

1. If 60% or more of a potential business unit's costs are allocated joint costs (i.e., costs shared with other units), then the unit should be combined with one or more others.
2. If 60% or more of a unit's sales are accounted for by "transfers" to other units of the same parent company, the units should be combined. The Federal Trade Commission used a similar rule in defining "Lines of Business." (See *Statistical Report: Annual Line of Business Report 1977,* Washington, D.C., Federal Trade Commission, April 1985, pp. 291-92.

The FTC's cut-off for combining vertically related LBs was 50%).

3. In defining the boundaries of a served market, an important criterion is the (actual or estimated) responsiveness of customers and competitors to the actions of the reporting business. For example, if the business were to increase marketing effort substantially, would a particular group of customers respond? If not, they may not belong in the served market. Similarly, if Competitor "X" would not respond at all, then X may not qualify as a competitor in the served market. (As many readers will recognize, this notion is an effort to apply the concept of "cross-elasticity" to the process of defining and measuring the extent of a served market.)

II. COMPOSITION OF THE DATA BASE

Exhibits 3-2 and 3-3 in Chapter 3 show the numbers of businesses in the data base classified in two ways: by "Type of Business" and by geographic location of served markets. There are many other ways to classify the businesses, several of which are shown in Exhibits A-1 to A-3.

As these exhibits suggest, the data base includes a wide variety of business units in terms of age, timing of market entry, and so on. The sample is not representative of *all* businesses in the sense of having the same proportions of new and old, etc. as the overall population. Mature businesses, market leaders, and large parent corpo-

EXHIBIT A-1
PIMS Businesses, by Year of Initial Sales

Year of Inital Sale	% of Businesses
Before 1930	17%
1930-1949	32
1950-1954	10
1955-1959	10
1960-1964	12
1965-1969	11
1970-1974	5
After 1974	1

EXHIBIT A-2
PIMS Businesses, by Order of Market Entry

Order of Entry	% of Businesses
Pioneer	52%
Early Follower	31
Late Entrant	17

rations are over-represented in terms of the numbers of such units in the data base. Small companies and newer products or industries are less well represented.

EXHIBIT A-3
PIMS Businesses, by Market Share Rank

Rank	% of Businesses
First	37%
Second	24
Third	15
Fourth	10
Fifth	5
Sixth or Lower	9

III. DESCRIPTIVE INFORMATION

Each business unit provides basic descriptive information about its products/services, customers, distribution channels, and production processes. The most important kinds of descriptive data are listed in Exhibit A-4.

EXHIBIT A-4
Descriptive Information About Each Business Unit's Operations
(Excerpts from PIMS Data Forms)

TYPE OF BUSINESS
This business is best described as . . .

CONSUMER-PRODUCTS MANUFACTURING:

. . . Durable Products

. . . Non-Durable Products

(cont.)

EXHIBIT A-4 *(cont.)*

INDUSTRIAL/COMMERCIAL/PROFESSIONAL-PRODUCTS MANUFACTURING:

... Capital Goods □

... Raw or Semi-Finished Materials □

... Components for Incorporation into Finished Products □

... Supplies or Other Consumable Products □

SERVICES □

RETAIL AND WHOLESALE DISTRIBUTION □

PRODUCTS AND SERVICES

AGE OF PRODUCT

When were these types of products or services, *using the current basic technology,* first introduced? *(Check one)*

Prior to 1930	1930-1949	1950-1954	1955-1959	1960-1964	1965-1969	1970-1974	1975-
□	□	□	□	□	□	□	□

"LIFE CYCLE" STAGE OF PRODUCT CATEGORY

How would you describe the stage of development of the types of products or services sold by this business during the last three years? *(Check one)*

... Introductory Stage: Primary demand for product just starting to grow; products or services still unfamiliar to many potential users □

... Growth Stage: Demand growing at 10% or more annually in real terms; technology or competitive structure still changing □

... Maturity Stage: Products or services familiar to vast majority of prospective users; technology and competitive structure reasonably stable □

... Decline Stage: Products viewed as commodities; weaker competitors beginning to exit □

What was this business's first year of commercial sales?*(Check one)*

Prior to 1930	1930-1949	1950-1954	1955-1959	1960-1964	1965-1969	1970-1974	1975-
□	□	□	□	□	□	□	□

At the time this business first entered the market, was it ... *(Check one)*

... One of the pioneers in first developing such products or services? □

... An early follower of the pioneer(s) in a still growing, dynamic market? □

... A later entrant into a more established market situation? □

PATENTS AND TRADE SECRETS

Does this business benefit *to a significant degree* from patents, trade secrets, or other proprietary methods of production or operation ...

Pertaining to products or services?	NO □	Pertaining to processes?	NO □
	YES □		YES □

STANDARDIZATION OF PRODUCTS OR SERVICES

Are the products or services of this business ... *(Check one)*

... More or less standardized for all customers? □

... Designed or produced to order for individual customers? □

FREQUENCY OF PRODUCT CHANGES

Is it typical practice for the business and its major competitors to change all or part of the line of products or services offered ... *(Check one)*

... Annually (for example, annual model changes)?

... Seasonally?

... Periodically, but at intervals longer than one year?

... No regular, periodic pattern of change?

TECHNOLOGICAL CHANGE

Have there been *major* technological changes in the products offered by the business or its major competitors, or in methods of production, during the last 8 years? *(If in doubt about whether a change was "major," answer NO.)*

NO

YES

DEVELOPMENT TIME FOR NEW PRODUCTS OR SERVICES

For this business and for its major competitors, what is the typical time lag between the beginning of development effort for a new product and market introduction? *(Check one)*

... Less than 1 year

... 1 - 2 years

... 2 - 5 years

... More than 5 years

... Not applicable; little or no new-product development occurs in this business

END USERS AND IMMEDIATE CUSTOMERS

Immediate customers are those from whom the business receives purchase orders. End users are individuals, households and other businesses that consume the products or services or incorporate them into other products or services. End users are those who make the final decision on which of the competing products or services to purchase.

If the immediate customers resell the products or services in the same form, then they are not end users. If the immediate customers change the form of the products or services, or incorporate them into other products, then this business's immediate customers and end users are identical.

Only the immediate customers and end users who actually purchased this business's products or services in the last year should be considered in answering these questions, not those who purchased competitors' products or services.

DISTRIBUTION OF USE AMONG END-USER GROUPS

Approximately what percentages (to the nearest 5%) of the output of the business are used by ...

PER CENT

... Households, individual consumers?

... Manufacturers (including use as components, materials, etc.)?

... Institutional, commercial, professional customers (including farms)?

... Government and public utilities?

... Contractors?

NOTE: Please enter a percentage for every one of the above lines even if the percentage is zero.   TOTAL = 100%

(cont.)

EXHIBIT A–4 (*cont.*)

NUMBER OF END USERS

Approximately how many end users purchased this business's products or services in the last year? *(Check one)*

19 or fewer	☐	100,000-999,999	☐
20-99	☐	1,000,000-9,999,999	☐
100-999	☐	10,000,000-24,999,999	☐
1,000-9,999	☐	25,000,000 or more	☐
10,000-99,999	☐		

NUMBER OF IMMEDIATE CUSTOMERS

Approximately how many immediate customers purchased this business's products or services in the last year?

(NOTE: If this business sold directly and exclusively to end users, your answer to this question is simply a more detailed estimate than that given in Line 117, immediately preceding.) *(Check one)*

3 or fewer	☐	1	50-99	☐
4-9	☐	2	100-999	☐
10-19	☐	3	1,000-9,999	☐
20-49	☐	4	10,000 or more	☐

CONCENTRATION OF PURCHASES — END USERS

What percentage of this business's end users accounted for 50% of total purchases of its products or services?

PER CENT
☐☐

During the last 5 years, has the degree to which the sales of this business depend on purchases by its larger end users . . . *(Check one)*

. . . increased? ☐

. . . remained stable? ☐

. . . decreased? ☐

Are this business's end users . . . *(Check one)*

. . . more concentrated than those of its three largest competitors? ☐

. . . about the same as those of its three largest competitors? ☐

. . . less concentrated than those of its three largest competitors? ☐

CONCENTRATION OF PURCHASES — IMMEDIATE CUSTOMERS

What percentage of this business's immediate customers accounted for 50% of its total sales?

PER CENT
☐☐

During the last 5 years, has the degree to which the sales of this business depend on purchases by its larger immediate customers . . . *(Check one)*

. . . increased? ☐

. . . remained stable? ☐

. . . decreased? ☐

Are this business's immediate customers . . . *(Check one)*

. . . more concentrated than those of its three largest competitors?

☐

. . . about the same as those of its three largest competitors?

☐

. . . less concentrated than those of its three largest competitors?

☐

PURCHASE FREQUENCY — END USERS AND IMMEDIATE CUSTOMERS

How often do this business's end users and immediate customers typically purchase its products or services? (Focus on purchase orders and not on delivery schedules.)*(Check one box in each column)*

	END USERS	IMMEDIATE CUSTOMERS
Weekly or more frequently	☐	☐
Between once/week and once/month	☐	☐
Between once/month and once/6 months	☐	☐
Between once/6 months and once/year	☐	☐
Between once/year and once/5 years	☐	☐
Between once/5 years and once/10 years	☐	☐
Other	☐	☐

TYPICAL PURCHASE AMOUNT — END USERS AND IMMEDIATE CUSTOMERS

Indicate the typical purchase amount per transaction or contract for this business's products or services for both end users and immediate customers. (When customers buy on a contract basis covering a period of time, the total amount covered by such a contract should be regarded as a *single* transaction.) *(Check one box in each column)*

THESE AMOUNTS ARE IN U.S. DOLLARS AND SHOULD NOT BE DISGUISED.	END USERS	IMMEDIATE CUSTOMERS
. . . Less than $1.00	☐	☐
. . . From $1 up to $9.99	☐	☐
. . . From $10 up to $99	☐	☐
. . . From $100 up to $999	☐	☐
. . . From $1,000 up to $9,999	☐	☐
. . . From $10,000 up to $99,999	☐	☐
. . . From $100,000 up to $999,999	☐	☐
. . . From $1,000,000 up to $9,999,999	☐	☐
. . . Over $10 Million	☐	☐

IMPORTANCE OF PRODUCTS OR SERVICES TO END USERS AND IMMEDIATE CUSTOMERS

Indicate the proportion of the typical immediate customer's and typical end user's total annual purchases accounted for by purchases of the types of products and services sold by this business. *(Check one box in each column)*

	END USERS	IMMEDIATE CUSTOMERS
. . . Less than 0.25%	☐	☐
. . . Between 0.25% and 1.0%	☐	☐
. . . Between 1% and 5%	☐	☐
. . . Between 5% and 25%	☐	☐
. . . Over 25%	☐	☐

(cont.)

EXHIBIT A-4 *(cont.)*

IMPORTANCE OF AUXILIARY SERVICES TO END USERS

Are installation, repair, customer education, and other product-related services provided to end users
... *(Check one)*

... Of relatively little or no importance?

... Of some importance?

... Of great importance?

RELIANCE ON PROFESSIONAL ADVISERS

In making buying decisions, do end users rely on outside advisers, such as physicians, architects, or
consulting engineers ... *(Check one)*

... Never?

... Occasionally?

... Usually or always?

DISTRIBUTION CHANNELS

Approximately what percentages of the sales of this business are made ...

PER CENT

... Direct to end users?

... To end users via company-owned retail or wholesale distribution facilities?

... To wholesalers?

... To retailers?

TOTAL = 100%

NOTE: Please enter a percentage for every one of the above lines even if the percentage is zero.

GROSS MARGINS — DISTRIBUTION CHANNELS

What is the approximate difference between the manufacturer's price and the selling price to end
users, expressed as a percentage of the selling price to end users? (Please estimate to the nearest 5
percentage points, e.g., 20%, 25%, etc. If all sales are made direct to end users, answer zero.)

PER CENT

VERTICAL INTEGRATION

Compare the degree of vertical integration of *this business* relative to its three largest competitors ...
Backward (toward raw materials) ... Forward (toward customer). *(Check one box in each column)*

DEGREE OF VERTICAL INTEGRATION
BACKWARD   FORWARD

... Less

... Same

... More

PRODUCTION PROCESS

What percentage of this business's sales were derived from ... (Accuracy within 10 percentage
points is adequate.)

Products manufactured singly or in small batches (production runs normally under 200)?

PER CENT

Products manufactured in large batches or in an assembly line?

PER CENT

Products manufactured using a continuous process?

PER CENT

Non-manufacturing activities? (Service and distribution businesses should enter 100% in this box.)

PER CENT

NOTE: Please enter a percentage for every one of the above lines even if the percentage is zero.　TOTAL = 100%

SUPPLY CONDITIONS

Of the total purchases this business makes from sources outside the corporation, what percentage are made from its three largest vendors?

PER CENT

What percentage of the sales of the three largest external vendors are made to this business?

PER CENT

PERCENTAGE OF EMPLOYEES UNIONIZED

Of the total employees in this business (managerial and non-managerial, salaried and hourly), what percentage are unionized? (If a significant number of the employees work for this business part time, the number of full-time-equivalent employees should be used in calculating this percentage.)

PER CENT

IV. FINANCIAL STATEMENT MEASURES

Our measures of many of the competitive position/strategy factors discussed in Chapter 3 are derived from financial statement information. This section gives more detailed definitions of the key financial measures. An important feature of all of the financial data is that the *amounts* reported by the business units are *disguised*. A business with sales of $10 million and a net profit of $1.5 million might, for example, disguise its actual figures by multiplying all of them by 0.2. The reported data would then show sales of $2 million and a net profit of $300,000. This system preserves all of the financial *ratios* for the business—ROS is 15% in both the actual and disguised versions of the financial statements.

Profit and Loss Statement

> *Net Sales.* Net sales are reported net of returns, allowances, and bad debts. Lease revenues and progress payments received in a year are included in sales revenue. *Temporary* price reductions are treated as promotional expenses (see below), but discounts and price concessions that continue for extended time periods are deducted from net sales.
>
> *Purchases.* Purchases include the costs of raw and semi-finished materials, components, sub-assemblies, supplies, packaging, fuels, and energy. Purchases made from other units of the same parent company are valued at (estimated) market prices. Not included in purchases are the costs of purchased services such as telephone & telegraph, advertising, royalties, etc.
>
> *Value Added.* Value Added equals Net Sales *minus* Purchases. It represents the market value of the services or functions performed by the business unit itself.
>
> *Profit-Adjusted Value Added.* As explained in Chapter 8, we use Value Added as a measure of vertical integration. For this purpose, an adjustment in actual value added is necessary. Actual value added includes pre-tax net profits. Consequently, if we relate ROI or ROS to actual value added, we automatically find a strong, positive relationship that has nothing to do with vertical integration *per se.* To remove this tautological relationship, we adjust value added as follows:

$$\text{Profit-Adjusted Value Added} = \frac{\text{Actual Value Added } \textit{minus} \text{ Net Profit } \textit{plus} \text{ Normal Profit}}{\text{Sales } \textit{minus} \text{ Net Profit } \textit{plus} \text{ Normal Profit}}$$

The "normal profit" which we substitute for a business unit's actual profit is simply the amount that the business would have earned in order to achieve the PIMS data base *average* rate of return on investment. As an approximation of the average, we used a 20% ROI to calculate "normal profits."

> *Manufacturing and Physical Distribution Expense.* For manufacturing businesses, includes all direct and indirect costs of production (assembly, processing, etc.), and physical distribution (freight, warehousing, etc.). Excludes depreciation expenses but includes royalty fees and the costs of product-related services such as installation. For non-manufacturing

businesses, "manufacturing" costs include direct and indirect costs of *operations,* e.g., transaction processing activities in a bank or store operations in a retail enterprise.

Gross Margin. Gross margin is equal to Value Added (actual, not adjusted) minus Manufacturing & Distribution and Depreciation expenses. Gross margin, defined in this way, is the amount available to cover discretionary expenses (R&D, Marketing, and General & Administrative Expenses) and pre-tax profits.

Research and Development Expenses. R&D expenses are reported separately for *Product* R&D and *Process* R&D. They do not include "basic" research, carried out at the corporate level, that is unrelated to the business unit's products or processes. Both company-funded and government-funded R&D are included.

Marketing Expenses. Separate figures are reported for:

- *Sales Force* includes compensation and expenses of salespeople, commissions paid to agents or brokers, and costs of sales force administration. When two or more business units share a sales force, the total cost is allocated among them.
- *Advertising Media* covers only the costs of media time and space (including advertising agency commissions).
- *Sales Promotion* includes costs of catalogs, exhibits, displays, premiums, samples, and revenue reductions associated with *temporary* price reductions.
- *Other Marketing Costs* covers all marketing outlays not included in sales force, media advertising, and sales promotion. Marketing administration and marketing research fall in this category.

Total marketing expense is the sum of the four sub-categories listed above.

Depreciation Expense includes depreciation allowances on tangible assets.

Other Expenses. This residual category includes business unit General & Administrative Expenses as well as allocated corporate or divisional overhead charges. It also includes depreciation on Goodwill, if any.

Pre-Tax Operating Income. Pre-tax operating income equals Sales minus Purchases and all operating expenses.

Balance Sheet Categories. All of a business unit's assets are reported at *book values* (but see the comments on Replacement Values, below). In cases where a unit was acquired at a price in excess of book value, the resulting goodwill is treated under "Other Assets." Plant and Equipment assets that are leased on a long-term basis are capitalized.

Accounts Receivable. Receivables are reported net of allowances for bad debts. The reported figure is the *average* balance during a year.

Inventories. Separate figures are reported for (1) Finished Goods and (2) Raw Materials, Components, & Work in Process. Each figure is an average balance for the year, net of any reserves for losses.

Plant and Equipment. Values of these assets are reported at original cost (Gross Book Value) and at current, depreciated value (Net Book Value).

Newness of Plant and Equipment. The ratio of Net Book Value of Plant & Equipment to its Gross Book Value.

Replacement Cost of Plant and Equipment. The estimated cost (as of the reporting year) of replacing the unit's Plant & Equipment. (The average ratio of Replacement/Book Value was 1.95, with a range from 0.75 to 4.00).

Cash and Other Assets includes the cash balance, if any, needed for normal operations. Other assets, as noted, include any net goodwill balance carried on the books.

Total Assets. The sum of Net Receivables, Inventories, Net Book Value of Plant & Equipment, and Cash & Other Assets.

Current Liabilities includes accounts payable, short-term borrowings, and other liabilities due within one year.

Investments equals Total Assets minus Current Liabilities. Equivalent to Equity plus Long Term Debt.

Capacity. "Standard Capacity" is the dollar value of the maximum output possible for the business unit under normal operating conditions, including hours or shifts of operation per day and days per week.

Capacity Utilization. The average rate of utilization during a year. The rate of utilization equals Net Sales plus or minus change in finished goods inventory, divided by Standard Capacity.

Inventory Valuation Method. Reported as LIFO (51% of the businesses), FIFO (26%) or Other (23%).

Sales and Value Added per Employee. These figures are reported in *non-disguised* dollars. The number of employees is calculated in terms of full-time equivalents. Adjusted Value Added per Employee, or Adjusted Productivity, is based on Profit-Adjusted Value Added as a measure of output (see p. 266).

V. MARKET AND COMPETITION

Information collected about each business unit's served market and competition is summarized in Exhibit A–5.

EXHIBIT A–5
Information About the Served Market and Competition

EXIT OF COMPETITORS

During the past 5 years, have any competitors with at least 5% market share dropped out of the served market?

NO ☐   YES ☐

MARKET SHARES

For each year, report the share of the *served* market accounted for by this business and by each of the three largest competing businesses. "Share of market" is defined as being the sales of a business as a percentage of the served market (defined on Line 301). Please report the market shares in prior years of the three competitors with the largest market shares in the most recent year.

THIS BUSINESS

SERVED MARKET

SIZE OF SERVED MARKET (D)

Indicate the total sales in the market actively served by this business. Your entry should be in current dollars (i.e., including price changes) and reflect the same disguise factor as on Line 201 (Net Sales).

Please note that whenever the largest value entered on Line 301 is less than four or more than five digits, all Form 2 and 3 data designated "(D)" will automatically be rescaled.

GEOGRAPHIC LOCATION OF SERVED MARKET

Was the served market for this business, as   primarily located in . . . *(Check one)*

Entire United States ☐   United Kingdom ☐

All of Canada ☐   Common Market ☐

U.S. and Canada ☐   Regional within Europe ☐

Regional within U.S. and/or Canada ☐   Other ☐

EXHIBIT A-5 (cont.)

NUMBER OF COMPETITORS

Relative to the last year of data being entered, approximately how many businesses were competing in the served market? Include this business in the total. Ignore competitors with less than 1% of the served market.

5 or fewer	6-10	11-20	21-50	51 or Higher
☐	☐	☐	☐	☐

ENTRY OF COMPETITORS

During the past 5 years, have any competitors with at least 5% market share entered the served market?

NO ☐   YES ☐

COMPARISON WITH COMPETITORS

The questions in this section deal with the quality, price and cost of the products and services offered by this business relative to the three major competitors referred to on Lines 307, 308 and 309. The standard of comparison in each question is the *average* of the three largest competitors, weighted by their sales volumes if their market shares are not approximately equal. *

RELATIVE PRODUCT QUALITY

For each year, estimate the percentage of this business's sales volume accounted for by products and services that *from the perspective of the customer* are assessed as "Superior," "Equivalent," and "Inferior" to those available from the three leading competitors. (**NOTE:** The sum of Lines 316-318 should be 100%.) In assessing quality, the customer's perception of both the intrinsic characteristics of the product or service and any associated services (delivery time, warranties, application assistance, etc.) should be taken into account where these are important in decisions to purchase. (Please see the *PIMS Data Manual* for a more detailed discussion of the procedure for estimating relative quality.)

RELATIVE PRICES (Weighted Average for Three Largest Competitors = 100%)

For each year, estimate the average level of selling prices of this business's products and services, relative to the average price of the three largest competitors. (Example: If this business's prices averaged 5% above those of leading competitors, report 105%.)

RELATIVE DIRECT COSTS PER UNIT (Weighted Average for Three Largest Competitors = 100%)

For each year, estimate the average level of this business's direct costs per unit of products and services, relative to the average level of the three largest competitors. Include costs of materials, production, and distribution, but *exclude* marketing and administrative costs.

RELATIVE HOURLY WAGE RATES (Weighted Average for Three Largest Competitors = 100%)

For each year, estimate the average level of hourly wage rates paid by this business relative to the average level paid by the three largest competitors, regardless of their locations. Include the cost of fringe benefits and pension plans in estimating this index.

RELATIVE SALARY LEVELS (Weighted Average for Three Largest Competitors = 100%)

For each year, estimate the average level of compensation paid to salaried workers by this business, relative to the average level paid by the three largest competitors, regardless of their locations. Include the cost of fringe benefits and pension plans in estimating this index.

NEW PRODUCTS, PERCENTAGE OF TOTAL SALES

For each year, estimate what percentage of the total sales was accounted for by products introduced during the 3 preceding years first for this business and then for the simple average of the three largest competitors. **NOTE:** For the

*Since 1985, SPI has collected data in the form of comparisons with *each* major competitor rather than the average of the Top 3.

distinction between new products and product-line extensions, please consult the *PIMS Data Manual*. (Example: for 1974, "New Products" should include those introduced in 1972, 1973 and 1974.)

RELATIVE BREADTH OF PRODUCT LINE

Relative to the weighted average of the product lines of the three largest competitors, estimate the breadth of the product line of this business.

... Narrower

... Same

... Broader

Estimate the breadth of this business's served market, relative to the weighted average of the three largest competitors.

	Narrower Than Competitors	Same As Competitors	Broader Than Competitors
... Types of Customers			
... Number of Customers			
... Size of Customers			

RELATIVE MARKETING EXPENDITURES

These questions call for comparisons of this business's level of marketing expenditures, expressed as percentages of sales, relative to the levels of its three largest competitors. In these questions "About the Same" is defined as within ± 1 percentage point; "Somewhat More or Less" means 1 to 3 percentage points more or less; "Much More or Less" means more than 3 points more or less. The percentages for the three largest competitors should be weighted by their sales volumes in calculating the average if their market shares are not approximately equal.

RELATIVE SALES-FORCE EXPENDITURES

Relative to the three largest competitors, did this business spend "About the Same" percentage of its sales on sales force effort? Or "Somewhat More" (or Less)? Or "Much More" (or Less)?

RELATIVE MEDIA-ADVERTISING EXPENDITURES

Relative to the three largest competitors, did this business spend "About the Same" percentage of its sales on media advertising? Or "Somewhat More" (or Less)? Or "Much More" (or Less)?

RELATIVE SALES-PROMOTION EXPENDITURES

Relative to the three largest competitors, did this business spend "About the Same" percentage of its sales on sales promotion efforts? Or "Somewhat More" (or Less)? Or "Much More" (or Less)?

RELATIVE QUALITY OF CUSTOMER SERVICES

Customer services are the supporting services which accompany the primary products or services. Was the quality of the customer services this business provided to *end users* "About the Same," "Somewhat Better" (or Worse) or "Much Better" (or Worse) than that provided by the three largest competitors?

RELATIVE PRODUCT IMAGE/COMPANY REPUTATION

Were *end users'* perceptions of product image and company reputation (for quality, dependability, etc.) for this business "About the Same," "Somewhat Better" (or Worse) or "Much Better" (or Worse) than their perceptions of the image/reputation of the three largest competitors?

VI. THE PIMS SATELLITE DATA BASES

In addition to the core PIMS Competitive Strategy Data Base that contains about 3,000 SBUs, SPI is developing several growing satellite data bases that focus on specific application topics:

- PIMS *Start-up Business* data base—200 SBUs
  (This data base is used to analyze strategies of new ventures.)
- PIMS *Portfolio* data base—60 portfolios
  (This data base is used to study the effects of synergy.)
- PIMS *Quality/Differentiation* data base—200 SBUs
  (This data base contains detailed information on attributes, importance weights, and performance ratings. It is used to help managers determine how to improve perceived quality and market differentiation, and to study the differences between management's opinions of customer perceptions and actual customer perceptions.)
- PIMS *OASIS* data base—60 SBUs
  (This data base was developed jointly with Hay Associates and the University of Michigan to study the links between *human resource* issues, competitive strategy, and business performance. OASIS stands for Organization And Strategy Information Service.)

Appendix B ———————————————

Statistical Methods

The statistical method used to determine how market conditions and strategies affect business performance is that of multiple regression analysis. This appendix presents detailed results of the multiple regression models on which the material discussed in this book is based. A series of models is described: one derived from the entire PIMS data base, including businesses of all kinds, and others which were developed for purposes of comparing specific categories of businesses. The latter include:

- Consumer Product Manufacturers versus Industrial Product Manufacturers versus Service and Distribution Businesses (for discussion, see Chapter 2)
- Businesses located in different regions of the world (see Chapter 2)
- Market leaders versus followers (see Chapter 9)
- Businesses participating in markets at various stages of evolution (see Chapter 10)

Exhibit B-8 lists some of the profit-influencing factors that are included in the Strategic Planning Institute's "PAR ROI" model, in addition to those that we have used in the simplified model described in Exhibits B-1, B-2, and B-3. As noted in Chapter 3, the PAR model includes several "interactive" terms that represent contingent relationships between strategic or market factors and profitability. One such factor is an interaction between Fixed Capital Intensity and

EXHIBIT B-1
Multiple Regression Equations for ROI and ROS
(Entire PIMS Data Base)

Profit Influences	Impact on:	
	ROI	ROS
Real Market Growth Rate	.18	.04
Rate of Price Inflation	.22	.08
Purchase Concentration	.02**	N.S.
% Unionization	−.07	−.03
Low Purchase Amount:		
—Low Importance	6.06	1.63
—High Importance	5.42	2.10
High Purchase Amount:		
—Low Importance	−6.96	−2.58
—High Importance	−3.84	−1.11**
Exports-Imports, %	.06**	.05
Customized Products	−2.44	−1.77
Market Share	.34	.14
Relative Quality	.11	.05
% New Products	−.12	−.05
Marketing, % of Sales	−.52	−.32
R&D, % of Sales	−.36	−.22
Inventory, % of Sales	−.49	−.09
Fixed Capital Intensity	−.55	−.10
Plant Newness	.07	.05
Capacity Utilization, %	.31	.10
Employee Productivity	.13	.06
Vertical Integration	.26	.18
FIFO Inventory Valuation	1.30*	.62
R^2	.39	.31
F	58.3	45.1
Number of Cases	2,314	2,314

NOTE: All coefficients, except those starred, are significant ($p < .01$).
  *Significance level between .01 and .05.
**Significance level between .05 and .10.

Capacity Utilization; it reflects the fact that profits are most sensitive to the rate of utilization in highly capital-intense businesses.

MEASURING RELATIVE MARKET SHARE

Which measure of relative share is best for calibrating competitive advantage? Among the possibilities are:

- market share rank
- share relative to single largest competitor
- share relative to three largest competitors

As shown in Exhibit 5-8, share relative to largest competitor is more precise than share rank. Businesses that are about 2, 4, or 8 times as large as their largest competitor all rank number 1, but their ROI performance differs significantly.

An even better measure of relative share is share relative to three leading competitors. It captures the scale and bargaining effects associated with a business's relative size in its served market in a more comprehensive way.

EXHIBIT B-2

Means, Ranges, and Standard Deviations of Key Profit Influences

Profit Influences	Mean	Standard Deviation	Minimum	Maximum
Real Market Growth Rate	3.62	10.98	−20	40
Rate of Price Inflation	8.02	6.17	−5	30
Purchase Concentration	42.39	26.65	5	100
% Unionization	42.22	33.57	0	100
Low Purchase Amount:				
—Low Importance	.08*	.28	0	1
—High Importance	.06*	.23	0	1
High Purchase Amount:				
—Low Importance	.03*	.17	0	1
—High Importance	.07*	.25	0	1
Exports-Imports, %	2.60	8.51	−25	35
Customized Products	.22*	.41	0	1
Market Share	23.82	18.17	1	75
Relative Quality	25.18	28.13	−25	85
% New Products	8.34	14.63	0	70
Marketing, % of Sales	9.22	7.01	1	40
R&D, % of Sales	2.05	2.50	0	12
Inventory, % of Sales	19.77	11.48	2	55
Fixed Capital Intensity	18.19	15.62	4	110
Plant Newness	54.33	15.12	20	90
Capacity Utilization, %	75.70	16.00	40	110
Employee Productivity	36.65	24.77	10	160
Vertical Integration	55.42	15.79	10	92
FIFO Inventory Valuation	.52*	.50	0	1

*Dummy variables. Mean values represent fraction of businesses falling into each group. For example, 22/100 of the businesses produce customized products or services.

EXHIBIT B-3
Correlation Matrix for Major Profit Influences
(Entire PIMS Data Base)

	ROI	ROS	Grow	Infl	Pur Con	Union	LPA/ LPI	LPA/ HPI	HPA/ LPI	HPA/ HPI	Ex- Im	Custom	Mkt Shr	Qual	% New	Mktg	R&D	Invty	FCI	PN	Cap Util	Prody	Vert Int	FIFO
ROI	1.00																							
ROS	.85	1.00																						
Grow	.07	.06	1.00																					
Infl	.04	.05	-.28	1.00																				
Pur Con	.03	-.01	.01	-.03	1.00																			
Union	-.13	-.12	-.10	.11	.00	1.00																		
LPA/LPI	.09	.03	.00	-.05	.06	-.03	1.00																	
LPA/HPI	.03	.02	-.07	-.02	.06	-.06	.00	1.00																
HPA/LPI	-.03	-.02	-.02	.01	-.02	.02	.00	.00	1.00															
HPA/HPI	-.05	-.02	.04	.07	-.02	.02	-.05	-.07	.16	1.00														
Ex-Im	.03	-.07	.08	.03	-.02	-.09	-.09	-.07	.04	.05	1.00													
Custom	-.02	-.05	-.01	.05	.01	-.05	.04	-.01	.08	.07	.03	1.00												
Mkt Shr	.38	.37	.08	.04	-.04	.01	-.01	-.07	.08	-.01	.06	-.04	1.00											
Qual	.27	.25	.07	-.06	-.04	-.15	.00	.01	.16	-.06	.01	.04	.30	1.00										
% New	-.10	-.12	.22	-.13	-.03	-.19	.30	.04	-.02	-.05	.08	-.04	-.06	.09	1.00									
Mktg	-.06	-.11	.08	-.15	-.03	-.15	-.06	-.08	-.03	-.18	.04	-.16	-.03	.04	.21	1.00								
R&D	-.10	-.04	.16	-.12	-.11	.04	-.03	.03	.03	.04	.22	.06	.10	.03	.33	.18	1.00							
Invty	-.30	-.17	-.01	-.02	-.06	.04	-.10	-.06	-.02	.00	.09	-.03	-.11	-.05	.10	.16	.31	1.00						
FCI	-.20	.03	.06	.05	-.02	-.14	-.03	.01	.02	.10	.00	-.03	-.04	-.06	-.08	-.20	.02	-.10	1.00					
PN	-.05	.02	.15	-.01	-.06	.05	-.01	-.02	.02	-.02	.05	-.02	-.05	.10	.12	.13	.03	-.04	.30	1.00				
Cap Ut	.17	.19	.07	.09	-.06	-.05	-.02	-.07	.02	.10	-.02	-.01	.06	.05	-.07	-.22	-.11	-.11	.33	.00	1.00			
Prody	.14	.14	.01	.04	.11	-.09	.07	-.06	.10	.08	.05	-.13	.07	-.01	-.08	.12	.01	-.10	.03	.04	.00	1.00		
Vert Int	.01	.16	.08	-.13	-.13	-.09	.01	.00	.00	-.06	.11	.07	.13	-.08	.10	.30	.35	.19	.24	.01	-.04	-.10	1.00	
FIFO	-.01	.01	-.02	-.01	.01	-.06	.03	.01	.01	-.02	-.04	-.06	.01	.00	-.03	.05	-.01	.10	.00	.06	-.05	-.04	.00	1.00

EXHIBIT B–4
Multiple Regression Equations for ROI
(By Type of Business)

Profit Influences	Consumer Product Mfrs.	Industrial Product Mfrs.	Service & Distribution
Real Market Growth Rate	.21	.12	.31
Rate of Price Inflation	.33	.21	N.S.
Purchase Concentration	.08	N.S.	N.S.
% Unionization	−.09	−.09	N.S.
Low Purchase Amount:			
—Low Importance	3.95	8.31	N.S.
—High Importance	N.S.	8.90	N.S.
High Purchase Amount:			
—Low Importance	N.S.	−6.94	N.S.
—High Importance	N.S.	−2.75**	−12.64**
Exports-Imports, %	N.S.	.09	N.S.
Customized Products/Services	N.S.	−2.48	−11.97**
Market Share	.52	.24	.43
Relative Quality	.05	.13	.25
% New Products	−.08	−.10	N.S.
Marketing, % of Sales	−.55	−.44	−1.17
R&D, % of Sales	N.S.	−.68	7.14
Inventory, % of Sales	−.39	−.55	N.S.
Fixed Capital Intensity	−.81	−.49	−.48
Plant Newness	.22	N.S.	N.S.
Capacity Utilization, %	.40	.27	.57
Employee Productivity	.10	.15	.14*
Vertical Integration	.24	.26	.15**
FIFO Inventory Valuation	2.69	N.S.	N.S.
R^2	.44	.39	.52
F	21.8	44.0	5.71
Number of Cases	649	1,523	139

N.S. = Relationship with ROI not statistically significant.
NOTE: All coefficients, except those starred, are significant (p 0.01).
   *Significance level between .01 and .05.
**Significance level between .05 and .10.

The common effect on ROI of share-relative-to-single-largest competitor and share-relative-to-three-largest competitors is seen along the diagonal in Exhibit B–9. When these two measures of share yield different competitive positions (the off-diagonal cells), the share-relative-to-three-largest competitors shows a strong, positive, systematic pattern with ROI.

We have used market share rank to show the general differences between share-leaders and their small-share competitors. We have

EXHIBIT B–5
Multiple Regression Equations for ROI
(By Market Location)

Profit Influences	Market Location	
	N. America	Other Countries
Real Market Growth Rate	.11	.36
Rate of Price Inflation	.24	N.S.
Purchase Concentration	N.S.	.06*
% Unionization	−.07	−.10
Low Purchase Amount:		
—Low Importance	3.94	N.S.
—High Importance	6.18	N.S.
High Purchase Amount:		
—Low Importance	−5.94	N.S.
—High Importance	−3.64	N.S.
Exports-Imports, %	.15	−.27
Customized Products	−4.01	−5.55
Market Share	.30	.26
Relative Quality	.10	.19
% New Products/Services	−.09	−.17*
Marketing, % of Sales	−.61	−.42
R&D, % of Sales	−.55	N.S.
Inventory, % of Sales	−.49	−.53
Fixed Capital Intensity	−.54	−.61
Plant Newness	.04**	.17
Capacity Utilization, %	.31	.28
Employee Productivity	.15	N.S.
Vertical Integration	.29	.24
FIFO Inventory Valuation	1.76	N.S.
R^2	.39	.44
F	53.9	13.6
Number of Cases	1,902	412

NOTE: All coefficients, except those starred, are significant ($p\ 0.01$).
  *Significance level between .01 and .05.
**Significance level between .05 and .10.

used share-relative-to-largest-competitor to test BCG's relative cost
ratios inferred from cumulative volume curves. In a case analysis
analyzing an individual business in its competitive environment, we
use the full knowledge of where the business stands with respect to
its leading competitors as a group and individually. And we calibrate
the share/profitability relationship to reflect whether the business is
marketing intensive or manufacturing intensive, whether investment
to sales is high or low, and whether market shares are stable or unstable.

EXHIBIT B-6
Regression Equations for ROI, by Stage of Market Evolution

Product Influences	Growth, Growth Maturity	Stable Maturity	Decline Maturity, Decline
Real Market Growth Rate	.10*	N.S.	.24*
Rate of Price Inflation	.32	N.S.	.24*
Purchase Concentration	.03**	N.S.	N.S.
% Unionization	−.06	−.09	−.09
Low Purchase Amount:			
—Low Importance	N.S.	6.77	10.66
—High Importance	6.60	5.74	N.S.
High Purchase Amount:			
—Low Importance	−6.76*	N.S.	−12.49
—High Importance	N.S.	N.S.	−8.57
Exports-Imports, %	N.S.	.21	N.S.
Customized Products	−4.22	−3.08*	3.45*
Market Share	.30	.39	.18
Relative Quality	.12	.10	.09
% New Products/Services	−.10	−.11*	N.S.
Marketing, % of Sales	−.56	−.48	−.57
R&D, % of Sales	−.49*	−.74	.89*
Inventory, % of Sales	−.48	−.46	−.59
Fixed Capital Intensity	−.55	−.54	−.53
Plant Newness	.06**	N.S.	.19*
Capacity Utilization, %	.33	.27	.33
Employee Productivity	.12	.09	.23
Vertical Integration	.22	.30	.30
FIFO Inventory Valuation	1.47**	N.S.	2.58**
R^2	.42	.39	.40
F	32.0	23.3	12.8
Number of Cases	1,016	830	451

NOTE: All coefficients, except those starred, are significant (p 0.01).
*Significance level between .01 and .05.
**Significance level between .05 and .10.

CONTROLLING FOR A THIRD FACTOR

In a recent study, Robert Jacobson and David Aaker suggested that the observed correlation between share and profitability might be due to a third factor rather than to a direct effect of market share. But then, to control for such third factors, they included past profitability as a factor to explain current profitability! In effect they were relating *change* in ROI to market share level.

The differences among (1) relating ROI to share, (2) relating

EXHIBIT B–7
Multiple Regression Equations for ROI
(Market Leaders vs. Followers)

Profit Influences	Market Leaders	Market Followers
Real Market Growth Rate	N.S.	.17
Rate of Price Inflation	N.S.	.26
Purchase Concentration	N.S.	.04*
% Unionization	−.08	−.07
Low Purchase Amount:		
—Low Importance	8.44	4.23*
—High Importance	6.68	4.68*
High Purchase Amount:		
—Low Importance	N.S.	−9.83
—High Importance	−6.26	−2.53**
Exports-Imports, %	N.S.	.09**
Customized Products	−3.07*	−1.79**
Market Share	.28	.36
Relative Quality	.12	.10
% New Products/Services	N.S.	−.15
Marketing, % of Sales	−.42	−.55
R&D, % of Sales	N.S.	−.44*
Inventory, % of Sales	−.65	−.40
Fixed Capital Intensity	−.68	−.50
Plant Newness	.10	.07*
Capacity Utilization, %	.39	.29
Employee Productivity	.19	.08
Vertical Integration	.28	.23
FIFO Inventory Valuation	1.83**	N.S.
R^2	.41	.29
F	26.6	26.2
Number of Cases	877	1,437

NOTE: All coefficients, except those starred, are significant (p 0.01).
 *Significance level between .01 and .05.
**Significance level between .05 and .10.

change-in-ROI to share, and (3) relating ROI to share and lagged ROI can be seen in the three equations shown in Exhibit B–10.

In relating ROI to market share alone (equation 1) we find a 5.3 point ROI differential per 10 points of market share. This is the overall average steady-state relationship for all businesses.

In relating *change*-in-ROI to market share (equation 2) we find a 0.3 point ROI differential per 10 points of market share. This relationship is essentially zero, which is what we would expect since large-share businesses do not continuously build their ROI differ-

EXHIBIT B–8

Additional Profit-Influencing Factors, and Factors with Contingent
Effects, Included in SPI's "Par ROI" Model

Factor	Impact on ROI	Impact Contingent On:
Industry Long-Term Growth Rate	+	% Unionization
Industry Concentration Ratio	+	
Market Share	+	% Unionization, Investment Intensity
Market Share Growth Rate	+	
Market Share Instability	−	Vertical Integration
Relative Quality	+	Market Growth Rate
Relative Price	−	Marketing/Sales (%)
Relative Compensation	+	Employee Productivity
% New Products	−	Investment Intensity
Vertical Integration	+	Market Growth Rate
Relative Vertical Integration	+	
Fixed Capital Intensity	−	Capacity Utilization
Newness of Plant & Equip.	+	R&D/Sales (%)
R&D/Sales	−	Industry Long-Term Growth Rate

ential over small-share businesses. It *doesn't* mean that ROI is not
related to market share. It merely means that *change*-in-ROI is not
related to market share and that the differential between large- and
small-share businesses is stable over time.

In relating ROI to market share and lagged ROI (equation 3, the
approach of Jacobson and Aaker) we find a 1.5 point ROI differential per 10 points of market share. Jacobson and Aaker interpret
1.5 points of ROI per 10 points of share as a better estimate of the
direct causal effect of share on ROI than the 5.3 points of ROI per
10 points of share found in equation 1.

But their interpretation is wrong. Using Jacobson and Aaker's
methodology and interpretation you would conclude that weight is
not related to height, as suggested in Chapter 5. As our comparison
of the three equations shows, by including lagged ROI one really
comes much closer to estimating the change-in-ROI/share relationship rather than the steady-state ROI/share relationship.

The general profit differential between businesses with a market
share of 20 and businesses with a market share of 30 is about 5 points
of ROI, not 1.5 points. If a business moves from a market share of

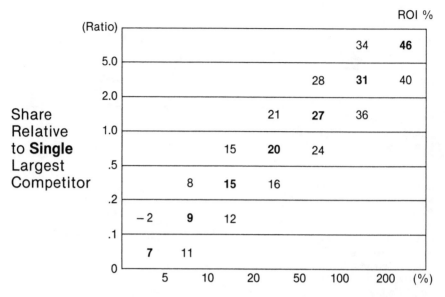

Answer: → Share relative to **3** largest competitors

EXHIBIT B-9
Which Measure of Relative Share Is Best for Calibrating Competitive Advantage?

20 to a new steady-state (after the transition costs have settled down) market share of 30 (with other profit-influencing factors changing in an "average" way) in general, we would expect its ROI to increase by about 5 points.

We have seen that including lagged ROI to control for third factors that might affect both ROI and share is a good way to obscure the relationship between ROI and share, and therefore not a good way to control for third factors.

How then should one control for third factors? By including in the ROI model any key profit drivers that are related to both share

EXHIBIT B-10
Alternate Approaches to Modeling the Market Share-ROI Relationship

(1) $ROI_t - 0.00\ ROI_{t-1}$ = Constant + 0.53 (Market Share)
(2) $ROI_t - 1.00\ ROI_{t-1}$ = Constant + 0.03 (Market Share)
(3) $ROI_t - 0.74\ ROI_{t-1}$ = Constant + 0.15 (Market Share)

and profitability. One key third factor is relative quality, which is positively related to both ROI and share.

When we relate ROI to market share and relative quality, we find a 4.7 point ROI differential per 10 points of market share. This is a better measure of the direct causal effect of market share on ROI than the 5.3 point differential that is estimated when quality is left out of the ROI model.

The general profit differential of 4.7 points of ROI per 10 points of market share is merely an overall average. Customized estimates of profit differentials (among a business and its key competitors or between a business's current and planned market share position) can be calibrated much more accurately for an individual business. This customization procedure takes into account the business's R&D and marketing cost versus manufacturing cost mix, its investment intensity, its share instability, and other business-unit specific characteristics.

SPI's Par ROI model is used together with an analysis of look-alike businesses for:

1. assessing an SBU's strategic position
2. reality-testing SBU plans
3. quantifying the profit payoff from improving quality or changing market share
4. assessing competitors
5. evaluating acquisition candidates

The findings shown here merely illustrate overall average relationships.

Procedures used to calibrate the parameters of SPI's current Par ROI model were designed to:

- prevent financial factors from distorting the effects of non-financial factors
- minimize distortions that might be caused by measurement errors
- build in contingent relationships that capture the differential effects of some factors on profitability, depending on whether the SBU
  —competes in a rapid-growth or slow-growth market
  —is capital-intensive or not capital-intensive
  —is unionized or not unionized

    —is vertically integrated or not vertically integrated
    —is high-tech or low-tech
    —operates at a high or low level of capacity utilization
    —is marketing-intensive or not marketing-intensive
- make each individual term in the equation comprehensible by minimizing the chance of multicollinearity.

In order to be included in the model, each term had to meet the following criteria:

- consistent with economic theory or business judgment
- statistically significant

These criteria were applied not only to the linear effects of each variable but also to non-linear effects and interaction effects that capture *contingent* relationships. (This is in contrast to many analyses where the researcher splits the overall sample into subgroups to test whether the effects of any variables differ from one subgroup to the next without having any hypotheses, or guiding theory, as to which variables will have a stronger effect in which subgroup.)

Notes and References

Chapter 1. Are There Any General Strategy Principles?

1. See Richard Hamermesh, *Making Strategy Work* (New York: John Wiley & Sons, 1986), for a brief overview of portfolio planning.
2. Richard A. Bettis and William K. Hall, "Strategic Portfolio Management in the Multibusiness Firm," *California Management Review,* XXIV (Fall 1981), pp. 23–38. (Italics added.)
3. Phillipe Haspeslagh, "Portfolio Planning: Uses and Limits," *Harvard Business Review,* January–February 1982, pp. 58–73.
4. Kenneth Andrews, "Corporate Strategy: The Essential Intangibles," *McKinsey Quarterly,* Autumn 1984, p. 43.
5. See "The New Breed of Strategic Planner," *Business Week,* September 17, 1984, pp. 62–68; and Walter Kiechel III, "Corporate Strategists Under Fire," *Fortune,* December 27, 1982, pp. 34–39.
6. Michael Lubatkin and Michael Pitts, "The PIMS and the Policy Perspective: A Rebuttal," *Journal of Business Strategy,* Summer 1985, pp. 88–92.
7. The earliest publications of PIMS results were Sidney Schoeffler, Robert D. Buzzell, and Donald F. Heany, "Impact of Strategic Planning on Profit Performance," *Harvard Business Review,* March–April 1974, pp. 137–45; and Robert D. Buzzell, Bradley T. Gale, and Ralph Sultan, "Market Share—A Key to Profitability," *Harvard Business Review,* January–February 1975, pp. 97–106.
8. The "spurious correlation" argument is used by Robert Jacobson and David A. Aaker in "Is Market Share All It's Cracked Up To Be?,"

Journal of Marketing, Vol. 49 (Fall, 1985), pp. 11–22. We explore this and other criticisms of the market share–profitability relationship in our working paper, "Does Market Share Still Matter?" Strategic Planning Institute (Cambridge, MA, 1986).

9. See Donald C. Hambrick and Ian C. MacMillan, "The Product Portfolio and Man's Best Friend," *California Management Review,* Vol. 25 (1982), pp. 84–95, and Bradley T. Gale and Ben Branch, "Cash Flow Analysis: More Important Than Ever," *Harvard Business Review,* July–August 1981, pp. 131–36.

Chapter 2. Linking Strategies to Performance

1. For discussions of the meaning of strategy, see Kenneth R. Andrews, *The Concept of Corporate Strategy* (Homewood, IL: Dow Jones–Irwin, 1971), Chapter 2; Bruce D. Henderson, *Henderson on Corporate Strategy* (Cambridge, MA: Abt Associates, 1979), pp. 3–44; and H. Igor Ansoff, *Corporate Strategy* (New York: McGraw-Hill, 1965).

2. Alfred D. Chandler, Jr., *Strategy and Structure* (Cambridge, MA: MIT Press, 1962).

3. William K. Hall, "SBUs: Hot New Topic in the Management of Diversification," *Business Horizons,* February 1978, pp. 17–25.

4. The Norton Company's approach to strategic planning, as of 1976, is described in Francis J. Aguilar's "Norton Company: Strategic Planning for Diversified Operations," Harvard Business School Case Services No. 9-377-044 (1976). Subsequent developments are described in Aguilar's "Norton Company: The Evolution of Strategic Management," HBS Case Services No. 9-384-024 (1984).

5. For a discussion of corporate culture, see Edgar H. Schein, *Organizational Culture and Leadership* (San Francisco: Jossey-Bass, 1985).

6. A bibliography compiled by the LB Research Program in February 1985 listed 26 published articles and 50 working papers based on LB data.

7. The use of ROI as a measure of divisional performance is discussed in Alfred Rappaport and Eugene M. Lerner, *Segment Reporting for Managers and Investors,* National Association of Accountants (New York: 1972); Richard F. Vancil, *Decentralization: Managerial Ambiguity by Design,* Financial Executives' Research Foundation (Homewood, IL: Dow Jones–Irwin, 1978). See also James S. Reece and William R. Cool, "Measuring Investment Center Performance," *Harvard Business Review,* May–June 1978, pp. 28–35.

8. See Robert Hayes and William F. Abernathy, "Managing Our Way to Economic Decline," *Harvard Business Review,* January–February 1979, pp. 133 ff. The connection between management performance measure-

ment and institutional investment practices is discussed by Richard R. Ellsworth, "Capital Markets and Competitive Decline," *Harvard Business Review,* September–October 1985, pp. 171–83.

9. The figures are taken from the *Forbes* magazine "37th Annual Report on American Industry," January 14, 1985. The ROE figures are after-tax.

Chapter 3. Learning from Experience: The PIMS Approach

1. Thomas Peters and Nancy Austin, *A Passion for Excellence* (New York: Random House, 1985), p. 53.

2. An account of General Electric's early experience with quantitative strategic planning models is given by C.H. Springer, "Strategic Management in General Electric," *Operations Research,* November–December 1973, pp. 1177–82.

3. See Sidney Schoeffler, Robert D. Buzzell, and Donald F. Heany, "Impact of Strategic Planning on Profit Performance," *Harvard Business Review,* March–April 1974, pp. 137–45.

4. A case study on Norton's strategic planning approach is cited in Note 4 to Chapter 1.

5. Comments on Hewlett-Packard appear in "Hewlett Bets the Store on Spectrum," *New York Times,* November 17, 1985, Section 3, p. 1 ff. 3M is discussed in "3M's Search for Strategic Identity," *Industrial Marketing,* February 1983, pp. 80 ff.

6. "How GE Bobbled the Factory of the Future," *Fortune,* Nov. 11, 1985, pp. 52–63.

7. The total number of businesses in the data base (as of August 1986) was around 2,900. Of these, 2,600 covered at least 4 years.

8. George J. Benston, "The Validity of Profits-Structure Studies with Particular Reference to the FTC's Line of Business Data," *American Economic Review,* Vol. 75 (March 1985), pp. 37–67. Benston questions the use of *any* accounting data, including corporate-level figures, for economic analysis.

9. William F. Long, "Impact of Alternative Allocation Procedures on Econometric Studies of Structure and Performance," Working Paper, Federal Trade Commission, July 1981.

10. See, for example, "Marketing: The New Priority," *Business Week,* November 21, 1983, p. 66.

11. Lynn W. Phillips, Dae Chang, and Robert D. Buzzell, "Product Quality, Cost Position, and Business Performance: A Test of Some Key Hypotheses," *Journal of Marketing,* Vol. 47 (Spring 1983), pp. 26–43.

12. John E. Prescott, "Competitive Environments, Generic Strategies, and Performance," Working Paper, University of Pittsburgh, 1984.

13. Alex Miller, John Guiniven, and Bill Camp, "Keys to Success for Adolescent Businesses," PIMSLETTER No. 35 (Cambridge, MA: Strategic Planning Institute, 1985).

14. Alex Miller, "An Empirical Typology of Technologies and Related Strategies," Working Paper, Virginia Polytechnic Institute, 1983.

Chapter 4.   Picking Profitable Markets

1. Thomas Peters and Robert Waterman, *In Search of Excellence: Lessons from America's Best-Run Companies* (New York: Harper & Row, 1982).

2. Bureau of Economics, Federal Trade Commission, *Statistical Reports* of the Annual Line of Business Program, 1974–77 (Washington: 1980, 1981, 1982, and 1985).

3. The term "strategic groups" is often used to describe sets of competitors within an industry that follow distinctly different strategies. Usually one group is significantly more profitable than the others. Examples include: producers of branded pharmaceuticals vs. generic producers and full-service department stores vs. discount department stores. For further discussion see Michael E. Porter, *Competitive Strategy: Techniques for Analyzing Industries and Competitors* (New York: The Free Press, 1980), Chapter 7.

4. The Life Cycle model of evolution has been a prominent feature of marketing textbooks since the 1960s. It was adopted by strategy consultants in the 1970s as one approach to evaluating the "attractiveness" of a business. There has been continuing debate over the years about the value of the life cycle concept. The debate has been confused by the question of whether life cycles apply to broad product categories (e.g., all cigarettes), to sub-categories (low-tar cigarettes), or individual products (Vantage brand cigarettes). For a recent survey of the topic, see the Special Section on Product Life Cycles in the *Journal of Marketing,* Vol. 45 (Fall 1981).

5. The PIMS measure of product age refers to the overall product *category,* based on current technology. For example, a producer of tufted carpeting would indicate that this type of carpeting was first produced and sold in the early 1950s, when modern tufting equipment was developed, not "in ancient times," when handmade carpets were first produced. An analysis of the PIMS businesses based on product age is reported in Hans B. Thorelli and Stephen C. Burnett, "The Nature of Product Life Cycles for Industrial Goods Businesses," *Journal of Marketing,* Vol. 45 (Fall 1981), pp. 97–108.

6. David J. Ravenscraft, 'Structure-Profit Relationships at the Line of Business Level," *The Review of Economics and Statistics,* Vol. 65 (February 1983), pp. 22–31. Ravenscraft's analysis relates operating profit as a percentage of *sales* to 23 factors. He also reports that a supplementary analysis using return on *assets* showed growth to have a significant positive impact.

7. The inflation adjustment procedure was developed by Mark J. Chussil. See "Inflation and ROI," PIMSLETTER No. 22 (Cambridge, MA: Strategic Planning Institute, 1980).

8. Procurement and supplier relations in the Japanese automobile industry are discussed in Michael A. Cusumano, *The Japanese Automobile Industry* (Cambridge, MA: Harvard University Press, 1985), pp. 241-61.

9. Same reference as Note 6, above.

Chapter 5. Market Position and Profitability

1. See Appendix B for a comparison of these two measures of relative market share.

2. David J. Ravenscraft, "Structure-Profit Relationships At The Line of Business and Industry Level," *Review of Economics and Statistics,* February 1983, pp. 22–31.

3. This general argument has been made in numerous books, articles and speeches dealing with antitrust economics; see, for example, Joe S. Bain, *Industrial Organization,* 2nd edition (New York: John Wiley & Sons, 1968), especially Chapter 6.

4. Boston Consulting Group, "The Experience Curve—Reviewed," *Perspectives* No. 135 (Boston: 1973).

5. Boston Consulting Group, "The Experience Curve Revisited," *Perspective* No. 229 (Boston: 1978).

6. "Unless You Can Be A Winner, Don't Play," *Forbes,* October 15, 1977.

7. Michael E. Porter, "Experience Curve," *The Wall Street Journal,* October 22, 1979.

8. Walter Kiechel III, "The Decline of the Experience Curve," *Fortune,* October 5, 1981.

9. Bruce D. Henderson, "Cross-Sectional Experience Curves," *Perspective* 208, The Boston Consulting Group, 1978.

10. Lynn W. Phillips, Dae Chang, and Robert D. Buzzell, "Product Quality, Cost Position, and Business Performance: A Test of Some Key Hypotheses," Harvard Business School Working Paper #83–13 (1982) and *Journal of Marketing,* Vol. 47 (Spring 1983) pp. 26–43.

11. Tom Peters' quoted passage summarizes key points from a Brad Gale speech on "Quality As A Strategic Weapon: Getting Closer to the Customer Than Your Competitors." Tom Peters and Brad Gale helped to kick off Milliken's fourth annual planning conference on quality at Pine Isle, Georgia on a Saturday morning in February, 1984. Whereas *In Search of Excellence* (1982) had only one chapter on quality, *A Passion For Excellence* (1985) by Tom Peters and Nancy Austin has five chapters on quality.

12. For the nonmanufacturing businesses in the PIMS sample, "manufacturing" was defined as the primary value-creating activity of the business. For example, processing transactions is the equivalent of manufacturing in a bank.

13. Richard G. Hamermesh, M. J. Anderson, Jr., and J. E. Harris, "Strategies for Low Market Share Businesses," *Harvard Business Review,* May–June 1978, pp. 95–102.

14. Carolyn Y. Woo and Arnold C. Cooper, "The Surprising Case for Low Market Share," *Harvard Business Review,* November–December 1982, pp. 106–13. In a sequel to this study, Woo compared the strategies of 41 market leaders with poor profitability and 71 high-profit leaders. See "Market-Share Leadership—Not Always So Good," *Harvard Business Review,* January–February 1984, pp. 2–4.

15. Michael E. Porter, *Competitive Strategy* (New York: The Free Press, 1980), pp. 42–43. Porter's U-shaped curve was reproduced in *Fortune* with the caption "Means to the Ends."

16. See "We Are The Target," *Forbes,* April 7, 1986, pp. 54.

17. Lynn W. Phillips, Dae R. Chang, and Robert D. Buzzell, "Product Quality, Cost Position, and Business Performance: A Test of Some Key Hypotheses," *Journal of Marketing,* Vol. 47 (Spring 1983), pp. 26–43.

18. See FTC study cited in footnote 2. For an earlier study that also measured share in relation to industry data and also found a significant *positive* relation between share and profitability see Bradley T. Gale, "Market Share and Rate of Return," *The Review of Economics and Statistics,* November 1972, pp. 412–423.

19. For an in-depth treatment of this topic, see Bradley T. Gale and Ben S. Branch, "Concentration vs. Market Share: Which Determines Performance and Why Does It Matter," *The Antitrust Bulletin,* Spring, 1982.

20. For the full load, see Richard E. Caves, Bradley T. Gale, and Michael E. Porter, "Interfirm Profitability Differences: Comment," *Quarterly Journal of Economics,* November, 1977 and Bradley T. Gale, "The Existence and Direction of Causality in Cross-Section Analysis of Hypotheses: A Paper in Research Strategy," *Proceedings of the American Statistical Association,* 1972.

21. Robert Jacobsen and David A. Aaker, "Is Market Share All That It's Cracked Up to Be?" *Journal of Marketing,* Vol. 49 (Fall 1985).

22. For a more technical discussion of the Jacobsen and Aaker study, see Appendix B.

23. *General Electric Monogram,* September–October 1981.

Chapter 6. Quality Is King

1. See Philippe Cattin & Dick R. Wittink, "Commercial Use of Conjoint Analysis: A Survey," *Journal of Marketing,* Summer 1982, pp. 44–53. David B. Montgomery, "Conjoint Calibration of the Customer/Competitor Interface in Industrial Markets," Marketing Science Institute Working Paper, December 1985. Allan D. Shocker and V. Srinivasan, "Multiattribute Approaches for Product Concept Evaluation and Generation: A Critical Review," *Journal of Marketing Research,* May 1979, pp. 159–80.

2. John M. Groocock, *The Chain of Quality* (New York: John Wiley & Sons, 1986).

3. Regardless of the size of the purchasing company, the most important factor in a microcomputer buying decision is the reputation of the manufacturer. Price, often thought of as an important factor, is a surprisingly minor consideration. *Infoworld,* November 25, 1985.

4. Theodore Levitt, *The Marketing Imagination* (New York: The Free Press, 1983).

5. *Forbes,* 1974.

6. Lawrence J. Utzig, "Quality Reputation—A Precious Asset," 34th Annual Quality Congress Transactions, ASQC, 1980 and Lawrence J. Utzig, "Customer-Based Measurements Close the Loop," 35th Annual Quality Congress Transactions, ASQC, 1981.

7. "Quality: The U.S. Drives To Catch Up," *Business Week,* 1982, pp. 68–69.

8. John J. Welch, Jr., "Where is Marketing Now That We Really Need It," General Electric executive speech reprint. Presented to the Conference Board's 1981 Marketing Conference, New York.

9. Market differentiation is measured as the weighted absolute rating difference among competitors.

10. The ROI contour lines show the combinations of market differentiation and relative perceived quality that yield a given level of ROI. They are based on a curvilinear regression of ROI on market differentiation and relative perceived quality.

11. "Detroit Runs on Empty," *Newsweek,* May 19, 1986, pp. 56.

12. The *Consumer Reports* ratings reflect testing rather than customer perception. And *Consumer Reports* did not cover service attributes nor provide importance weights. To calculate relative quality scores, SPI staff provided rough estimates of importance weights and the data on service attributes.

13. David A. Garvin, "Quality on The Line," *Harvard Business Review,* September–October 1983, pp. 65–75.

14. "Jaguar" *Research,* February/March 1986. "Roger Smith's Troubled Second Act," *New York Times,* January 12, 1986.

15. Damon Darlin, "Although U.S. Cars Are Improved, Imports Still Win Quality Survey," *Wall Street Journal,* December 16, 1985.

16. Philip B. Crosby, *Quality Is Free* (New York: Mentor Books, 1979), pp. 14, 15.

Chapter 7.   Capital Intensity Can Upset the Applecart

1. The Compustat data base was used to sort companies by their fixed- and working-capital intensity. Companies listed in Exhibit 7-1 had rates of return on equity that were near the average of their investment category.

2. When data on replacement cost (as distinct from original or book cost) are available (as they are in the PIMS data base), they can be used as well. Earlier PIMS research indicates that adjusting for replacement cost does not change the relationship to ROI. See Mark J. Chussil, "Inflation and ROI," *PIMSLETTER* No. 22, The Strategic Planning Institute (Cambridge, MA: 1980).

3. For an early treatment of this topic see Sidney Schoeffler, "Capital-Intensive Technology versus ROI: A Strategic Assessment," *Management Review,* September 1978, pp. 8–14.

4. For a study of barriers to exit based on the PIMS data base, see Michael E. Porter, "Please Note Location of Nearest Exit: Exit Barriers and Planning," *California Management Review,* Winter 1976, pp. 21–33.

5. See David J. Ravenscraft, "Structure-Profit Relationships at the Line of Business and Industry Level," *Review of Economics and Statistics,* February 1983, pp. 22–31.

6. Michael E. Porter, "Capital Expansion: Should You Play the Preemption Game?" *Journal of Business Strategy.*

7. For a description of the titanium dioxide case see Pankaj Ghemawat, "Capacity Expansion in the Titanium Dioxide Industry," *Journal of Industrial Economics,* December 1984, pp. 145–163.

8. Joseph L. Bower, *When Markets Quake* (Boston: Harvard Business School Press, 1986).

9. Value added represents the amount that purchased raw materials, components and energy increase in value when they have been converted into the products of the business or—stated another way—a firm's sales minus its purchases. For a discussion of when does mechanization to improve labor productivity pay off, see Bradley T. Gale, "Can More Capital Buy Higher Productivity?" *Harvard Business Review,* July-August 1980, pp. 78–86. For a discussion of measuring employee productivity and tracking it relative to a benchmark that reflects capital inputs see Bradley T. Gale, "A Strategic Approach to Productivity Management," *Planning Review,* March 1981.

10. Peter F. Drucker, *Management: Tasks, Responsibilities, Practices* (New York: Harper & Row, 1974), p. 112.

Chapter 8. When Does Vertical Integration Pay Off?

1. This chapter is based primarily on Robert D. Buzzell, "Is Vertical Integration Profitable?" *Harvard Business Review,* January–February 1983, pp. 92–102.

2. Robert H. Hayes and William J. Abernathy, "Managing Our Way to Economic Decline," *Harvard Business Review,* July–August 1980, p. 72.

3. "Roger Smith's Troubled Second Act," *New York Times,* January 12, 1986, p. F-23.

4. Dennis W. Carlton, "Vertical Integration in Competitive Markets Under Uncertainty," *Journal of Industrial Economics,* XXVII (March 1979), p. 189.

5. David J. Tecce, "Vertical Integration in the U.S. Oil Industry," in Edward J. Mitchell (ed.), *Vertical Integration in the Oil Industry* (Washington: American Enterprise Institute, 1976), pp. 105–90.

6. Quoted in "Du Pont's Costly Bet on Conoco," *Business Week,* July 20, 1981, p. 52.

7. Edwin Mansfield and Samuel Wagner, "Organization and Strategic Factors with Probabilities of Success in Industrial Research and Development," *Journal of Business,* 48 (April 1975), pp. 180–98.

8. Robert A. Leone, William J. Abernathy, Stephen P. Bradley, and Jeffrey Hunker, "Regulation and Technological Innovation in the Automobile Industry," Report to the Office of Technology Assessment, July 1981, p. 43.

9. Reported in *The New York Times,* March 20, 1982, p. 33.

10. David J. Tecce, "Vertical Integration in the U.S. Oil Industry," in Edward J. Mitchell (ed.), *Vertical Integration in the Oil Industry* (Washington: American Enterprise Institute, 1976), p. 129.

11. Edward T. Bowman, "Strategy, Annual Reports, and Alchemy," *California Management Review,* XX (Spring 1978), p. 70.

12. Robert D. Buzzell, "Vertical Integration—Does It Increase Profits in Chemicals?" *Chemical Strategies,* Vol. 2, C.H. Kline Company (1984), pp. 20–32.

13. We use the rate of change in selling prices, rather than material costs, as a measure of high vs. low inflation. The reason is that if there *is* any advantage associated with a high (or low) degree of vertical integration under high-inflation conditions, it would be reflected in a business unit's reported rate of change in material costs, which might appear to be low even when industry *average* costs are rising rapidly.

14. Robert H. Hayes and William J. Abernathy, "Managing Our Way to Economic Decline," *Harvard Business Review,* July–August 1980, p. 73.

Chapter 9.   Strategies for Market Leaders and Followers

1. In the PIMS data base, each business is classified as "One of the Pioneers," "An Early Follower," or "A Late Follower" in terms of the timing of its entry into the market. We cannot distinguish between *the* pioneer and others who entered at about the same time. In fact, there is usually some ambiguity about who was first to develop or introduce a given product or service. For example, Amana, Litton, and General Electric all might claim to be the first to have introduced the consumer version of the microwave oven.

2. The advantages and risks of early market entry have been explored by William Robinson, using the PIMS data base. See W. T. Robinson and C. Fornell, "The Sources of Market Pioneer Advantages in Consumer Goods Industries," and W. T. Robinson, "Market Pioneering and Sustainable Market Share Advantages in Industrial Goods Manufacturing Industries," Working Papers Nos. 866 and 869, Krannert Graduate School of Management, Purdue University, 1984.

3. Michael E. Porter, "Strategic Interaction: Some Lessons from Industry Histories for Theory and Antitrust Policy," in Robert B. Lamb (ed.), *Competitive Strategic Management* (Englewood Cliffs, NJ: Prentice-Hall, 1984), pp. 415–445.

4. Docutel's early history is summarized in a case study, "Docutel Cor-

poration," in Derek F. Abell and John S. Hammond, *Strategic Market Planning: Problems and Analytical Approaches* (Englewood Cliffs, NJ: Prentice-Hall, 1979), pp. 65–102. The company's later difficulties are described in "Docutel: Trying for a Comeback by Dovetailing the New with the Old," *Business Week,* October 30, 1978, pp. 179–80.

5. See "Note on the Motorcycle Industry—1975," Harvard Business School Case No. 478-210, in John F. Cady and Robert D. Buzzell, *Strategic Marketing* (Boston: Little, Brown & Co., 1986), pp. 17–44.

6. Heinz's market position in the mid-1960s is described in "The H. J. Heinz Company (A)," Harvard Business School Case Services No. 569-011. Subsequent changes in the marketing program for catsup are described in "H. J. Heinz Company: Plastic Bottle Ketchup (A)," Harvard Business School Case Services No. 586-035.

7. Paul Bloom and Philip Kotler suggest that there is an "optimal" market share for the leader that is usually smaller than the maximum possible one, partly because of the risks of antitrust action. See "Strategies for High Market Share Companies," *Harvard Business Review,* November–December 1975, pp. 63–72.

8. See Robert D. Buzzell, "Are There Natural Market Structures?" *Journal of Marketing,* 45 (Winter 1981), pp. 42–51.

9. For a comment on Sterling's tardy response to Tylenol, see the *Wall Street Journal,* January 7, 1983, p. 5. Estimates of 1985 market shares are taken from *Advertising Age,* September 14, 1986, pp. 118, 156.

10. See Thomas V. Bonoma, "Marketing Success Can Breed Marketing Inertia," *Harvard Business Review,* September–October 1981, p. 117.

11. Based on "The Limits of Tradition," *Forbes,* May 20, 1985, pp. 112, 115.

12. Michael E. Porter, "Strategic Interaction: Some Lessons from Industry Histories for Theory and Antitrust Policy," in Robert B. Lamb (ed.), *Competitive Strategic Management* (Englewood Cliffs, NJ: Prentice-Hall, 1984), p. 436.

13. Kimberly-Clark's challenge to P&G is described in *Advertising Age,* July 29, 1985, pp. 1, 50.

14. A statistical model of market-share changes is outlined in Robert D. Buzzell and Frederick D. Wiersema, "Modelling Changes in Market Share: A Cross-Sectional Analysis," *Strategic Management Journal,* Vol. 2 (1981), pp. 27–42. See also the same authors' "Successful Share-Building Strategies," *Harvard Business Review,* January–February 1981, pp. 27–42.

15. See Richard G. Hamermesh, M. J. Anderson, Jr. and J. E. Harris, "Strategies for Low Market Share Businesses," *Harvard Business Review,* May–June 1978, pp. 95–102; and Carolyn Y. Woo and Arnold

Cooper, "The Surprising Case for Low Market Share," *Harvard Business Review,* November–December 1982, pp. 106–113.

16. The focus strategy is one of the three so-called generic strategies identified by Michael Porter. See his *Competitive Strategy* (New York: The Free Press, 1980), Chapter 2.

17. Savin's strategy is discussed by Roberto Buaron, "How to Win the Market-Share Game? Try Changing the Rules," *Management Review,* January 1981, pp. 8–17.

18. Based on Toni Mack, "Pizza Power," *Forbes,* September 23, 1985, pp. 106 ff.

19. See Barry Stavro, "Strategic Withdrawal," *Forbes,* February 10, 1986, pp. 34–35.

Chapter 10.   Market Evolution and Competitive Strategy

1. A useful overview of the product life cycle (PLC) concept is provided by a collection of articles on the subject in the *Journal of Marketing,* Vol. 45 (Fall 1981). In one of the articles in this collection, George S. Day reviews differing viewpoints on the question of the "level of aggregation" for life cycle models. Different authors have attempted to apply the PLC model to individual brands (e.g., Merit cigarettes), product sub-categories (low-tar cigarettes), product categories (all cigarettes), and broadly defined industries (automobiles). In this chapter we use the PLC model to describe the evolution of *served markets,* as defined in Chapter 2.

2. See Michael Porter, *Competitive Strategy* (New York: The Free Press, 1980), Chapter 8.

3. The General Foods guidelines are described in a case study, "General Foods Corporation: Dessert Toppings Strategy," in John F. Cady and Robert D. Buzzell, *Strategic Marketing* (Boston: Little, Brown and Co., 1986), pp. 463–85.

4. See, for example, Nariman K. Dhalla and Sonia Yuspeh, "Forget the Product Life Cycle Concept," *Harvard Business Review,* January–February 1976, pp. 102–12, and Michael Porter, *Competitive Strategy,* pp. 158–62.

5. R. A. Thietart and R. Vivas, in an analysis based on PIMS data, used the PLC stages designated by the business units' managers, with one exception: they reclassified "mature" markets that were declining at a 5% or faster rate into the "decline" stage. See their article, "An Empirical Investigation of Success Strategies for Businesses Along the Product Life Cycle," *Management Science,* Vol. 30 (December 1984), pp. 1405–23. A different approach was used by Hans Thorelli and Ste-

phen Burnett, who analyzed PIMS industrial products businesses strictly in terms of market *age*. See "The Nature of Product Life Cycles for Industrial Goods Businesses," *Journal of Marketing,* Vol. 45 (Fall 1981), pp. 97–108.

6. In an earlier study of product life cycles in the food industry, one of the authors distinguished between product categories in the "growth maturity" stage (such as peanut butter at the time) and those in the "stable maturity" stage (e.g., flour). See Robert D. Buzzell, "Competitive Behavior and Product Life Cycles," in John S. Wright and Jac L. Goldstucker (eds.), *New Ideas for Successful Marketing* (Chicago: American Marketing Association, 1966), pp. 46–68.

7. James M. Utterback and William J. Abernathy, "A Dynamic Model of Process and Product Innovation," *Omega,* Vol. 3 (1975), p. 631.

8. See "This Is the House That Jack Built," *Forbes,* May 25, 1981, p. 92 ff.

9. William A. Sahlman and Howard H. Stevenson, "Capital Market Myopia," *Journal of Business Venturing,* Vol. 1, No. 1 (1985), p. 25.

10. *Fortune,* November 25, 1985, p. 47.

11. Philip Kotler, "Harvesting Strategies for Weak Products," *Business Horizons,* August 1978, pp. 15 ff.

12. Du Pont's approach is described in John B. Frey, Jr., "Pricing and Product Life Cycles," *CHEMTECH,* January 1985, pp. 15 ff.

Chapter 11. Managing for Tomorrow

1. Robert H. Hayes and William J. Abernathy, "Managing Our Way to Economic Decline," *Harvard Business Review,* July–August 1980, pp. 67–77. In a sequel to this article, Hayes and David A. Garvin focus on the role of capital budgeting techniques in (as they see it) distorting management choices. See "Managing As If Tomorrow Mattered," *Harvard Business Review,* May–June 1982, pp. 71–79.

2. For a survey of public policies that affect "competitiveness," see Bruce Scott and George Lodge (eds.), *U.S. Competitiveness in the World Economy,* (Boston: Harvard Business School Press, 1985).

3. See Richard R. Ellsworth, "Capital Markets and Competitive Decline," *Harvard Business Review,* September–October 1985, pp. 171–83.

4. The use of DCF measures is described, and criticized, in Robert Hayes and David Garvin, same reference cited in Note 1.

5. A useful area for future research would be the development of varying discount rates for each business. These discount rates might vary, for

example, as a function of market stability vs. volatility as well as prevailing interest rates and other macroeconomic conditions in different time periods.

6. For discussions of *value-based planning,* see Alfred Rappaport, "Selecting Strategies that Create Shareholder Value," *Harvard Business Review,* May–June 1981, pp. 139–49; and Enrique R. Arzac, "Do Your Business Units Create Shareholder Value?" *Harvard Business Review,* January–February 1986, pp. 121–26. A company system based on this approach (developed by the Dexter Corporation) is outlined in Worth Loomis, Bela Chakravarthy, and John M. Vrabel, "A Value-Based Strategic Planning and Control System," presentation to the Fifth Annual Strategic Management Society Conference, October 1985. The pros and cons of alternative measures of long-term performance are explored in Kenneth A. Merchant and William J. Bruns, Jr., "Measurements to Cure Management Myopia," *Business Horizons,* May–June 1986, pp. 56–64.

7. Ben Branch and Bradley T. Gale, "Linking Stock Price Performance to Strategy Formulation," in Robert B. Lamb (ed.), *Competitive Strategic Management* (Englewood Cliffs, NJ: Prentice-Hall, 1984), pp. 611–33.

8. The market valuation model calculates a ratio of (1) the market value of equity plus the book value of long-term debt to (2) the book value of equity plus long-term debt. Implicitly, the company-wide ratio of debt to equity is applied to each business unit.

9. Correspondence with the authors, 1986.

10. Dexter's system is described in Worth Loomis, Bala Chakravarthy, and John M. Vrabel, "A Value-Based Strategic Planning and Control System," presentation to the Strategic Management Society Conference, Barcelona, October 1985.

Chapter 12.   Integrating Strategies for Clusters of Businesses

1. Donald F. Heany and Gerald Weiss, "Integrating Strategies for Clusters of Businesses," *Journal of Business Strategy* (Summer 1983, pp. 3–11).

2. John R. Wells, "In Search of Synergy," Doctoral Thesis, Harvard Business School, 1984.

3. Richard P. Rumelt, *Strategy, Structure and Economic Performance,* Boston: Division of Research, Graduate School of Business Administration, Harvard University. (For a summary of the follow-on research, see Wells, pp. 95–108.)

4. E. Ralph Biggadike, *Corporate Diversification: Entry, Strategy and Per-*

formance, Cambridge, MA: Harvard University Press 1976. (See Chapter 7, "The Impact of Relatedness on Performance.")

5. Worth Loomis, "Strategic Planning In Uncertain Times," *Chief Executive* (Winter 1980/81).

6. Russell Mitchell, "Dow Chemical's Drive to Change Its Market—and Its Image," *Business Week,* June 9, 1986, pp. 92–96.

Select Bibliography

The publications listed in this Select Bibliography include books, articles, and reports based on research utilizing the PIMS data base. It does not include privately-circulated working papers, conference presentations, or similar materials.

GENERAL DESCRIPTIONS/OVERVIEWS

Branch, Ben, "The Laws of the Marketplace and ROI Dynamics," *Financial Management* (Summer 1980), pp. 58–65.

Burgess, Arthur R., "The Modelling of Business Profitability: A New Approach," *Strategic Management Journal,* 3 (1982).

Gale, Bradley T., "Planning for Profit," *Planning Review* (January 1978), pp. 4–7, 30–32.

Gale, Bradley T., "Cross-Sectional Analysis—The New Frontier in Planning," *Planning Review,* Vol. 6, No. 2 (1978), pp. 16–20.

Gale, Bradley T. and Ben Branch, "Cash Flow Analysis: More Important than Ever," *Harvard Business Review,* July–August 1981, pp. 131–36 (Reprint #81407).

Hambrick, Donald C. and Ian C. MacMillan, "The Product Portfolio and Man's Best Friend," *California Management Review,* Vol. 25 (Fall 1982), pp. 84–95.

Hambrick, Donald C., and Ian C. MacMillan, and Diana L. Day, "Strategic Attributes and Performance in the BCG Matrix—A PIMS-Based

Analysis of Industrial Products Businesses," *Academy of Management Journal,* Vol. 25 (1982), pp. 510–31.

Loomis, Worth, "Strategic Planning In Uncertain Times," *Chief Executive* (Winter 1980/81).

MacMillan, Ian C., Donald C. Hambrick, and Diana L. Day, "The Product Portfolio and Profitability—a PIMS-Based Analysis of Industrial Products Businesses," *Academy of Management Journal,* Vol. 25 (1982), pp. 733–55.

Schoeffler, Sidney, "The PIMS Program," Ch. 23 in Kenneth J. Albert, *The Strategic Management Handbook* (New York: McGraw-Hill, 1983).

Schoeffler, Sidney, Robert D. Buzzell, and Donald F. Heany, "Impact of Strategic Planning on Profit Performance," *Harvard Business Review,* March–April 1974, pp. 137–45. (Reprint #74210).

MARKET STRUCTURE, MARKET SHARES,
AND COMPETITIVE STRATEGIES

Buzzell, Robert D., "Are There Natural Market Structures?" *Journal of Marketing,* 45 (Winter 1981), pp. 42–51.

Buzzell, Robert D., Bradley T. Gale, and Ralph G. M. Sultan, "Market Share—A Key to Profitability," *Harvard Business Review,* January–February 1975, pp. 97–106. (Reprint #75103).

Buzzell, Robert D. and Frederik D. Wiersema, "Successful Share-Building Strategies," *Harvard Business Review,* January–February 1981, pp. 135–44. (Reprint #81101).

Buzzell, Robert D. and Frederik D. Wiersema, "Modelling Changes in Market Share: A Cross-Sectional Analysis," *Strategic Management Journal,* 2 (1981), pp. 27–42.

Caves, Richard E., Bradley T. Gale, and Michael E. Porter, "Interfirm Profitability Differences," *Quarterly Journal of Economics* (November 1977), pp. 667–675.

Caves, Richard E. and Michael E. Porter, "Market Structure, Oligopoly, and The Stability of Market Shares," *Journal of Industrial Economics,* XXVI (June 1978), pp. 289–313.

Caves, Richard E. and Michael E. Porter, "Barriers to Exit," in *Essays In Industrial Organization In Honor of Joe S. Bain,* ed. by Robert T. Masson and P. D. Qualls (Cambridge, MA: Ballinger, 1976), pp. 39–69.

Galbraith, Craig S. and Curt H. Stiles, "Firm Profitability and Relative Firm Power," *Strategic Management Journal,* Vol. 4 (1983), pp. 237–49.

Gale, Bradley T. and Ben Branch, "Concentration Versus Market Share: Which Determines Performance and Why Does It Matter?" *Antitrust Bulletin,* Vol. 27 (Spring 1982), pp. 83–106.

Lillis, Charles, James Cook, Roger Best, and Del Hawkins, "Marketing Strategy to Achieve Market Share Goals," in Howard Thomas and David Gardner, *Strategic Marketing and Management* (New York: John Wiley & Sons, 1985), pp. 181–92.

Porter, Michael E., "Please Note Location of Nearest Exit: Exit Barriers and Planning," *California Management Review,* XIX (Winter 1976), pp. 21–33.

Thietart, R. A. and R. Vivas, "An Empirical Investigation of Success Strategies for Businesses Along the Product Life Cycle," *Management Science,* Vol. 30 (December 1984), pp. 1405–23.

Thorelli, Hans B. and Stephen C. Burnett, "The Nature of Product Life Cycles for Industrial Goods Businesses," *Journal of Marketing,* 45 (Fall 1981), pp. 97–108.

Varadarajan, Poondi and W. R. Dillon, "Competitive Position Effects and Market Share: An Exploratory Investigation," *Journal of Business Research,* Vol. 9 (1981), pp. 49–64.

Varadarajan, Poondi and W. R. Dillon, "Intensive Growth Strategies," *Journal of Business Research,* Vol. 10 (1982), pp. 503–22.

Woo, Carolyn Y., "Evaluation of the Strategies and Performance of Low ROI Market Share Leaders," *Strategic Management Journal,* Vol. 4 (1983), pp. 123–35.

Woo, Carolyn Y., "Market-Share Leadership—Not Always So Good," *Harvard Business Review,* January–February 1984, pp. 50–54 (Reprint #84119).

Woo, Carolyn Y. and Arnold C. Cooper, "The Surprising Case for Low Market Share," *Harvard Business Review,* November–December 1982, pp. 106–113. (Reprint #83613).

Woo, Carolyn Y. and Arnold C. Cooper, "Corporate Settings of Effective Low-Share Businesses," in Howard Thomas and David Gardner, *Strategic Marketing and Management* (New York: John Wiley & Sons, 1985), pp. 465–81.

Yip, George S., "Gateways to Entry," *Harvard Business Review,* September–October 1982, pp. 85–92. (Reprint #82512).

Yip, George S., *Barriers to Entry: A Corporate Strategy Perspective* (Lexington, MA: Lexington Books, 1982).

Zeithaml, Carl P. and Louis W. Fry, "Contextual and Strategic Differences Among Mature Businesses in Four Dynamic Performance Situations," *Academy of Management Journal,* Vol. 27 (1984), pp. 841–60.

MARKETING COSTS

Buzzell, Robert D. and Paul W. Farris, "Marketing Costs in Consumer Goods Industries," in *Strategy + Structure = Performance,* Hans Thorelli (ed.), Bloomington, IN: Indiana University Press (1977), pp. 122–45.

Farris, Paul W. and Robert D. Buzzell, "Why Advertising and Promotional Costs Vary: Some Cross-Sectional Analyses," *Journal of Marketing,* 43 (Fall 1979), pp. 112–22.

Farris, Paul W. and David J. Reibstein, "How Prices, Ad Expenditures, and Quality are Linked," *Harvard Business Review,* November–December 1979, pp. 173–84 (Reprint #79606).

Farris, Paul W. and Robert D. Buzzell, "A Comment on 'Modelling the Marketing Mix Decision for Industrial Products'," *Management Science,* 26 (January 1980), pp. 97–101.

Meisel, John B., "Demand and Supply Determinants of Advertising Intensity Among Convenience Goods," *Southern Economic Journal,* July 1979, pp. 233–43.

Zif, Jehiel, Robert F. Young, and Ian Fenwick, "A Transnational Study of Advertising-to-Sales Ratios," *Journal of Advertising Research,* Vol. 24 (June–July 1984), pp. 58–63.

VERTICAL INTEGRATION

Buzzell, Robert D., "Vertical Integration: Does It Increase Profits In Chemicals?" *Chemical Strategies,* May 1984, pp. 20–32 (Charles H. Kline & Co., Inc., 330 Passaic Avenue, Fairfield, NJ 07006).

Buzzell, Robert D., "Is Vertical Integration Profitable?" *Harvard Business Review,* January–February 1983, pp. 92–102 (Reprint #83103).

Vesey, Joseph, "Vertical Integration: Its Effect on Business Performance," *Managerial Planning* (May–June 1978).

PRODUCTIVITY AND UNIONIZATION

Clark, Kim B., "Unionization and Firm Performance: The Impact on Profits, Growth and Productivity," Harvard Business School Working Paper #83-16 (January 1982).

Clark, Kim B. and Zri Grilliches, "Productivity Growth and R&D at the

Business Level: Results from the PIMS Data Base," Harvard Business School Working Paper #83-03 (January 1982).

Gale, Bradley T., "Can More Capital Buy Higher Productivity?" *Harvard Business Review,* July–August 1980, pp. 78–86 (Reprint #80403).

Gale, Bradley T., "A Strategic Approach To Productivity Management," *Planning Review* (March 1981), pp. 12–18.

PRODUCT AND SERVICE QUALITY

DeSouza, Glenn and Phillip Thompson, "Quality Management and the CFO," *Financial Executive,* January/February 1985, pp. 65–70.

Gale, Bradley T. and Richard Klavans, "Formulating A Quality Improvement Strategy," *Journal of Business Strategy,* Vol. 5 (Winter 1985), pp. 21–32. (See also PIMSLETTER No. 31.)

Guiniven, John, "How to Compete By Quality," *Management Today,* December 1985.

Luchs, Robert, "Successful Businesses Compete on Quality—Not Costs," *Long Range Planning,* Vol. 19, No. 1, pp. 12–17, 1986, printed in Great Britain.

Phillips, Lynn W., Dae Chang, and Robert D. Buzzell, "Product Quality, Cost Position, and Business Performance: A Test of Some Key Hypotheses," Harvard Business School Working Paper #83-13 (1982) and *Journal of Marketing,* Vol. 47 (Spring 1983), pp. 26–43.

Thompson, Phillip, Glenn DeSouza, and Bradley T. Gale, "The Strategic Management of Service Quality," *Quality Progress,* June 1985, pp. 20–25. (See also PIMSLETTER No. 33.)

Vinson, William D. and Donald F. Heany, "Is Quality Out of Control?" *Harvard Business Review,* November–December 1977, pp. 114–22. (Reprint #77611).

PLANNING SYSTEMS AND APPLICATIONS

Collier, Donald W., "Strategic Planning Systems Design and Operation," *Journal of Business Strategy,* 1 (Fall 1980).

Heany, Donald F. and Gerald Weiss, "Integrating Strategies for Clusters of Businesses," *Journal of Business Strategy,* Vol. 4 (Summer 1983), pp. 3–11.

Hobbs, John M. and Donald F. Heany, "Coupling Strategy to Operating Plans," *Harvard Business Review,* May–June 1977, pp. 119–26. (Reprint #77308).

Product Innovation, Research and Development

Collier, Donald W., John Monz, and James Conlin, "How Effective is Technological Innovation?" *Research Management,* September–October 1984, pp. 11–16.

Heany, Donald F., "Degrees of Product Innovation," *The Journal of Business Strategy,* Spring 1983, pp. 3–14.

Meisel, John B. and Steven A. Y. Lin, "The Impact of Market Structure on The Firm's Allocation of Resources to Research and Development," *Quarterly Review of Economics and Business,* University of Illinois, Vol. 23 (Winter 1983), pp. 28–43.

Ravenscraft, David and F. M. Scherer, "The Lag Structure of Returns to Research and Development," *Applied Economics,* Vol. 14 (December 1982), pp. 603–20.

New Ventures

Biggadike, Ralph E., *Corporate Diversification: Entry, Strategy, and Performance,* (Division of Research, Harvard Business School: Harvard University Press, 1979), (based on his doctoral dissertation).

Biggadike, Ralph E., "The Risky Business of Diversification," *Harvard Business Review,* May–June 1979, pp. 103–11. (Reprint #79303).

DeSouza, Glenn, "The Best Strategies for Corporate Venturing," *Planning Review,* Volume 14, Number 2, March 1986, pp. 12–14.

Capital Investments

Hambrick, Donald C. and Ian C. MacMillan, "Asset Parsimony-Managing Assets to Manage Profits," *Sloan Management Review,* Winter 1984, pp. 67–74.

Wagner, Harvey, "Profit Wonders, Investment Blunders," *Harvard Business Review,* September–October 1984, pp. 121–35 (Reprint #84516).

Miscellaneous Topics

Branch, Ben and Bradley T. Gale, "Linking Corporate Stock Price Performance to Strategy Formulation," *Journal of Business Strategy,* Vol. 4, Summer 1983, pp. 40–50. Reprinted in Robert B. Lamb (editor)

Competitive Strategic Management, Englewood Cliffs, NJ: Prentice-Hall, 1984, pp. 611-33.

Buzzell, Robert D. and Mark J. Chussil, "Managing for Tomorrow," *Sloan Management Review,* Summer 1985, pp. 3-14.

Carroll, Charles, "Winner and Losers in the Food Processing Sector," *Business and Finance* (Ireland), November 29, 1984, pp. 33-36.

Carroll, Charles, *Building Ireland's Business: Perspectives from PIMS,* Irish Management Institute (Dublin, 1985).

Cvar, Margaret, "Evaluating Your Foreign Business: Finally, Some Facts," *Planning Review* (November 1982), pp. 8-13, pp. 38-43.

FitzRoy, Peter T., "Effects of Buyer/Seller Concentration on Profitability," in Howard Thomas and David Gardner, *Strategic Marketing and Management* (New York: John Wiley & Sons, 1985), pp. 151-66.

Guiniven, John, "Establishing An Acquisition Policy," *European Journal of Management,* Vol. 3 (Summer 1985), pp. 79-84.

Heany, Donald F., "Businesses in Profit Trouble," *Journal of Business Strategy,* Vol. 5 (Spring 1985), pp. 4-12.

Wind, Yoram, Vijay Mahajan, and Donald J. Swire, "An Empirical Comparison of Standardized Portfolio Models," *Journal of Marketing,* Vol. 47 (Spring 1983), pp. 89-99.

REVIEWS AND CRITIQUES OF PIMS

Aikawa, Katsuo and Tsuneo Yahagi, "Market Share: Key Determinant of Corporation Profitability," *Keio Business Forum,* Vol. 5, March 1984, pp. 71-79 (in Japanese).

Anderson, C. R. and F. T. Paine, "PIMS: A Re-Examination," *Academy of Management Review,* Vol. 3 (1978), pp. 602-11.

Lubatkin, Michael and Michael Pitts, "PIMS: Fact or Folklore?" *Journal of Business Strategy,* Vol. 3 (Winter 1983), pp. 38-44. See also Mark J. Chussil, "PIMS: Fact or Folklore—Our Readers Reply," *Journal of Business Strategy,* Vol. 4 (Spring 1984), pp. 90-96.

Lubatkin, Michael and Michael Pitts, "PIMS and the Policy Perspective," *Journal of Business Strategy* (Summer 1985), pp. 88-92.

Naylor, Thomas H., "PIMS: Through A Different Looking Glass," *Planning Review,* Vol. 6 (1978), pp. 15-16, 32. See also Bradley T. Gale, "Cross-Sectional Analysis—The New Frontier in Planning," *Planning Review,* Vol. 6 (1978), pp. 16-20.

Ramanujam, V. and N. Venkatraman, "An Inventory and Critique of Strategy Research Using the PIMS Data Base," *Academy of Management Review,* Vol. 9 (1984), pp. 138-51.

Wensley, Robin, "PIMS and BCG: New Horizons or False Dawn?" *Strategic Management Journal,* Vol. 3 (1982), pp. 147-58.

DOCTORAL DISSERTATIONS

The PIMS data base has been used by advanced graduate students in business and economics as a source of information for doctoral dissertation research. Some of these dissertations are available through University Microfilms.

Anderson, Patricia, "Capacity Utilization and Investment in Manufacturing: A Theoretical and Empirical Explanation," University of Massachusetts, 1977.

Bennett, Gerald F., "The Determinants of Relative Price Change—An Empirical Investigation," Manchester Business School (England), 1985.

Biggadike, Ralph E., "Entry, Strategy and Performance," Harvard University, 1980.

Burnett, Stephen, "An Empirical Investigation of the Product Portfolio Concept Within the Strategy-Structure-Performance Research Paradigm," Indiana University, 1980.

Catry, Bernard, "A Comparison of the Role of Advertising and Sales Force for Industrial and Consumer Goods," Harvard University, 1977.

Christensen, H. Kurt, "Product, Market & Company Influence Upon the Profitability of Business Unit R&D Expenditures," Columbia University, 1976.

Cvar, Margaret, "Competitive Strategies in Global Industries," Harvard Business School, 1984.

Farris, Paul, "Advertising Intensity in Consumer Goods Marketing: An Analysis of Variations in Advertising-to-Sales Ratios," Harvard University, 1976.

Harrigan, Kathryn, "Strategies for Declining Businesses: A Thesis," Harvard University, 1979.

Miller, Alex, "Technology's Impact on Strategy, Performance, and Strategy-Performance Relationships: An Investigation Employing A Taxonomic Approach to Model-Building," University of Washington, 1983.

Nunn, Kenneth, "The Strategic Determinants of Working Capital," University of Massachusetts, 1979.

Prescott, John E., "Competitive Environments, Strategic Types, and Business Performance: An Empirical Analysis," Pennsylvania State, 1983.

Varadarajan, Poondi, "An Empirical Investigation of the Relationship Between Market Share and the Competitive Market Position of a Firm,'' University of Massachusetts, 1978.

White, Roderick, "Structural Context, Strategy and Performance," Harvard University, 1981.

Wiersema, Frederik, "Price-Cost Dynamics: An Empirical Study," Harvard University, 1983.

Yip, George, "Barriers to Entry: A Corporate Strategy Perspective," Harvard University, 1980.

Zeithaml, Carl, "An Examination of the Contingency Relationship between Environmental Uncertainty, Business Strategy, and Performance," University of Maryland, 1980.

The PIMSLETTER Series

PIMSLETTERs are brief summaries of research findings on various aspects of business strategy, published by The Strategic Planning Institute.

No.	Title	Author(s)	Year
1	*Nine Basic Findings on Business Strategy*	Sidney Schoeffler	1977
2	*The Unprofitability of Modern Technology*	Sidney Schoeffler	1977
3	*Market Position: Build, Hold or Harvest?*	Sidney Schoeffler	1977
4	*Product Quality*	Robert D. Buzzell	1978
5	*Pricing High-Quality Products*	Mark J. Chussil Sidney Schoeffler	1978
6	*Unions and Profits*	Valerie Kijewski Sidney Schoeffler	1978
7	*How Price Premiums and Discounts Affect Performance*	Stephen B. Land	1978
8	*Does It Pay to Follow PIMS Signals?*	Stephen B. Land	1978
9	*Market Share Strategy: Beliefs vs. Actions*	Valerie Kijewski	1978
10	*The Senior Executive Tight-Wire Act: Balancing the Portfolio of Businesses*	Paul Nowill	1978
11	*Good Productivity vs. Bad Productivity*	Sidney Schoeffler	1979

(cont.)

No.	Title	Author(s)	Year
12	*How Price Controls Affect Businesses*	Stephen B. Land	1979
13	*How Much to Spend on R&D*	Mark J. Chussil	1979
14	*Recession: Who Gets Hurt? How to Cope?*	Sidney Schoeffler	1979
15	*Relatedness*	Robert D. Buzzell	1979
16	*"Social Benefit" and Profitability*	Stephen B. Land	1979
17	*Entry of New Competitors: How Safe Is Your Industry?*	George Yip	1979
18	*When Value Helps*	Mark J. Chussil Steve Downs	1979
19	*The Dispute About High-Share Businesses*	Bradley T. Gale Ben Branch	1979
20	*Impacts of Business Strategy on Stock Prices*	Sidney Schoeffler	1980
21	*Productivity Benchmarks*	Bradley T. Gale	1980
22	*Inflation and ROI*	Mark J. Chussil	1980
23	*Coping with Double-Digit Inflation*	Mark J. Chussil Sidney Schoeffler	1980
24	*Brand Awareness and Profitability*	William L. Burke Ruth G. Newman	1980
25	*Strategic Determinants of Cash Flow*	Bradley T. Gale Ben Branch	1980
26	*Above-Par or Below-Par Profitability*	Ben Branch	1981
27	*Hard-Working Capital?*	Keith Roberts	1981
28	*New Products and Market Position*	Richard M. Morrison Donald Tavel	1982
29	*Is R&D Profitable?*	David Ravenscraft F. M. Scherer	1982
30	*The Full Potential of Your Business*	Robert D. Buzzell Mark J. Chussil	1983
31	*Formulating a Quality Improvement Strategy*	Bradley T. Gale Richard Klavans	1984
32	*Beating the Cost of Capital*	Bradley T. Gale Ben Branch	1984
33	*Strategic Management of Service Quality*	Phillip Thompson Glenn DeSouza Bradley T. Gale	1985

No.	Title	Author(s)	Year
34	*How Much Autonomy Should Business Units Have?*	Rod White	1985
35	*Keys to Success for Adolescent Businesses*	Alex Miller John Guiniven Bill Camp	1985
36	*Sales Promotion vs. Advertising in Consumer Goods Marketing*	John Quelch Dae Chang	1985
37	*Calibrating the Cost (?) of Gaining Market Share*	Robert D. Buzzell	1986
38	*Entering New Industrial Businesses: Aggressive Strategies That May Pay Off*	Ian MacMillan Diana Day	1986
39	*Market Pioneering and Sustainable Market Share Advantages*	William Robinson Claes Fornell	1986
40	*Margins and Buyer/Seller Power in Capital-Intensive Businesses*	Peter Cowley	1986

TEXTBOOK REFERENCES AND COMMENTARIES

The authors of various textbooks in Strategic Management, Marketing, and Economics have included PIMS research findings in their works. The list below is not comprehensive, but illustrates the extent to which the research results have been recognized and incorporated into courses.

Abell, Derek F. and John S. Hammond, *Strategic Market Planning* (Englewood Cliffs, NJ: Prentice-Hall, 1979).

Abell, Derek F., *Defining the Business: The Starting Point of Strategic Planning* (Englewood Cliffs, NJ: Prentice-Hall, 1980), esp. pp. 243–44.

Cravens, David W., *Strategic Marketing* (Homewood, IL: Richard D. Irwin, 1982), pp. 79–88, 96–105.

Day, George S., *Analysis for Strategic Market Decisions* (St. Paul, MN: West Pub. Co., 1986), pp. 115–65. (An extensive description of PIMS including a detailed case example of its application.)

Hofer, Charles W. and Dan Schendel, *Strategy Formulation: Analytical Concepts* (St. Paul, MN: West Pub. Co., 1978), pp. 126–30.

Jacoby, Jacob and Jerry C. Olson, *Perceived Quality: How Consumers View Stores and Merchandise,* Institute of Retail Management, New York University (Lexington, MA: Lexington Books, 1985), Chapter 4.

Jain, Subhash G., *Marketing Planning and Strategy* (Cincinnati: South-Western Pub. Co., 1981), pp. 472–79.

Schendel, Dan and Charles W. Hofer, *Strategic Management* (Boston: Little, Brown & Company, 1979), pp. 206–12.

Scherer, F. M., *Industrial Market Structure and Economic Performance* (Chicago: Rand McNally, 1980), pp. 283–85, 293–94.

Wind, Yoram J., *Product Policy: Concepts, Methods, and Strategies* (Reading, MA: Addison-Wesley Pub. Co., 1982), pp. 531–33.

CASE STUDIES

Several case studies have been developed to illustrate the application of PIMS-based analysis to specific situations.

Abell, Derek F., "Tex-Fiber Industries—Petroloid Division (A), (B), (C), (D), and (E)," Harvard Business School Case Services Order Numbers 576-188, 576-189, 577-039, 577-040, and 578-132.

Aguilar, F. J., "Norton Company—Strategic Planning," and abridged version of same, Harvard Business School Case Services Order Numbers 377-044 and 380-003.

Biggadike, Ralph E., "Scott Air Corporation (B)," University of Virginia Number UVA-M-166R.

Bradley, S. P., "Sterling Industries, Inc. (A), (B)," Harvard Business School Case Services Order Numbers 178-163, 178-164.

Hamermesh, Richard G., "Dexter Corporation," Harvard Business School Case Services Order Number 379-112.

Name Index

Aaker, David, 92, 93–96, 279
Abernathy, William, 163, 179–80, 202, 211
Allis-Chalmers, 27
Amana microwave ovens, 201
American Chicle, 189
American LaFrance, 189
Anderson, M. J., 84
Andrews, Kenneth, 5
Anheuser-Busch, 116
Atlanta Hawks, 88
Austin, Nancy, 30

Bayer aspirin, 74, 188
Bettis, Richard, 4
Biggadike, Ralph, 233–34
Black & Decker, 175
Bonoma, Thomas, 188–89
Boston Consulting Group, 3, 76–78, 278
Bower, Joseph, 152
Bowman, Edward, 170
Bowmar Instrument Company, 163
Briggs & Stratton, 86
Burroughs, 84, 85, 101
Buzzell, Robert D., 81, 86, 93–96

Caterpillar Tractor Company, 52
Caves, Richard, 89, 90
Chandler, Alfred, 19
Chang, Dae, 81, 86
Chicago Board of Trade, 114
Chussil, Mark, 211
Coca-Cola, 73, 184
Compustat data base, 141–43
Conoco, 167
Cooper, Arnold, 84, 85
Crosby, Philip, 8, 118, 131
Crown Cork & Seal, 101
Cushman, Robert, 19

Deere & Company, 27
Deming, W. E., 118
Dexter Corporation, 73, 227, 228, 242
Docutel Corporation, 184
Dow Chemical, 247
Dr. Scholl, 73
Drucker, Peter, 156
du Pont de Nemours, E. I., 19, 25, 151, 167, 209–10

Emergency One, 189
Evinrude, 255

Subject Index